Th

THE BUSINESS OF POLITICS IN THAILAND

Thaksin

THE BUSINESS OF POLITICS IN THAILAND

"A company is a country. A country is a company.
They're the same. The management is the same."
—Thaksin Shinawatra, November 1997

Pasuk Phongpaichit
Chris Baker

SILKWORM BOOKS

Set in 10 pt. Jenson by Silk Type

ISBN 974-9575-55-5

First Published by Silkworm Books in 2004

Silkworm Books
104/5 Chiang Mai–Hot Road, Suthep
Chiang Mai 50200, Thailand
E-mail <silkwormbooks@loxinfo.co.th>
www.silkwormbooks.info

Printed in Thailand by O. S. Printing House

7 9 10 8 6

CONTENTS

v

Appendices

PREFACE

He won the country's biggest ever election victory under a new constitution hailed as the most democratic in the country's history. Then his government controlled the media, harassed civil society, and used state violence in ways that recalled Thailand's past military dictators. He launched "populist" economic policies that critics predicted would roll back IMF-imposed reforms and bring a "second crisis." Yet the economy revived without a "lost decade" and the IMF became an admirer. He claims to be "beyond ideology," and yet constantly lectures the Cabinet, officials, and people at large on his ideas for transforming everything. He prioritizes a "war on poverty," while his family business delivers an annual profit equivalent to the total income of a moderate Thai provincial city.

Thaksin Shinawatra's impact on Thailand is not simple to understand, but it is important to do so. He has put back money in many people's pockets but also broken a lot of rice bowls. He has raised people's expectations but also stifled dissent and debate. He aspires to create a new, cleaner politics but is accused of conflict of interest over his business empire. We have heard him described by two long-standing observers of Thai affairs as "the best premier Thailand has ever had" and "another grubby businessman."

This book is an attempt to explain where he comes from, and what he is trying to do. We make no claim to neutrality, but suspect we will disappoint his fierce critics just as much as his fervent fans. We look at him as both politician and businessman, because in Thaksin's Thailand these two spheres are joined at the hip, like Siamese twins. The first three chapters are about where he comes from—the political and economic background, his family history, the growth of his business, and his rise to power. The next three are about what he is trying to do—to the economy, to the society, and to the political system. The final chapter looks at the family business. The appendices include his Cabinets, his statutory asset statement upon becoming prime minister, and our translation in full of his speech launching the war on drugs. Many of his important speeches are available in English but not this one, which is among the most passionate and revealing.

We owe a very big debt to Kevin Hewison and Ukrist Pathmanand for sharing their own research and engaging us in a running conversation about the interpretation of Thaksin and Thailand's political economy.

We would also like to thank Ammar Siamwalla, Andrew Brown, Daniel Lewis, Kavi Chongkittavorn, Michael Connors, Nualnoi Treerat, Peter Warr, Porphant Ouyyanont, Sakkarin Niyomsilpa, Somkiat Tangkitvanit, Thani Chaiwat, Thanong Khanthong, and Viengrat Nethipo for sharing research and ideas; Chayodom Sapasri, Isra Santisart, Suthiphand Chirathiwat, and Vorawait Suwanrada for help on the economics; Kasian Tejapira and Pitch Pongsawat for some good ideas; Ben Anderson for demanding a cultural footnote; Peter Warr, John Sidel, and Eva-Lotta Hedman for pushing us to write earlier versions of some chapters; Akapat Bunyaratavej, Chantra Thanawatthanawong, Jirayu Tulyanond, Kane Sarika, Nitinai Srismattakan, Nopparit Ananapibut, Panya Lertsukprasert, Pairin Plaikaew, Shawn Crispin, Shigeyuki Abe, Somchai Sujjapongse, Takashi Shiraishi, Tatchakorn Pongroj, Tomas Laarson, Veerayooth Kanchoochat, and Yukio Ikemoto for help with sources in finding information; the *Bangkok Post* for the cover photo, and for permission to reproduce a Wallop cartoon; and Trasvin Jittidecharak, Susan Offner, and Silkworm Books for their professionalism and friendship.

For English spelling of Thai personal names, we have used the person's own version where known, or else the version used in the Bangkok English-language press where consistent, or else a transcription by the RI system.

All the quotations introducing chapter sections are from Thaksin. The sources for these are listed on pages 273–4.

PROLOGUE:
4:30 P.M., 3 AUGUST 2001

Inside the Everlasting Thailand Building in the Government House compound, the chaos and confusion was even greater than outside. Ministers, advisers, senior officials, and others were rushing in and out of the prime minister's office to offer their congratulations on his escape from a political trap. The waiting crowds overflowed onto the path outside. The sounds of congratulation and laughter competed with the ringing of mobile phones, making listening impossible. The atmosphere was like a miniature epic. Then everything began to happen very fast. The groups broke up and rushed to fight for space on the staircase. The prime minister emerged to make his speech to the press gathered outside. In the scene behind him, faces of that special breed of human known as politicians jostled to appear in the historic photograph. (Surathian 2003, 19–21)

Around a month before the January 2001 election that returned Thaksin Shinawatra as prime minister of Thailand, the National Counter Corruption Commission (NCCC) charged that he had concealed assets on three occasions over 1997–8 when he had been obliged to file statements as a minister. The amounts involved were 2.4 billion baht, 1.5 billion baht, and 0.6 billion baht.[1] They had been registered in the names of his housekeeper, maid, driver, security guard, and business colleagues. Two of these domestic servants had for some time figured among the top ten holders of shares on the stock exchange. If found guilty, Thaksin faced a ban from politics for five years.

The issues in the case divided sentiments—not just over Thaksin as a leader, but also over the practice of politics and the future of the country.

For the liberal press and public opinion, the case was a test for the much vaunted "People's Constitution" of 1997. This charter had created Thailand's first-ever Constitutional Court and a much strengthened NCCC with precisely the aim of reining in the country's profit-oriented business politicians. The NCCC charged: "There is ground to believe that the use of nominees by Thaksin and his wife was part of a dishonest scheme, or there would have been no need to use the nominees in the first place" (*TN*, 27 December 2000). For this camp, the case was about advancing the rule of law another small step. By the time of Thaksin's judgment, the Constitutional Court had ruled on nine similar cases, and each time had upheld the NCCC's charges. The most recent ruling, just hours before Thaksin's verdict, resulted in a political ban on one of Thaksin's big business friends (Prayuth Mahakitsiri).

For Thaksin's camp and supporters, the issues were very different. Thaksin repeatedly argued that he had made his enormous fortune before entering politics, and was a new type of politician who did not need to use power to make money. The case was an attempt to remove from politics an honest man who had been elected by a huge majority and was dedicated to work "for the people."

One of Thaksin's entourage who wrote a memoir about the case took this argument further. In a brilliant passage of atmospheric writing, Surathian Chakthranont (2003) painted the case as a contest between the future and the past. He described the offices of the NCCC as cramped, old-fashioned, and dreary. He sketched the apparently aimless confusion inside these offices as the standard of bureaucratic culture. He used a term for the NCCC officials (*khun nang*) that made them leftovers from the feudal order. He contrasted all this with the soaring office towers and modern management culture of the Shinawatra business empire.

He also presented the case as nothing more than a scheme by the opposition to win the election. He treated the content of the charges as totally irrelevant. The affair was just dirty politics or worse—not about right or wrong, but us and them. In this presentation, the 1997 constitution's idea of independent bodies serving as tribunes of the people to monitor the tricky activities of politicians and their business friends was turned absolutely on its head. Rather, the independent bodies became remnants of the old feudal-bureaucratic order, which "stole power away from the people" and tried to prevent the people from having their own chosen leader. In Surathian's summary, "the people wanted someone to serve them and work for them, not some pure, unsullied angel who would rule and lord over them" (Surathian 2003, 32).

The case was fought as much in the public space of the press as in the confines of the courtroom. In his first public statements, Thaksin effectively admitted he knew about the nominees but claimed it was "normal business practice." Later he claimed the judges were ignorant of commercial law. But as the hearings approached, he switched to the argument that he knew nothing about the nominees. His wife had handled such transactions, and her secretary who drafted the asset declaration had not understood these holdings should be included. It was just an "honest mistake" by the women around him. Thaksin's lawyers added technical points, in particular, that Thaksin had not actually needed to make these asset declarations at all.

To buttress these legal arguments, Thaksin courted public popularity in a way that no previous Thai prime minister had found necessary. He promised to bring prosperity: "I will lay down a pipe from where 600 billion baht is stored and send 300 billion baht to our people" (*BP*, 15 June 2001). He dramatized his appearances at the court by arriving on foot and walking through the crowds, shaking hands. He attended a temple where 1,017 monks in the presence of nine Buddha images and 30,000 onlookers conducted a chanting rite to ward off evil influences (another prominent monk described this as "voodoo") (*BP*, 15 and 16 June 2001). The Assembly of the Poor, followers of the popular monk Luangta Mahabua, a ninety-year-old former minister, and a prominent politician separately announced they would collect signatures in his support. The nonagenarian ex-minister delivered 1.4 million signatures a few days before the verdict (*BP*, 1 August 2001). Thaksin's former classmates from the military cadet school turned up on his doorstep in full uniform, along with the entire press corps. An MP declared: "the people believe Thaksin is the only one who can solve their problems" (*TN*, 28 June 2001). Thaksin claimed he alone could boost economic growth and rid Thailand of poverty:

> The people want me to stay and the people know what's right for Thailand. And who should I be more loyal to? The people? Or to the Court? I love people. I want to work for them. (*Time*, Asia edition, 13 August 2001, 19)

In effect, he challenged the court to risk the public discontent that would flare up if he were removed.

As the verdict approached, the press divided the fifteen judges into two camps. On one side were the "legalists" who would decide the case on grounds of law alone; on the other were the "political scientists" who would make a judgment on the costs and benefits of removing Thaksin or leaving him in place. But legal thinking was not the only force in play. One judge later said he had been "unsuccessfully lobbied" on the case: "I witnessed many subtle attempts by politicians to sway judges. The attempts were so discreet as to leave no tangible evidence . . . I had to admit I felt strong pressure from the pro-Thaksin mob" (*TN*, 4 and 21 October 2002).

The denouement confirmed this confusion between a political trial and a legal trial. The final statements to the court by plaintiff and defendant were run on live television. On the day of the verdict, Government House was mobbed by media and on-lookers. Before the chairman of the court was due to present his judgment to the TV cameras, another judge leaked the decision to the awaiting press—possibly timed to allow fast punters a few minutes before the stock market closed to take advantage of the expected surge in Shinawatra shares on the following day (the index rose ten points in

4

the remaining twenty minutes of trading). When the chairman of the judges did appear, he seemed paralyzed by emotion, and needed time and prompting before he could read the official verdict.

The judges decided in Thaksin's favor by an 8–7 split decision. The judgment was curious in several ways. The court ruled on seventeen comparable cases both before and after the Thaksin ruling, and in every other case endorsed the NCCC's findings. The 8–7 result was a combination of two divisions which both went against Thaksin. First, the court rejected by 11–4 a technical legal argument that Thaksin actually had no need to make the asset declarations in question. Then the remaining 11 divided 7–4 to reject Thaksin's argument that the concealment was an "honest mistake." By the conventions of the court, this meant only 7 voted Thaksin guilty and were outnumbered by the 4+4=8 who had been the minority in each of the divisions (Klein 2003).

Surathian called the acquittal "the minute that changed history." Certainly it deepened the division of political attitudes. The Thaksin side celebrated the acquittal as a victory for the popular will. Thaksin said: "I believe I can lead all of you to our goal which is happiness and prosperity." He went on to challenge the "checks and balances" thinking behind the 1997 constitution:

> It's strange that the leader who was voted by 11 million people had to bow to the ruling of the NCCC and the verdict of the Constitutional Court, two organisations composed of only appointed commissioners and judges, whom people do not have a chance to choose. This is a crucial point we have missed. (*BP*, 5 August 2001)

Three months later he returned to the same theme:

> What kind of political figures do you want to solve the nation's problems? If you say that for the nation to survive they must be pure from the beginning and not have done anything at all, then they have to administer the country and solve the nation's problems without any experience. For that you pass one kind of [anti-corruption] law. But if you say the people to administer the country must have

experience and abilities like the criteria used by companies when selecting a company president—namely knowledge, ability and experience—then the law must be of another type. So to write a law, we must ask what kind of political figures are wanted. (Thaksin 2001f)

On the other side, liberal opinion predicted exactly where this train of thinking was running:

> For reform activists, the ruling and the PM's subsequent commentary raised fears that Constitution reforms could be reversed and the nation forced down the path of Malaysia and Singapore, where authoritarian CEO-types with strong parliamentary majorities are able to control the media, stifle dissent, and impose a rule-by-law regime. (*TN*, 10 August 2001)

Three weeks later, the chairman of the court, Prasert Nasakul, published a summary of his verdict which deepened the confusion about what was being judged. He went far beyond legal argument into a political and moral assessment of Thaksin's leadership:

> An aspiring politician can never identify the public interest if he or she still clings to self or vested interest. The heart of political reform is to nurture politicians who uphold sound moral principles and aspire to observe stricter *dharma* than other laymen. . . . What the accused did shows he is a product of the past. He still thinks the same old way and acts the same old way, like other businessmen in the Thai-style capitalist system. He only propagated that he had achieved enormous business success through honest means, but he never explained exactly why he managed such a big success in such a short period of time. Nor did he explain how he would solve the conflict of interest stemming from his own fortune and that of the country. . . . Politicians who are inclined to put their selfish interest before the public interest cannot be expected to make a positive contribution to the society they are supposed to serve. (*TN*, 31 August and 1 September 2001)

The aftershocks continued for some time.[2] One of the pro-Thaksin judges threatened to sue political parties whose members criticized the judgment (*TN*, 17 August 2001). One of the anti-Thaksin judges claimed "My wife was moved out from her job soon afterwards" (*TN*, 21 October 2002).[3] Sanan Kachornprasart, a veteran Democrat who had been banned from politics for five years for an incorrect asset declaration, collected fifty thousand signatures to petition the NCCC to investigate four of the pro-Thaksin judges. These four responded by challenging the validity of the signatures. The Constitutional Court thus had to decide whether it was constitutional for it to make a ruling about the constitutionality of proceedings against members of the Constitutional Court. Two years later, this case was still becoming more convoluted.

The meanings of Thaksin's acquittal were complex and conflicting. Thaksin undoubtedly represented a new force in Thai politics at a time when so much of the old system had been discredited, especially by the crisis of 1997. A large majority of the population welcomed the acquittal. Yet, the case pitched Thaksin against the spirit of the constitution that had been so heralded on its passage four years earlier, and under which Thaksin had risen to power. The conflict between the "legal" and "political" aspects of the case signaled how much Thaksin represented a departure from the reform trends of the 1990s.

Even more strikingly, the case dramatized the intimate connections between profit and power, between big money and high politics. The subject of the case was some truly massive shareholdings. One almost instant result of the verdict was a flurry of speculative profiteering on the stock market.

Thaksin had closed the gap between business and politics. He had invoked popularity against the rule of law. His followers had vaunted the success represented by Shin Corporation against the principles enshrined in the 1997 constitution. The interplay of these themes is the story of this book.

1

THE BACKGROUND

In February 2001, Thaksin Shinawatra, one of Thailand's richest businessmen, became prime minister and appointed a Cabinet studded with other leading business figures. This was new. Although businessmen had dominated Thailand's parliament as electoral politics developed over the previous two decades, big business figures had remained slightly aloof. Thaksin had won the election on a platform of measures appealing directly to the rural mass. This too was new. Previous elections had been won by local influence. Party platforms had not been taken seriously (Arghiros 2001; Callahan and McCargo 1996). The foreign press described Thaksin and his program as "populist." This was so new that a Thai term had to be invented, while Thai academics helpfully wrote press articles to explain populism's meaning and history (e.g., Kasian 2001). Thaksin's party had won just short of an absolute majority. In no previous election since 1979 had any party reached one third. Over the coming year, Thaksin implemented all the major elements of his electoral platform. This was very new indeed. By mid 2002, Thaksin was predicting he would remain in power for several four-year terms. No previous elected premier had survived one.

Of all these many novelties, two were especially striking: first, Thaksin's own wealth and the big business interests clustered in and around his Cabinet; second, Thaksin's electoral platform of "populist" measures, and the commitment to implement them. The first of these reflected the spectacular rise of big business in recent decades, and its politicization by the crisis of 1997. The second reflected how much mass politics had developed over the 1990s and begun to demand more from the state. These two trends, and the conflicts between them, are the background for understanding Thaksin.

THE RISE OF BUSINESS

The expansion of Thailand's modern urban business dates back to the development policies initiated around 1960. At that time Bangkok was a government-dominated city of three million people. Agriculture was the main sector of the economy, the main source of exports, and the occupation of 80 percent of the population. Over the following decades, economy and society were totally transformed. Guided by the World Bank and helped by US aid, Thai governments built modern infrastructure, incentivized investment, and controlled labor. The Thai economy grew at an average of 7 percent a year for almost forty years. Per capita GDP increased from US$100 in 1961 to US$2,750 in 1995. Industry overtook agriculture as the main contributor to GDP and exports in the early 1980s. By 2000, the total population had doubled since 1960, and Greater Bangkok's size had multiplied almost four times.

This long phase of urban-biased growth climaxed in the decade-long boom which began in 1985–6. For four years, the economy grew at double-digit rates, and over the decade as a whole, the economy multiplied in size two-and-a-half times. Businesses that had been growing gradually for two or three generations suddenly made profits on a scale not previously imagined. Many new entrepreneurs built business empires in a short length of time. Thaksin Shinawatra was the most outstanding example. Surathian (2003, 22) described his excitement on first meeting someone who had built in a few years "a business empire so huge it would earlier have required three generations." Over the boom decade, the urban middle class more than tripled in size and greatly changed in character; its dominant segment was no longer government officials but business employees.

This long forty-year boom changed not only the economy but also the society, culture, and politics. Back at the start of this period, Fred Riggs (1966) had characterized Thailand as a "bureaucratic polity" and its businessmen as "pariah entrepreneurs" because their Chinese origins made them vulnerable to political repression. The "pariah" bit was greatly exaggerated, but the term "bureaucratic polity" captured how much Thailand in 1960 remained a semi-traditional culture in which social status (and to a lesser extent, wealth and power) depended on official position. The rise of business over the next four decades changed this culture and politics.

Chinese had migrated to settle in Thailand over many centuries. In the early nineteenth century, families of Chinese origin were very prominent in Bangkok, and Chinese products and culture were highly fashionable in the court and upper-class society. This changed when the court began to admire the West, when the concept of a characteristically Thai "nation" replaced older political ideas, and when China became identified as a source of revolutionary movements. In the early twentieth century, the Chinese were marginalized. The new nation-state was dominated by civilian and military officials that used ethnic politics to limit the political impact of commercial wealth.

But the Chinese were useful because they made money—for themselves, for the state, and for the old elite. The state developed techniques to merge them into local society. It imposed some restrictions on the civil rights of the first two generations, but removed these from the third. The old elite denigrated newcomers for being "too Chinese," but absorbed their descendants who showed commitment to their adopted home, and who learned the language and basic cultural practice. Big surges in the immigration numbers tended to be followed by phases of anti-Chinese sentiments and policies, but these phases were quite short. The last surge of Chinese immigration was in the 1920s when arrivals averaged around one hundred thousand a year. There were smaller spurts each side of the Second World War, ending in 1949. By the

1980s, only a handful of Chinese-origin families had not reached the crucial third generation.

Thailand's major Chinese-origin big business families fall into two groups. The first had arrived in the nineteenth century and become established by the early twentieth. The second group originated from the last inter-war surge of immigration. Many of those who succeeded in the "development era" came from this last group. Their success was based on the self-exploitation, high rates of saving, and mutual camaraderie of the classic migrant. In the 1950s and 1960s, they faced some social and political resistance. But over the next thirty years, this faded away completely. The families progressed through one or two changes of generation. The children passed through the elite channels of the education system in lockstep with children of more established families. Marriages between old status and new money became easier by the early 1970s, and unremarkable by the 1990s. Many children of wealthy families were schooled in the US and returned to take leading roles in the technocracy, universities, and professions. The division between Thai officialdom and Chinese business blurred and dropped away.

By the end of the twentieth century, it was not just urban business families that could claim some Chinese origin, but an overwhelming majority of the whole urban upper and middle classes. Of course, that Chinese origin had become more remote and often compromised by intermarriage. The new generations had grown up educated in Thai. Contacts with kin in China had been difficult during the Maoist period. Many families only vaguely remembered or cared about their Chinese roots. But within the business community, Chinese origins retained some significance. In some sectors, Chinese remained the language of business dealing. In many others, connections based on family or origin were still a commercial asset.

The growing wealth and social confidence of urban business and middle class resulted in a repositioning of those of Chinese origin within the culture. In the 1970s, intellectuals still complained that the Chinese were written out of the nation's history, and excluded from an ethnically rigid definition of the nation. Against the background of the urban boom, this changed. Books celebrated the rise of the great business families. Fictionalized versions were broadcast as TV drama serials of great popularity. China's reopening to the world in the 1980s, and its emergence as an economic power in the 1990s, legitimized pride in Chinese origins. Families traveled back to visit their birthplace and resume links with relatives. The Charoen Pokphand (CP) conglomerate became one of the largest foreign investors in China's opening economy, and several other Thai-Chinese firms followed the example. Learning a Chinese language became popular for reasons of both ethnic pride and practical business. The Chamber of Commerce published a bilingual journal to promote Mandarin language skills. Jitra Konuntakiat became a media personality and bestselling author by explaining Chinese customs, ceremonies, and culture to those whose families had lost the memory over the past generations.

Wealth also meant power. Estimates of the proportion of the successful MPs at the 2001 election who might claim some Chinese origin range between 60 and 90 percent.

In a 1987 book, Sujit Wongthet described himself as *chek pon lao*, Chinese mixed with Lao, suggesting such mixing was typical of the true reality of "Thai" ancestry. In 1996, a singer who emphasized his Chineseness by dressing in pyjamas, sporting a pigtail, and calling himself Joey Boy, was hugely successful. In the late 1990s, looks that would earlier have been called "too Chinese" became the fashion for actors, singers, and even the winner of the Miss Thailand World contest. In a deconstruction of Thai identity unimaginable only a few years earlier, a leading businessman described his origins as "100 percent Cantonese born in Thailand" (Sawat Horrungruang, *TN*, 7 April 2003). Chinese had "become Thai," but they were also changing what "Thai" meant.

BUSINESS AND POLITICS

In the era of military dictatorship, big business was closely connected to politics. The businessmen shared some of their profits with the generals, who in return constructed a friendly environment for business, and rewarded their particular friends with contracts, favors, and other profit-generating advantages. Around 1980, the business leaders attempted to push this mutually advantageous alliance to another level. The banker and Cabinet minister, Boonchu Rojanastien, promoted the idea of Thailand Inc., meaning a replication of the active government support for big business that had leapfrogged the economies of the four East Asian "tigers." Boonchu said: "We should run the country like a business firm" (Yos 1985, 196).

This dream was blocked by the generals who, even in the fading years of the Cold War, feared that capitalism rampant would provoke communism militant. Instead, the relationship between business and politics remained looser than in the East Asian pattern, and economic policy remained business friendly rather than more actively developmentalist.

Big business gave cautious support for the transition from military dictatorship to parliamentary rule, which began in 1973 and proceeded fitfully over the next quarter century. Meanwhile, because the early stages of this transition took place while communism was still deemed a threat, the authorities continued to smash grassroots organizations, with the result that popular interests and causes played virtually no role in the new electoral politics. Instead, Thailand evolved a parliamentary system that represented money rather than people. Elections were fought through vote buying, patronage, pork barrel, and professional violence. Parties were ideologically neutral, undifferentiated coalitions of business interests maneuvering for access to power. This pattern delivered the political system into the hands of business. At each election from 1979 onwards, more of the MPs were businessmen, until in the 1990s virtually all described themselves either as businessmen or professional politicians.

These new business politicians gradually eased the generals out of their positions of power and privilege. The critical point came in 1991–2, when an ambitious military faction opposed this trend and staged a coup. Their government was brought down in May 1992 by massive street demonstrations and public revulsion against the generals' use of violence to cling to power.

The new politicians also clawed power away from the influential senior bureaucracy, but here the result was more of a compromise. The politicians threatened to overhaul the semi-colonial, centralized, hierarchic, and highly self-regarding bureaucracy but once in control of the executive, they found this structure very useful. Instead, formulas for power and profit sharing between the new politicians and the old bureaucrats were negotiated at every level from the central ministries down to the provinces and districts. Under this new disposition, the nature of corruption changed. Classic bureaucratic squeeze—charging informal fees for public services—became less important. Meanwhile conspiracies between bureaucrats, politicians, and businessmen to make super-profits from manipulation of government rules, budgets, and mechanisms enjoyed a boom. By the early 1990s, this system had been dubbed "money politics."

In the 1970s and early 1980s, Bangkok big business played a big role in this new parliamentary politics. Business profits helped finance elections and coalition building, while several prominent business figures like Boonchu entered parliament. They could not realize Boonchu's dream of a more developmentalist state, but they gained privileged access to power both through formal means and informal links. They were able to preserve the advantages earlier secured through relations with the generals, while at the same time diverting more of the government's budget and energies to developing the economy, especially the modern urban economy.

Through the 1980s, Bangkok big business withdrew into a more backseat role in parliamentary politics. In part, this was a consequence of electoral demography. Ninety percent of the seats were returned by provincial constituencies where the majority of voters were rural. Once local business factions came to understand the potential of this new representative politics, they deployed their local knowledge and patronage to displace outsiders. In part, however, the political withdrawal by big business was strategic. Particularly once the boom began in 1985–6, they concentrated their energies on making money. The existing political system looked after big business interests without the need for direct intervention. Government managed the macroeconomy well, kept labor under control, built lots of infrastructure, maintained social peace, and did not interfere much with big business itself. Only the crisis of 1991–2 gave rise to concerns that political instability could undermine economic growth, prompting many businessmen to feel they should take a more active political role. But once the crisis was resolved and the economy survived virtually unscathed, these fears dissolved.

Moreover, the state seemed to be of declining importance for the fortunes of big business compared to the rising influence of globalization. External markets, external finance, foreign partnerships, new technology, and new ideas were increasingly the keys to business profit. Many big business groups plunged into joint ventures with foreign partners, and some ventured overseas themselves, especially into the liberalizing markets of the Southeast Asian region. Big business families sent their sons and daughters out for education—especially to the fount of globalization, the USA—from where they returned with new technical knowledge and new business ideas. In the mid 1980s, big business lobbies pressed for trade liberalization and a shift towards export industrialization on East Asian lines. At the end of the 1980s, they embraced financial liberalization and reveled in the resulting flood of cheap credit. In the 1990s, they tacitly welcomed the influx of cheap, mostly illegal, foreign workers who supplemented Thailand's faltering labor supplies. The great boom, which began in 1985–6 and for a decade made Thailand into one of the world's most dynamic economies, was seen in large part as a gift of globalization. Without doubt, globalization was good for big business, and businessmen welcomed it with enthusiasm.

This confidence cracked in the economic crisis of 1997. After forty years during which the Thai economy had averaged 7 percent growth and had never fallen below 4 percent, it shrank a shocking 11 percent in one year (fig. 1.1). Thousands of companies were technically bankrupt. Many paper fortunes disappeared. Some of the largest business groups, built over three or four generations, were wrecked, and several never recovered.

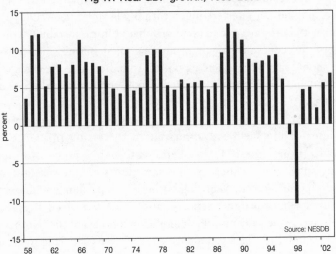

Fig 1.1 Real GDP growth, 1958–2003

The crisis had two dramatic effects on business thinking. First, globalization was no longer an unqualified friend, but in part a powerful threat.

The threat came from the ruthless behavior of international financial markets, which Thai firms had failed to predict and protect themselves against. It also came from new ideologies. The US had earlier helped to boost Thailand's modern capitalism. Now it wanted to buy it out. The neoliberal interpretation popular in the US blamed the crisis firmly on Asia's defective, cronyist capitalism, and argued that the solution must be to overhaul the institutional framework which nurtured Asian capitalism, and replace Asian capital with its more sophisticated Western counterpart. One US policy maker predicted that after the crisis "there is going to be a significantly different Asia in which Americans have achieved much deeper market penetration." The IMF "rescue" package largely accorded with that interpretation. Over 1998 to 2000, foreign investment flooded into Thailand in far larger volume than ever previously seen to buy up the wreckage of bankrupt companies. The Cabinet, headed by the Democrat Party, largely fell in with these policies. For big business, which had come to expect government to provide a generally protective and friendly environment, this amounted to treachery (Pasuk and Baker 2000; Hewison 2000).

As Richard Higgott (2000) and others recognized at the time, this neoliberal aggression provoked a "politics of resentment" in the crisis economies, and nowhere more so than in Thailand's business-dominated polity. Tycoons suddenly remembered their political science courses on US campuses decades earlier, and began railing against "neocolonialism." Enthusiasm for globalization dissolved into nationalism (see chapter 3). But most of the participants in these noisy politics were small and medium business figures. The big businessmen were more cautious. Their interests were too locked into globalization to contemplate any serious withdrawal. Public figures like Anand Panyarachun, former prime minister, protagonist of liberalization, and chairman of a major conglomerate, cautioned against rejecting globalization. But Anand and others agreed that Thailand's involvement with globalization needed to be better managed.

The second impact of the 1997 crisis was a wave of distrust in the system of "money politics" which had developed over the previous two decades. This distrust, and the associated pressure for "political reform," had been growing through the 1990s, but had remained an affair mainly of intellectuals and activists, not businessmen. From 1995, the failure of governments composed of loosely allied provincial factions to manage the national economy became increasingly evident. Respected technocrats were sacked, and others fled. The financial system was shaken by the crash of a bank looted by political gangs. Prime minister Banharn Silpa-archa (1995–6) had a limited grasp of economics but deep interest in the distribution of the government budget. His successor Chavalit Yongchaiyudh (1996–7) responded to pressure for his resignation by trying to stir up a movement of anti-urban and anti-Chinese populism. Big business began to want political reform, and a political role.

In sum, by the end of the twentieth century, after four decades of spectacular growth, Thailand's big business had big interests to protect. It was more socially dominant, as signaled by the revised evaluation of Chineseness in the national culture. After the 1997 crisis, it was motivated to control the state—in order to recover the protection that the Thai state had traditionally provided for big business, and to manage globalization.

OPENING UP POLITICAL SPACE

Apart from the rise of business, the second major sociopolitical trend of the 1990s was the opening up of political space after the end of the Cold War and the collapse of military rule.

In the decades of "development," the society was dramatically and jarringly transformed. The strains of this transformation were bottled up by a security state that interpreted all forms of political assertion as illegitimate, and made free use of violence. New ideas, new leaders, and new organizations began to appear in the late 1980s. But the critical event was the May 1992 political crisis, which seemed to mark the end of Thailand's military era, and which sparked hopes of widespread reform to sweep away the detritus of half a century of military dominance.

During the 1991–2 crisis, when the army took power by coup and was then ejected by street demonstrations, two political movements came of age. The first was a rural movement protesting against the decline of the agrarian economy and urban encroachment on natural resources. The second was a movement of largely urban, middle-class activism demanding reforms in politics, bureaucracy, media, rights, social welfare, and much else. The interplay between these two movements shaped a new public politics through the 1990s.

The upsurge of rural protest was a function of agrarian decline and political liberalization. Until the 1980s, agriculture was still growing because of an expanding land frontier, heavy investment both public and private, and rising international prices. At the same time, rural society was kept under firm political control. The army destroyed political organizations, and rural leaders simply got shot. Over the 1980s, all this changed. Agriculture lost its buoyancy because the land frontier ran out, investment was diverted to industry, and the world terms of trade turned against agricultural goods. With the ending of the Cold War, the army's role in Thai politics diminished, and the attempts to suppress rural politics relaxed. In a frank interview, a senior army officer explained that whereas the army simply used to shoot rural dissident leaders, they now only sent people round to intimidate their wives. General Panlop Pinmanee said:

> In the past, we had a "hunting unit." It was easy. We got a list of communist leaders, then . . . bang!, that's it, then we went home and rested. . . . We are not killing them like in the past. We have our methods, as I have said, and use psychology. . . . If a core member comes from Isan, we send our men to their family every day. When we arrive there we don't have to do anything. We talk to their wife and children, we take our meals at their houses. When we finish our meals we talk to their family. In only three or four days, they (the leaders) will come home because they are worried about their families. (*KT*, 3 August 2002; *BP*, 1 September 2002)

By the early 1990s, two streams of rural protest emerged. The first was located among more market-oriented farmers who protested against falling crop prices and rising rural debt. In short, they complained that market-oriented agriculture was no longer profitable. The second stream of protest was located among marginal farmers at the edge of the land frontier whose access to land, water, and other natural resources was threatened by dams, government forest policies, and industrialization. They protested to defend their own *withi chiwit*, way of life (Pasuk 2002).

In 1978, the government counted forty-two incidents of protest. In 1994, the figure was almost one thousand. Most of these protests were rural, and around half about the control over natural resources. In 1992, farmers marched on Bangkok like an invasion, and repeated the same tactic in most years following. Many new rural organizations were formed including the Small-scale Farmers of the Northeast, the Northern Farmers' Network, the Thai Farmers' Federation, and the Assembly of the Poor. In 1997, some twenty thousand protesters under the Assembly of the Poor camped outside Government House for ninety-nine days while their leaders negotiated with ministers on a 125-point agenda. The government conceded 4.7 billion baht in compensation, mostly for farmers displaced by dams, and promised key changes in forest and land management (Praphat 1998; Baker 2000; Somchai 2001; Missingham 2003).

This historic agreement came to nothing. A few months later, the Cabinet fell and its successor countermanded everything. Yet even the partial victory had great symbolic significance. Over the late 1990s, protests increased in intensity, especially against large projects that displaced people or encroached on local resources. The electricity authority was forced to abandon all future plans to build hydro dams. Two proposed power plants on the peninsula coast had to be indefinitely delayed. Protesters also targeted an experimental nuclear facility, several waste disposal projects, and a gas pipeline on the Thai-Malaysia border. While the state had, only a few years earlier, commanded natural resources at will, it now faced protests against major projects as a matter of course.

The protest groups began to forge international links, allying with equivalent organizations across the world, and importing new ideas and techniques of protest. A late-1990s movement for land reform was explicitly modeled on Latin American experience. Also, protest organizations edged nearer to domestic politics. Especially after the countermanding of the Assembly of the Poor's concessions in 1997, some argued that rural groups needed their own political party. But most rural leaders believed forming a party would worsen factional conflict and provoke attempts to co-opt or suppress rural organizations. They preferred to bargain their support to political parties in return for specific concessions.

In parallel to this rural wave, urban middle-class activism promoted reforms of the overpowerful and overcentralized state shaped by a history of absolute monarchy and military dictatorship. From the 1980s, NGOs campaigned for reform in media, law, rights, decentralization, bureaucracy, education, and social welfare. In 1991–2, many of these organizations joined in alliance to oust the coup junta. Through the 1990s, an aggressive daily press, multiplication of new media, cheap book and magazine publication, a growing culture of public seminars and conferences, a new cadre of "public intellectuals," and increasing access to broadcast media created a lively and expanding public space.

In terms of political ideas, this reform movement fell into two camps. The first was broadly liberal. It supported economic liberalization to undercut monopolies and privileges. It believed in rights, the rule of law, transparency, and a political system of checks and balances as the means to make the political system more accessible and fair. This camp looked on globalization in a largely favorable light. Its models were the advanced urban societies of the West, especially of Europe, with strong civil societies and embedded liberalism.

The second camp was usually dubbed localist or communitarian. Proponents argued for a dramatic decentralization of power, away from the central state to local communities. They wanted to rescue and enhance rural society in the belief that it enshrined social values that could serve as a counterweight to those of urban capitalism. They urged communities and local economies to be more self-reliant or "sufficient," rather than rushing to be absorbed, dominated, and perhaps devastated by capitalism. This camp was wary of globalization, and had a strong streak of cultural nationalism.

While the ways of thinking of these two camps were very different and often directly in conflict, the two shared a common opposition to the strong, overpowerful state, and thus could cooperate while ignoring their differences. Also, this largely urban middle-class activism and the rural protest movements lived off one another. The rural protests tapped the services of NGO workers, journalists, and intellectuals to organize their campaigns, articulate their demands, and add a touch of legitimacy to their projects. The urban activists allied with the rural campaigners out of conviction but also out of a need for numbers to create political weight.

Although these groups were locked out of the parliamentary "money politics" by the price level, politics *nok rabop* (literally, "outside the system") grew rapidly in influence. In the late 1990s, this resulted in four victories.

First, and most importantly, in 1995–6 the reform and NGO coalition, fronted by the health activist Dr. Prawase Wasi, forced the parliament to allow the drafting of a new constitution. The drafting process was removed from parliamentary control, although approval still required a parliamentary vote. Some reformers invaded the drafting process, and many more lobbied from outside. The draft that emerged in early 1997 was a blend of several agendas. The recasting of the political system was designed to move beyond the age of money politics by upweighting the franchise of the capital, strengthening the power of the prime minister, and creating new semi-judicial "independent bodies" to act as checks and balances on the power of executive and legislature. Other parts of the lengthy charter were shaped by the reform and NGO lobbies. The draft contained a long list of civic rights, including community rights over natural resources. The chapter on "Directive Principles of Fundamental State Policies" was virtually a manifesto of the 1990s reform movement with provisions for decentralization, greater popular participation, liberalization of broadcast media, and education reform (Klein 1998; Connors 1999; McCargo 2002a).

Second, in 1997, the eighth in the sequence of five-year plans begun in the development era proposed to shift "from growth orientation to people-centred development." It argued that the main barrier to this goal was the state itself because of its "very centralized power structure, administrative inefficiency, lax law enforcement, lack of popular participation, unethical and unfair use of administrative power, lack of administrative accountability, and lack of continuity in policy and implementation" (GoT, n.d., 121).

Third, in 1999, a decentralization act arising out of the new constitution proposed to transfer 245 responsibilities and 35 percent of the national budget from the central administration to local government by 2006, mostly to some seventy thousand elective Tambon Administrative Organizations.

Fourth, proposals for education reform, which had been researched and drafted by activists outside the state machinery, were translated into a major education act. Apart from changing the ideology of education, the act aimed to decentralize control. Apart from these major victories, there were several lesser ones. Even the National Security Council embraced principles of decentralization and participation (Connors 2003b). Together, these reforms constituted a major attempt to change the Thai state. By exploiting the new public space and negotiating directly with the bureaucracy, activists were able to bypass the business-dominated parliament and translate their agenda into legislation and policy commitments.

The 1997 crisis had a mixed impact on these trends. Most importantly, it clinched the passage of the new constitution. The draft was initially opposed as too radical by almost everybody with formal power including ministers, political parties, senators, judges, generals, and village officers. But against the backdrop of the crisis and the collapse of faith in the existing political system, particularly among big business and the urban middle class, the new constitution was transformed into a beacon of hope and passed into law with little opposition. The Eighth Plan suffered an opposite fate. Its ambitious proposals were ignored as the economic priority became simple survival. But at the same time, many government departments engaged in combating the crisis embraced the principles of decentralization and participation out of desperation. Meanwhile, in public space, the crisis magnified the voice of reformers, especially those with a communitarian or otherwise anti-globalist message.

CONCLUSION: GLOBALIZATION AND DEMOCRATIZATION

Thailand's big business reached a new stage of maturity in the 1990s. The 1997 crisis persuaded big business leaders that they needed to control politics in order to restore state support for capital, and manage globalization. But the strongest political movements of the 1990s wanted to level down the state, and replace its business orientation with other social agendas—better distribution of wealth, protection of the environment, people-centered development, human and community rights, participation in decision making.

2

FAMILY AND BUSINESS

In a speech delivered in Manila in 2003, Thaksin said: "Through my modest family background . . . I learned the hardship of poverty in the rural areas. I learned the importance of earning rewards by working hard" (Thaksin, 2003f). In fact, by the time of his birth, the Shinawatra were one of the most prominent families in Thailand's second city, Chiang Mai. They were big in both business and politics. Thaksin returned from his overseas education to be immediately appointed private secretary to a Cabinet minister. Thaksin grew up in an environment of wealth, power, and privilege.

Like many of his generation, he moved from provinces to capital initially for education, and then never left. Also like many privileged students of his generation, he returned from a US education with new ideas that had a business application—in his case, a fascination with computer technology. Then, unlike others, he made a billion dollars in a handful of years. This was not a normal level of profit. It came from the unique combination of new technology, high demand, new forms of financing, and—above all—a politically constructed oligopoly.

Thaksin constructed his life story as a *tamnan* (legend) for political purposes. The early part of his autobiography (Thaksin 1999)[1] positions Thaksin as a man of the people, starting from rural origins, and rising by a struggle patterned on the stories of first-generation Chinese migrants. The reality is actually a more interesting tale stretching over four generations.

TAX FARMS AND CARAVANS

> From the start of the family, there has been a fighting spirit.
> (Autobiography, 1998–9)

Thaksin's great-grandfather, Seng sae Khu (or Khu Chun Seng), was a Hakka Chinese who migrated to Siam in the late nineteenth century. He probably came from Kwangtung and arrived in the late 1860s, aged ten to twelve, which means he may have accompanied his father, but these early details are unclear.

People from coastal southern China had been coming to Siam since at least the fourteenth century. The numbers increased steadily from the eighteenth century. After the old Siamese capital of Ayutthaya was sacked by the Burmese in 1767 and a new capital founded at Thonburi-Bangkok, the kings welcomed Chinese to rebuild the economy and generate a base for government revenue. By the 1860s, the annual arrival was around ten thousand people, almost all male, of which two-thirds would settle permanently. Most arrived with nothing more than the proverbial "one pillow and one mat," and worked initially as coolie labor in Bangkok's port, rice mills, and saw mills. If they could generate some seed capital, they would then open a trading business of some kind. As Bangkok became more crowded, more of these fledgling merchants fanned out into Siam's upcountry towns.

Nothing is known of Seng's early life. By 1890 he was a gambling tax farmer in the small port of Chanthaburi on the eastern coast of the Gulf of Siam, and had married a local girl, Thongdi. Since the 1820s, the Siamese government had auctioned the right to collect taxes on various goods and services, and allowed the tax farmers to profit by collecting more than their auction bid. Most of the tax farmers were immigrant Chinese, and several became very rich. By the end of the century, government had replaced most of the tax farms by centralized collection, but not those on gambling, opium, and liquor. The consumers of these products were mainly Chinese; and government found it efficient to allow Chinese entrepreneurs to collect these dues.

Seng sae Khu

Some time around 1900, Seng's tax farm expired and he moved to trade at Talat Noi in Bangkok's Chinese commercial district. Then around 1908 he moved to Chiang Mai to become a gambling tax farmer again. There are two versions of how he secured this concession. The first comes from a book entitled *Pioneers of Chiang Mai*, compiled in 1980 from interviews with descendants of the city's commercial dynasties:

In 1908, Akon Seng and Thongdi received good news from one of Thongdi's relatives, who was a genuine Thai from Chanthaburi town. He said another relative who held a government post in Bangkok had secured for Akon Seng another gambling tax farm monopoly in Chiang Mai. The relative also advised Seng and Thongdi to travel to Chiang Mai and settle there rather than staying in Bangkok because many Chinese traders and their locally born descendants had already settled in the north and made their fortunes. (Prani 1980, 174)

In the other version, Seng traveled to Chiang Mai on his own accord and became a subsidiary tax farmer under Ma Nikhonphan, a major tax farmer in the northern region with the official title of Luang Nikhon Jinkit, and a big patron in the region's Chinese community (Ariwat 2003, 22–3).

Chiang Mai had formerly been a semi-independent state. Bangkok had gradually imposed control from the 1870s onward. In 1898, the local rulers were finally sidelined, and a Bangkok-style administration installed. Seng was among many Chinese traders and tax farmers who flocked to the city in this era to take up the opportunities presented by this change in rule. He and Thongdi collected taxes from gambling houses in Mae Rim, Sansai, and Doi Saket districts. In 1910, there was a disaster:

> One day Thongdi and a servant from the locality were traveling by cart in Amphoe Mae Rim which at that time, unlike today, still had no good roads, only tracks for elephants and carts. As they were going to collect taxes from the owners of gambling dens, Thongdi was attacked by robbers who took the considerable sum of money she had already collected. Although the robbers did not touch her at all, Thongdi was so shocked she had a heart attack and died in the forest beside the road.[2] The robbers made off with a large sum of money. The servant fled unhurt. (Prani 1980, 187–8)

Following this incident, Seng moved to Sankamphaeng, a settlement twelve kilometers east of Chiang Mai where there was a market for caravan traders. He bought a plot of three rai[3] next to this market, and entered into the caravan trade across the borders from Siam into Burma and China.

Seng had six children with Thongdi and another three with a second wife named Noja. Chiang, Thaksin's grandfather, was the second child and first son, born in Chanthaburi in 1890. After the family moved to Bangkok, Chiang (aged around fifteen) entered Assumption School which was already one of the most renowned missionary schools, especially popular with well-to-do Chinese. According to different versions, Chiang either left to move to Chiang Mai with his parents in 1908, or was summoned in 1911 after Thongdi's death. He married Saeng, daughter of Nai Mun Somna, a big landowner, trader, and village headman of Sankamphaeng. Chiang and Saeng joined Seng in the caravan trade.

> The couple worked together, trading and bartering with the Chinese Ho and Shan who brought goods from Yunnan, Sipsongpanna, and the British Shan States. . . . The Shan and Ho came in horse or bullock caravans in the cool season. . . . Chiang and Saeng also transported goods like kerosene, salt, matches, candles, and pickles from Chiang Mai to sell to villagers who came to Sankamphaeng

Chiang and Saeng

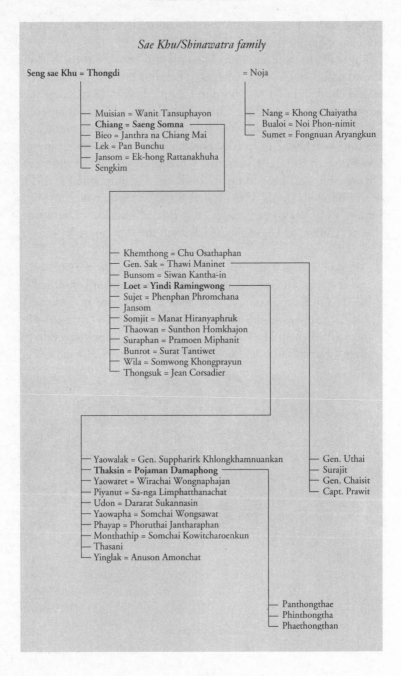

Sae Khu/Shinawatra family

Seng sae Khu = Thongdi

= Noja

— Muisian = Wanit Tansuphayon
— **Chiang = Saeng Somna**
— Bieo = Janthra na Chiang Mai
— Lek = Pan Bunchu
— Jansom = Ek-hong Rattanakhuha
— Sengkim

— Nang = Khong Chaiyatha
— Bualoi = Noi Phon-nimit
— Sumet = Fongnuan Aryangkun

— Khemthong = Chu Osathaphan
— Gen. Sak = Thawi Maninet
— Bunsom = Siwan Kantha-in
— **Loet = Yindi Ramingwong**
— Sujet = Phenphan Phromchana
— Jansom
— Somjit = Manat Hiranyaphruk
— Thaowan = Sunthon Homkhajon
— Suraphan = Pramoen Miphanit
— Bunrot = Surat Tantiwet
— Wila = Somwong Khongprayun
— Thongsuk = Jean Corsadier

— Yaowalak = Gen. Suppharirk Khlongkhamnuankan
— **Thaksin = Pojaman Damaphong**
— Yaowaret = Wirachai Wongnaphajan
— Piyanut = Sa-nga Limphatthanachat
— Udon = Dararat Sukannasin
— Yaowapha = Somchai Wongsawat
— Phayap = Phoruthai Jantharaphan
— Monthathip = Somchai Kowitcharoenkun
— Thasani
— Yinglak = Anuson Amonchat

— Gen. Uthai
— Surajit
— Gen. Chaisit
— Capt. Prawit

— Panthongthae
— Phinthongtha
— Phaethongthan

market. . . . They also purchased cloth woven by the Sankamphaeng villagers for sale in the city. They made loans to the villagers too. . . . Before long they became steadily richer. (Prani 1980, 191–3)

As one part of their caravan business, the Sae Khu family imported plain silk from Burma, dyed it, and reexported it back to Burma as sarongs. This business underlay the family's next stage of growth.

SILK

Shinawatra Thai silk became famous all over the country. It was popular among royalty, officials, even villagers. . . . It made the family name widely known. (Autobiography, 1998–9)

In this era, Chiang Mai was part of the Thai state but still very remote from Bangkok. The journey by a combination of riverboat and horse or elephant took at least three months. The completion of a railway connection in 1921 changed that. Chiang Mai's external commerce reoriented towards Bangkok. The old caravan routes across the northern borders into Burma and China withered. The Sae Khu family rode this transition on the silk trade.

In Sankamphaeng at that time, women wove cotton cloth for their own use, using locally grown cotton, but they did not sell it. . . . Chiang had the idea that the cloth could be improved and sold. He consulted older Chinese merchants in Chiang Mai, some of whom knew about silk production from China, and about local dyeing methods. . . . Chiang started to buy the Sankamphaeng cotton cloth for sale, and the business developed rapidly. . . . The Chinese Ho who came to Sankamphaeng market brought lengths of Chinese silk from Yunnan. . . . The women weavers were not interested in copying the Chinese silk . . . but Chiang and Saeng decided to buy silk yarn from the Ho, install looms in their house, and hire skilled weavers. . . . Chiang had silk samples of many different types sent from Bangkok to imitate. . . . He bought and dyed silk yarn from Isan, and traveled to Kengtung to buy Burmese silk. . . . The business was successful. They invested the profits in buying land. (Prani 1980, 199–203)

A small but growing middle class of high officials, professionals, and traders in Chiang Mai and more especially Bangkok created a new market for silk goods. Other Chinese-origin entrepreneurs from the Chiang Mai region recognized the opportunity, but the Sae Khu family was ultimately the most successful. Around 1932, they established a factory in Sankamphaeng that eventually carried out weaving, dyeing, and tailoring ready-made silk clothes (Plai-or 1987, 53–4). Chiang and Saeng had twelve children. From the early 1930s, the children began to reach an age when they could contribute to the business.

The roles of sons and daughters were initially rather different. The daughters went straight into the trade. Khemthong, the first child and eldest daughter, quit school after the compulsory four years of primary and worked in the family business. She opened the family's first retail outlet in a shophouse close to Chiang Mai's main Warorot market. Her two younger sisters, Jansom and Somjit, worked in the shop and later branched into managing the factory and wholesale silk trading, respectively. The sons, meanwhile, were given higher education. Of the first three, Sak went to army cadet school, Loet to Thammasat University, and Sujet to Chulalongkorn University.

As the family finances improved, the later children, male or female, were sent abroad and gained skills that helped to develop the family silk business. Suraphan studied engineering and cloth printing in Germany. He returned to manage the retail business and improve the production technology. Bunrot studied as a technician in Japan and returned to manage the factory. Thongsuk studied business administration in France and opened another factory to make clothing for export. Sumet, a son of Seng sae Khu by his second wife, retired from a career in teaching to help with the financial side of the business. After the Second World War, the elder daughter Khemthong moved to Bangkok with her husband.

After his death in 1957, she turned their house on Sukhumwit Soi 23 into a factory and retail outlet for silk and cotton goods. Later she added a larger factory on the Bangkok outskirts.

Unlike many other Chinese migrant lineages, Seng sae Khu and his descendants seem never to have looked back to China. There is no record of any of the family members returning, or even paying a visit. Both Thaksin's great-grandfather and grandfather married Thai wives. Until 1938, they continued to use the family's Chinese name. On 17 October 1938, Chiang's eldest son, Sak, registered a Thai surname he had chosen himself, Shinawatra, meaning "does good routinely" (Jitra 2004). Other descendants of Seng adopted Shinawatra as both a surname and branding for their various silk businesses.

But the family did not fade into Thai society and culture. Rather it became part of the distinctively hybrid Thai-Chinese *lukchin*[4] culture which developed in twentieth-century Siam. In *Pioneers of Chiang Mai* and other biographies, the wives of Seng and Chiang are portrayed as working alongside their husbands with the same motivation and aptitude for commerce as a Chinese immigrant— they become honorary *lukchin* as much as or more than the men "become Thai." From Chiang's generation onwards, the family built connections with other rising Chinese-origin commercial families in Chiang Mai. Chiang's elder sister Muisian married into a branch of the Chutima family which had risen on the riverine trade down the Ping River and become one of the city's most eminent dynasties. Muisian's daughter married into the Osothaphan clan, which owned rice mills and saw mills. Her granddaughter married Thawat Tantranont who built the city's first department store (Tantraphan). In the next generation, Khemthong married Chu Osothaphan of the same rice and timber family, and Sujet married into the Phromchana family, owners of rice land, orchards, a school, and later property developments around Sankamphaeng. By the 1950s, the Shinawatra were established as one of the premier commercial families of Chiang Mai (Prani 1980, 182–6).

At the same time, not all the lineage concentrated on commerce. From the third generation onwards, several went into the army. In the traditional social order, an official career had more prestige than commerce. Compared to the civilian bureaucracy where advancement depended heavily on patronage and connections, the military offered more chance to rise through personal achievement. In addition, after 1938, army generals occupied the premiership for forty-two of the next fifty years, adding to the power, glamour, and privilege of the officer elite.

Among Chiang's younger brothers, Bieo put one of his sons in the army, and Lek put both of his sons. Chiang's eldest son Sak also entered the army and rose to the rank of general. All four of Sak's sons entered the armed services. One was killed fighting in Laos and another left the air force to become a pilot in Thai Airways, while the remaining two, Uthai and Chaisit, rose to the rank of general.

EDUCATION

> My nursery school was not really a nursery school. The teacher washed the monk's begging bowls and ate from them. . . . The school was in a *sala* of Wat Sankamphaeng. The teaching aids were broken slates and a cane. He would rap on the slate to frighten each child into studying. (Speech, 3 March 2003)

In the autobiography published as part of his political campaign in 1999, Thaksin presents himself as a "backwoods kid" with a tough childhood (Thaksin 1999). This was a partial truth. By the time of Thaksin's birth on 26 July 1949, the Shinawatra clan was both well off and well connected. His uncle would shortly become a municipal councilor; his father would be a Chiang Mai MP; and another uncle would be an MP and deputy minister. One fifth of the book *Pioneers of Chiang Mai* is devoted to the Shinawatra clan. Yet it was true that the fortunes of Thaksin's immediate family were rather wayward.

Thaksin's father, Bunloet sae Khu, later known as Loet Shinawatra, was born in 1919. He studied secondary school at Yupharat College in Chiang Mai and entered Thammasat University, but left

34

after one term because the family wanted him in the business. He followed the pattern of his father and grandfather by marrying a local girl, Yindi from Sansai. But Yindi does not seem to have shown the same business affinity and migrant spirit as her predecessors, and scarcely appears in the accounts of the family by Thaksin or his biographers. Loet's younger brother, Sujet, completed engineering at Chulalongkorn University and returned to Chiang Mai to become a construction contractor. He recruited Loet to help him. Their main business was a government concession—erecting poles for electricity lines.

In the early 1950s, Loet was set to become head of the Shinawatra *kongsi* or family business through seniority; of his elder siblings, Khemthong had followed her husband to Bangkok, Sak had entered the army, and Som (Bunsom) had married a former Miss Chiang Mai and shown no aptitude for commerce. But at this point, Loet separated himself from the *kongsi* and opened a small coffee shop by Sankamphaeng market. Thaksin explained that his father "seemed not so interested in his material inheritance" (Thaksin 1999, 31), but the real reasons for this split can only be imagined.

The family's slump was short-lived. Loet soon dabbled in trading. His mother gave him thirty-six rai of land, which he developed into an orange orchard. In the 1950s, Thailand launched into the age of "development," including growth of a new bank-based finance system. Loet's brother, Sujet, rose to be a major property developer, municipal councilor of Chiang Mai, and in 1957 the manager of the Chiang Mai branch of Siam City Bank. Sujet invited Loet to become the bank's compradore or head of its loan department. With the contacts made in this role, Loet came to own two cinema houses, a bus service, motorcycle agency, the BMW dealership, a gas station, and several tracts of land. By the mid 1960s he was wealthy and well connected enough to be a political force. He became part of the "Chiang Mai Progress" group, led by Suriya-wong na Chiangmai, a descendant of the old Chiang Mai ruler, and Kraisri Nimmanhaeminda, a banker, intellectual, and the most prominent local figure of his generation (Rattaphong and Prajak 2003, 79). Loet was elected to the provincial council in 1967, became its president in 1968, and was elected MP for Chiang Mai in 1969. In the parliament he joined a group of non-party MPs who called themselves the Independent Party (*phak issara*) led by Kosol Krairiksh, a Bangkok financier and businessman. Most of the group were rising businessmen. Four had children or younger siblings who later entered politics and became ministers under Thaksin.[5] Loet was the party's deputy leader and then leader after Kosol resigned. The assembly disappeared when the military premier, General Thanom, performed a coup against his own government in 1971. When parliament was restored in 1975, Loet was elected MP again under the military-connected right-wing Chat Thai Party.

But at elections a year later, he stood aside and let his younger brother Suraphan assume the seat. Probably this was because Loet's fortunes had again dipped. Biographies mention only that he was "cheated" by a partner and lost all his assets except one cinema house and a small amount of land (Ariwat 2003, 91). Suraphan remained a Chiang Mai MP under the Chat Thai Party until 1988, and became deputy minister for transport and communications in 1986–8.

Loet's excursion into the coffee shop coincided with Thaksin's early schooling. As a result, Thaksin went to a nursery in a shabby *sala* of the local *wat* and started primary at the local school in Sankamphaeng. He helped his father in the coffee shop, and later in his cinema and other businesses. But in truth, the hard times were relatively brief. After just three years at primary school, Thaksin moved to Montfort College, one of Chiang Mai's most established, prestigious, and expensive schools, for the remainder of his primary and secondary schooling.[6] On finishing, he toyed with the idea of civil engineering like his uncle, but ultimately chose the military cadet school. He explains:

> Thirty years ago, the career that almost every Thai boy wanted to follow was in the armed forces or police. Apart from the glamour of the uniform and external appearance which I myself fell in love with, there was the admiration for men who were patriotic, self-sacrificing, strong, and full of fighting spirit. Also, the fact that the big people

Loet as an MP, Sujet as a municipal councilor

with power and influence in the society were all people in uniform made this the ideal career for Thai youth. (Thaksin 1999, 55)

After graduating from two years of cadet school in 1969, he had to choose in which service to complete his study. His father (now an MP) favored the army: "Like Field Marshal Praphat and Field Marshal Thanom.[7] They are army from the military staff college (*cho po ro*)." (Thaksin 1999, 57). But Thaksin explains that he "had little expectation of a future in government service," and did not want to follow his several Shinawatra cousins into the army. So he chose the police.

By his own account, at the Police Academy Thaksin hated learning law and other "uncreative" subjects. He wanted to quit, but his father dissuaded him. However, he enjoyed the physical training, the camaraderie, and especially the discipline. In his account of the earlier two years at cadet school, he noted, "the most impressive thing was that everyone had to respect those in command, and listen to those with seniority, without exception." At the Police Academy he discovered "the most valuable thing in my life," the motto for the armed forces invented by King Rama V: "1. Nothing is impossible; 2. death rather than defeat; 3. death rather than failure in duty. The path to pride and glory is not strewn with alluring fragrant flowers." (Thaksin 1999, 56, 59). In 1973 he graduated top of his class of ninety police cadets. He spent an uneventful six months attached to the Border Patrol Police before taking the scholarship granted for his top position to study an M.A. in criminal justice at Eastern Kentucky University in the US.

On his return to Thailand in 1975, his father had just been reelected MP for Chiang Mai along with Prida Patthanathabut from the same local faction (now called Santichon). Prida had been appointed minister in the Prime Minister's Office in Kukrit Pramoj's government. Prida immediately had Thaksin assigned to his staff. Although nominally a police guard, Thaksin worked more as a secretary. He wrote parliamentary speeches and helped in negotiations between the minister and student activists. He acted as bagman for the delivery of payments from the government's secret fund to ensure coalition partners voted the right way in house divisions: "I was used for collecting money from some big army figures, borrowing from certain ministers, and distributing the money to MPs and ministers whose 'hand' or vote the government needed." (Ariwat 2003, 103)[8] Later, he reflected:

> The politics I found twenty-five years ago was totally different from
> my past experience. This was the first time I realized that politics was
> about interest in a big way. Money was becoming a major factor in
> politics, and would gradually have a bigger and bigger role. (Thaksin
> 1999, 96)

After Kukrit's government fell in January 1976, Prida lost his ministerial post. Thaksin was assigned to a police station in Bangkok. In July, he married Pojaman Damaphong. He had met her in 1970 when she was a secondary school girl and the younger sister of Phongphet, a friend at the cadet school. She came from a rather well-established family with service connections. Her great-grandfather had come from Nong Khai and later settled in rural

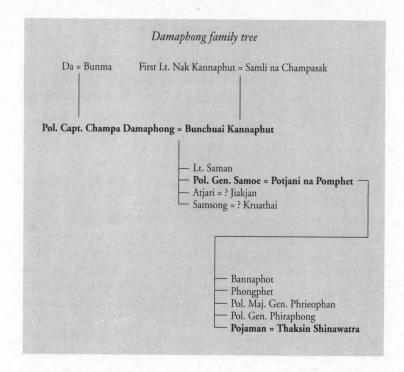

Damaphong family tree

Da = Bunma   First Lt. Nak Kannaphut = Samli na Champasak

Pol. Capt. Champa Damaphong = Bunchuai Kannaphut

— Lt. Saman
— **Pol. Gen. Samoe = Potjani na Pomphet**
— Atjari = ? Jiakjan
— Samsong = ? Kruathai

— Bannaphot
— Phongphet
— Pol. Maj. Gen. Phrieophan
— Pol. Gen. Phiraphong
— **Pojaman = Thaksin Shinawatra**

Chaiyaphum. His only son, Champa, entered the police, rose to the rank of captain, and married very well. His wife's father had been a general who led an army against the Lao state of Champasak in the late nineteenth century, and who married the sister of the Champasak ruler. Their daughter Bunchuai served as a royal lady-in-waiting in Bangkok before marrying Champa. The first son of Champa and Bunchuai became a naval lieutenant while the second, Samoe, entered the police. Samoe graduated from the cadet school in 1945 and rose rapidly through the ranks because of "an outstanding record for both suppression and investigation work." He married into the illustrious na Pomphet family, and put two of his own sons in the police (*Anuson* 1999, 58–9). By the time his youngest child, Pojaman, married Thaksin, Samoe was the police commander of Bangkok South (he would retire as the deputy director general).

By his own account, Thaksin tangled with his superiors at the police station who were running protection rackets for illegal businesses in their jurisdiction. His father-in-law had to intervene, and this incident prompted Thaksin's decision to take a Civil Service Commission scholarship for a doctorate in criminal justice at Sam Houston State University in Huntsville, Texas.

By this time, his father's fortunes were in another downturn. In Thaksin's account, both he and Pojaman had to work at various odd jobs in Huntsville (newspaper delivery, babysitting, fast food service) to supplement the scholarship. But they could still afford to buy an aging Mercedes, and ship it back to Thailand.

Thaksin's doctoral thesis begins from the fascinating question of why "criminal justice practioners" tend to break the law. The opening page reproduces press reports of police, judges, and jailers beating and otherwise abusing people. His research examines whether education may help. He tests whether studying criminal justice at Sam Houston State University improves the students' attitude to the rule of law. The answer, based on 860 questionnaires, is that it does, but only a very little bit (Thaksin 1979).[9]

Thaksin received his doctorate in May 1979. He had already returned to Thailand in 1978. He was put in charge of the police office of planning, and later moved to the police information collection center. In parallel, he also taught in various police educational institutions.

But these posts seemed to interfere little with a plunge into entrepreneurship. At first he did what he knew from family experience. He and Pojaman opened a silk shop at the Trocadero Hotel. But sales were abysmal and they had to close the shop within a month. Next he drew on his experience helping his father's cinemas. He bought the rights for distributing some Thai films in the provinces. After an initial success (with the hit film *Ban sai thong*), this business also languished. In 1979, he bought up an old cinema house in central Bangkok. When this failed, he tore down the cinema and converted it into apartments. This also failed. Pursued by angry clients and creditors, he had to downsize the project and then sell it off at a loss. By this time he was 200 million baht in debt.

In 1981 he started a business leasing IBM computers to government offices. His first clients were Chulalongkorn University and the State Railways. Over the next three years, the business expanded gradually to other government departments and state enterprises. His position improved but only slowly, and in 1984, he incurred a 19 million baht loss when the government devalued the baht. He was bailed out by the Thai Military Bank—a relationship which continued through his business career. In 1986, he drafted a plan for installing computers in the police information center, and then won the bid to implement his own plan (Sorakon 1993, 36–7). With this contract, the business began to grow. In the same year, he secured his first government telecommunications concession—to offer paging services in a joint venture with Pacific Telesis. In 1987, he resigned from the police with the rank of lieutenant colonel.

THE CONCESSIONS

> Politics and business are inseparable. We have to accept this reality. Politics is like the sun, and business like the earth. If the earth goes close, it will be too hot, and if it moves far away it will be too cold. But they are inseparable. (Interview, 22 March 1992)

Three interlocking developments made telecommunications a focus of business and political competition from the late 1980s onwards. First, from 1985 Thailand's economy accelerated and shifted towards industrialization and urbanization, creating a demand for much new infrastructure including telecommunications. Second, rapid changes in technology made possible a range of new products and services, and hence new business opportunities. Third, Thailand's political transition from military rule to parliamentary democracy created a fluid environment for competition over both power and profits.

Two government agencies oversaw telecommunications—the Communications Authority of Thailand (CAT) and the Telephone Organization of Thailand (TOT). During the years of military rule, generals occupied the heads of these and most other state agencies, and continued to defend their place in TOT and CAT into the 1980s on grounds that communications were a matter of national security. Both agencies reported to the Ministry of Transport and Communications. With its large budget for sophisticated equipment and infrastructure projects, the ministry had a reputation for corruption and was rated among the three most corrupt agencies in opinion surveys. Until the early 1980s, the ministership was also usually captured by military figures,[10] but from 1983 under "semi-democracy," elected politicians took the post. Originally CAT looked after external matters and TOT after internal matters, but the division was never precise and became more blurred with changes in technology. The competition between these bodies created opportunities for both politicians and businessmen. Meanwhile, the changing political background made telecoms a focus of negotiation between bureaucrats (civilian and military), elected politicians, and businessmen.

Elected ministers pushed for some liberalization and privatization of communications services on grounds of efficiency and speed, but also undoubtedly to get access to the corruption revenue on communications investments. The wrangling between the politicians on the one side, and CAT/TOT bureaucrats and their military patrons on the other, brought some of the internal workings of the ministry and its agencies into the light of day. Those involved talked to newspapers about the "consolidated TOT mafia," about executives who would "ask for material benefits from business directly without fears," and about attempts to buy positions in the agencies for many million baht (Sakkarin 2000, 149, 155).

This rivalry also created openings for private businessmen to gain part of the expanding telecom business. But to succeed, they had to operate in a political environment that was unstable. And they had to pay. While researching the book *Corruption and Democracy in Thailand* in the early 1990s, we asked Thaksin what the going rate was for kickbacks on projects. It is a measure of his openness that he replied that 10 percent was normal but could drop down to 3–5 percent on projects with a very large budget. He was of course talking generally, not in reference to any particular project, payee, or recipient.

The two agencies failed to keep up with the demand for telephone services. New subscribers had to wait ages or pay a large bribe to get a connection. As the economy accelerated in the mid 1980s, this shortfall rapidly worsened. In 1986, the elected minister of transport and communications (Samak Sundaravej) pushed the two agencies to open up new projects to private investment. The military heads of the agencies at first resisted fiercely, but were eventually persuaded that any benefits could be equitably shared. As a pioneer experiment, CAT invited bids for a build-transfer-operate (BTO) concession to offer paging services (CAT already provided paging services but could not meet the rising demand).

The US company, Pacific Telesis, was interested in becoming a supplier of hardware to the Thai telephone agencies. The company had earlier contacted IBM in Thailand, which passed them on to one of their dealers, Thaksin. When the paging concession was announced, Thaksin suggested this was an entry point. He did most of the work on their successful joint bid, but had only a small minority share in the venture (known by the brand name Paclink). Within months, Thaksin fell out with the partner. According to his version, he withdrew from the venture, but equally possibly he was eased out now his services as a contact man were no longer needed. He was still deeply in debt and looking, in his own words, for "something big to clean up all the old mess" (Thaksin 1999, 118).

Though he quit the Paclink venture, it convinced Thaksin of the potential of businesses based on wireless communications. He founded a company to start a cable TV service, and applied for a license from the Mass Communications Organization of Thailand (MCOT) which oversaw broadcasting, but repeatedly failed to get a positive response. He persuaded the Bangkok bus authority to license a system for broadcasting a radio channel to buses, but the sound quality was poor and the advertising demand low. He persuaded the police to license a pager-like system for people to make SOS calls, but there was no consumer interest. He floated a village radio service to CAT, which at the time was under his uncle

Suraphan as deputy minister of communications (Sorakon 1993, 45). None of these ventures succeeded.

In July 1988, the political system underwent one of the dramatic shifts of these transitional years. The military premier, General Prem Tinsulanond, stepped down. He was succeeded by Chatichai Choonhavan, the first elected occupant of the post since 1976. Chatichai set out to shift power away from the generals and bureaucrats towards elected politicians. The Communications Ministry was allotted to Montri Phongphanit, one of the most ambitious businessmen-politicians. The military heads of the two telecom agencies were replaced by more compliant technocrats, especially Paibun Limpaphayom at the head of TOT. Montri initiated many telecom projects himself, including data communications, a telephone project, and satellites. Chatichai created a young policy advisory team, headed by the former journalist, Pansak Vinyaratn, which advocated further liberalization of communications investments to increase efficiency and help make Thailand a leader in mainland Southeast Asia (Sakkarin 2000, 69–70).

In this environment, both CAT and TOT launched new concessions, often in competition with one another for the visible and invisible revenues. TOT offered a paging concession to compete with the Paclink venture. Both TOT and CAT solicited bids for mobile phone services (both had launched their own services earlier but could not keep up with demand). Thaksin won both the paging and mobile concessions from TOT, while Ucom, a company founded by former agents for Motorola equipment, won the CAT mobile phone concession. TOT gave its new paging service an advantage against the established Paclink service: it levied a charge from CAT/Paclink for each access to the landline telephone network which it controlled, while sparing its own concessionaire, Thaksin, from any equivalent charge. In addition, TOT allowed the subscribers to its own paging system to dial a three digit number, while those using Paclink had to dial seven.

The same vital advantage of the access charge was also built into the mobile phone concession. From the start, Ucom had either to charge its users a higher rate, or accept a lower profit and marketing budget. Ucom also believed that TOT biased the market in other ways, such as delaying installation of equipment needed for the CAT-TOT linkage (Sakkarin 2000, 172–3).

With these advantages, Thaksin dominated both the paging and mobile phone markets. With his technical advantages and some aggressive advertising, his Phonelink pager overtook Paclink in little more than one year. In the vastly more lucrative mobile phone segment, he benefited from a one-year first-mover advantage, and huge pent-up demand in the booming economy. Initially he thought he had underestimated the start-up costs and expected another bankruptcy. But within months the cash flow surpassed his wildest dreams. Lots of people wanted a phone. Under the duopoly, he could charge high prices and make a profit rate of 25 percent. With the built-in advantages of his TOT concession, he had twice as many subscribers and twice the revenues of Ucom. The profits were 445 million baht in 1992, and rose to 3 billion baht by 1995 (table 2.2). He was rich.

In all, the Chatichai government issued twenty-two telecom concessions over 1988–91 (table 2.1). Shinawatra won seven of them including card phones, data networks, and satellites (on which more below). Over the same period, Thaksin also finally gained the cable TV license when a friend and fellow ex-policeman, Chaloem Yubamrung, became deputy interior minister overseeing broadcasting. In a house no-confidence debate, Chaloem was arraigned for corruption over this deal. Thaksin also took over the contract for yellow- and white-page phone directories, originally subcontracted from AT&T, and then extended under the Shinawatra name. In addition, he helped to "arrange matters nicely" (Sorakon 1993, 41) between Minister Montri and the CP business conglomerate, which, as a result, won the largest ever infrastructure contract in Thai history to install 3 million landlines.

Between 1988 and 1991, Thaksin had been transformed from owner of a struggling computer leasing business into a major entrepreneur in government concessions, with a special relationship with TOT and the new politicians.

The earlier venture into computer leasing had not been in vain, as it had given Thaksin the vital experience in dealing with government agencies. Thaksin explained: "Because of my understanding of government rules and regulations which my competitors do not comprehend, I therefore have an edge over them in a bid" (Sakkarin 2000, 87–8). One of Thaksin's right-hand men explained that, "Thaksin knows lots of people" and "has no problem dealing with senior officials because he knows how to show respect" (Sorakon 1993, 83–4). His major competitors had similar backgrounds. Ucom had earlier been a supplier of hardware to the two telecom agencies. Its head, Bunchai Benjararongkun, noted: "Connections are always important . . . people open their doors to us when we knock." Adisai Bodharamik of Jasmine said: "I have good relations with TOT because I used to work there" (Sakkarin 2000, 76, 153).

Table 2.1 Shinawatra concessions, 1989–91

Concession	Company	Issuer	Date	Value (m. baht)	Length (years)
cable TV	IBC	MCOT	Mar 89		20
paging	Digital Paging Services*	TOT	19 Dec 89	200	15
datanet	Shinawatra Telecom	TOT	19 Sep 89	400	10
card phone	Advanced Info Service (AIS)	TOT	27 Mar 90	3000	20
mobile phone	AIS	TOT	27 Mar 90	3000	20
phone point	Fonepoint	TOT	30 May 90	965	10
satellite	Shinawatra Satellite	MOTC	11 Sep 91	6500	30

Source: Sakkarin 2000, 64   *later renamed Shinawatra Paging

In 1991, the political system underwent its next shift. In February, a clique of generals seized power by coup, citing the corruption of the Chatichai government as justification. To increase its own legitimacy, the military junta installed a former foreign service official, Anand Panyarachun, as prime minister. Anand brought several technocrats into his Cabinet and made "transparency" his watchword. In terms of the telecom concession business, this political shift created a very delicate situation involving two directly conflicting forces: Anand's technocrats and the junta generals.

Anand's team believed that more radical and transparent liberalization was needed in telecoms and other areas to increase efficiency and reduce corruption. Several figures in the former government were arraigned for being "unusually rich," including both of the ministers who had granted Thaksin key concessions—Montri and Chaloem. An investigating committee found them guilty of amassing 336.5 million baht and 32 million baht respectively while in office. The permanent secretary of the Communications Ministry, who had been a key figure in granting the TOT concessions, was one of three senior bureaucrats immediately transferred to an inactive position. Anand later also removed Paibun Limpaphayom from the headship of TOT. The huge landline contract, over which Thaksin had "arranged matters nicely" for CP, was recalled for investigation. The Shinawatra satellite concession was subjected to scrutiny. Anand's Cabinet passed an Act on Private Participation in State Economic Affairs in 1992 to "ensure transparency, consistency, and fairness in the privatization programmes, especially for large-scale concession projects" (Sakkarin 2000, 95). The Cabinet also drew up bills to abolish the monopoly power of TOT and CAT in order to stop the grant of monopolistic concessions which generated super-profits for businessmen and their patrons.

But while Anand pursued this housecleaning, the generals in the military junta had older and simpler ideas. They did not want to stop the concession business but rather gain control over it. They fought bitterly for the post of communications minister in the Cabinet, and settled finally for two deputy posts in this ministry. They resisted the investigations of past concession deals and almost ejected Anand over the CP landline contract (one of the junta member's close relatives was married into the CP family). The generals also blocked Anand's attempts to reform CAT and TOT, and sabotaged other reform measures by stonewalling inside the ministry and agencies. The Anand Cabinet then proposed to set up a national communications commission to act as a regulator, taking over many powers from TOT and CAT. The generals delayed this proposal until Anand's term came to an end with new elections. The two generals serving as deputy communications ministers hatched up a slew of new concessions and were trying to rush ten projects worth 5 billion baht through the Cabinet when the junta was felled by street demonstrations in May 1992 (Sakkarin 2000, 151).

Thaksin initially faced major difficulties because of the benefits he had received from the Chatichai Cabinet, and because of his relationship with Chaloem. Some army units threatened to revoke contracts with the Shinawatra computer business. Under grilling in parliament over the grant of the cable TV concession, Chaloem admitted that Thaksin was his "very good friend" (*phuean rak*) (Sorakon 1993, 90). Much more significant was the threat to the Shinawatra satellite contract.

CAT had invited bids for launching satellites since 1985 but without concluding any result. In September 1990, Montri opened a new bid. Thaksin competed against four other groups including one headed by the Thai-Hong Kong property entrepreneur, Khiri Kanchanapas. The Shinawatra bid offered government a higher guaranteed return and was approved by CAT and Montri in December. But Khiri challenged that the decision was unfair because his bid had offered the government free use of a transponder. He also intimated there had been corrupt dealing because Montri had signed the deal just one day before ceasing to be a minister.[11] A review board was appointed but the issue had not been resolved before the 1991 coup. Khiri appealed again to the junta. Eventually Thaksin was able to rescue the deal, but only by lobbying for almost two years, increasing the benefits offered to government, and agreeing that Shinawatra would have the exclusive right for only eight years rather than thirty. When the first satellite was launched in December 1993, Thaksin said: "I could not have this day without Big Jod," meaning General Sunthon Kongsompong, the head of the 1991 coup junta (quoted in *TN*, 28 March 2001).[12]

After the junta was felled and parliament restored, the pressure towards further liberalization had another lease of life. Anand briefly returned to power in mid 1992. He removed military figures from many old sinecures, and installed reformers in the boards of TOT and CAT. Liberalization and privatization remained on the agenda through the early 1990s. After long discussions, in 1995 the TOT board passed a resolution to move towards privatization within one year. But nothing came of this. Reality was that the business politicians were now firmly in control. In September 1992, Somsak Thepsuthin, a protégé of Montri, became deputy minister of communications. In 1993, he sacked the entire CAT board, removing Anand's appointees, and installing more pliant allies. TOT was compromised more gradually but no less effectively. Somsak returned to the vision of launching more grand projects on the justification of making Thailand a telecom center for the region.

In 1994, Thaksin upgraded his mobile phone concession to the new digital technology (as did Ucom). He ventured out into the region by extending the cable TV service into Laos and Cambodia, and winning mobile phone concessions in Laos, Cambodia, the Philippines, and Gujarat (India). He also moved into another form of concession business under the Communications Ministry. His family and businesses acquired around 10 percent of the shares in Bangkok Expressway Consortium Limited, which built and managed Bangkok's freeways (Ukrist 1998, 71–2). He gradually shed some of the less profitable ventures including the bus radio, peripheral phone services, and overseas cable ventures.

Most importantly, he launched the main businesses into the stock market. Listing such concessionaire companies required the permission of the Finance Ministry and involved another round of political lobbying. Shinawatra Computer was listed in 1990, Advance Info Services (AIS, mobile phones) in 1991, IBC cable TV in 1992, and Shinawatra Satellite in January 1994 (a month after the first launch). The stock market in this era was boosted by foreign inflows following financial liberalization. The index rose from 613 at the end of 1990 to 1683 three years later. With the added help of the high profit rates of the oligopoly concessions, the value of the listed Shinawatra companies, in Thaksin's own words, "soared upwards, multiplying in worth several times over" (Thaksin 1999, 126). The share price of AIS (adjusted for stock splits) multiplied eight times from 1991 to a peak in early 1996 (fig 2.1). In 1994, the Shinawatra companies' combined annual revenues were 25 billion baht, and their total asset value was 56 billion baht, or US$ 2.4 billion (table

Fig 2.1 Shinawatra stock prices, 1991–2004

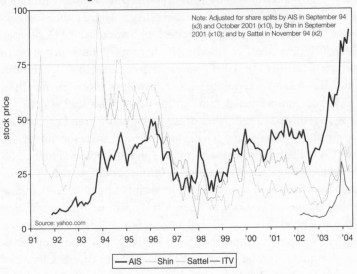

Note: Adjusted for share splits by AIS in September 94 (x3) and October 2001 (x10), by Shin in September 2001 (x10); and by Sattel in November 94 (x2)

Source: yahoo.com

— AIS — Shin — Sattel — ITV

Table 2.2 Shinawatra listed companies' results, 1992–1998 (baht million)

		1992	1993	1994	1995	1996	1997	1998
Shin	assets	10,796	18,863	30,398	39,907	45,339	59,900	57,788
	revenue	6,312	10,439	16,191	21,051	21,231	25,009	28,933
	profit	512	1,472	2,765	3,296	2,631	-5,644	-1,088
	market cap	22,730	60,984	75,953	85,932	42,966	17,464	16,632
AIS	assets	4,704	8,319	15,527	20,109	21,798	35,238	41,526
	revenue	1,891	3,862	6,478	10,551	13,315	15,575	17,284
	profit	445	949	1,545	2,994	3,563	2,523	2,966
	market cap	15,500	87,828	81,432	104,364	51,012	54,288	49,608
Satellite	assets	3,019	6,238	6,591	11,430	14,010	13,513	11,117
	revenue			379	1,787	2,098	2,620	4,317
	profit			-157	467	241	-4,495	1,835
	market cap			10,238	14,263	10,150	1,400	6,388
IBC	assets	1,385	1,813	3,460	3,539	2,561	4,186	7,970
	revenue	1,781	1,956	2,465	3,003	2,022	1,341	2,854
	profit	160	124	149	-331	-427	-1,320	-4,485
	market cap	4,176	19,512	9,636	3,103	2,884	1,993	12,778

Source: Company reports. Note: The 1998 figures here differ from those in Table 7.1 because the group was restructured. This table shows the reported figures for 1998. Table 7.1 shows the 1998 figures as they appear in the 1999 reports reworked for comparison with later years.

2.2). This value had virtually all been generated in just four years since the mobile phone business began generating cash flow.

In 1996, Thaksin began to rationalize the business structure by converting the old computer company into a holding company (renamed as Shinawatra Corporation in 1997). In 1995 and 1997, he launched two more satellites.

BUSINESS AND POLITICAL COMPETITION

> When we enter politics, everything is a loss. The only profit lies in doing something that challenges our abilities. If we succeed it makes us proud. We have a feeling of giving something back to the country, to the nation. That's the profit. But for sure, it's a loss of image, reputation, and cash—for sure. (Speech, 3 March 2002)

In the mid 1990s, the competitive situation of the telecom industry changed in two ways. First, multinational companies became more interested in acquiring a part of the rapidly growing business. They added their weight to the pressure for liberalization and privatization by lobbying through international forums and through the usual channels of economic diplomacy.

Second, and more pressingly, competition between the Thai companies in the segment increased. In the first phase of growth, a handful of companies shared out most of the opportunities. A "Big Four" emerged (Ukrist 1998, 2002, 2004). Shinawatra and Ucom shared most of the projects involving wireless transmission. Loxley/ Jasmine and TelecomAsia specialized in landlines. But by the mid 1990s, these dividing lines were increasingly transgressed. In particular, TelecomAsia and Shinawatra became rivals.

TelecomAsia was a venture by Thailand's largest business conglomerate, the Charoen Pokphand (CP) group. CP's foundations were in agribusiness but it had extended into many areas and by the mid 1990s had identified telecoms as its springboard into the future. The CP head, Dhanin Chiaravanont, said in 1991:

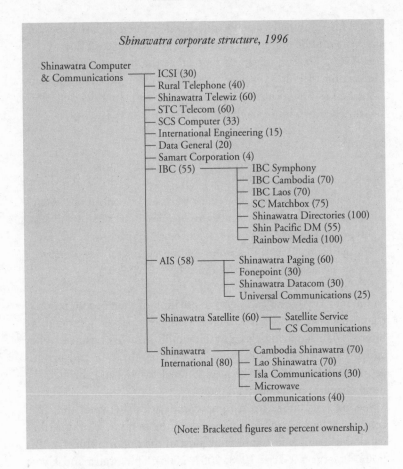

Shinawatra corporate structure, 1996

Shinawatra Computer & Communications
- ICSI (30)
- Rural Telephone (40)
- Shinawatra Telewiz (60)
- STC Telecom (60)
- SCS Computer (33)
- International Engineering (15)
- Data General (20)
- Samart Corporation (4)
- IBC (55)
  - IBC Symphony
  - IBC Cambodia (70)
  - IBC Laos (70)
  - SC Matchbox (75)
  - Shinawatra Directories (100)
  - Shin Pacific DM (55)
  - Rainbow Media (100)
- AIS (58)
  - Shinawatra Paging (60)
  - Fonepoint (30)
  - Shinawatra Datacom (30)
  - Universal Communications (25)
- Shinawatra Satellite (60)
  - Satellite Service
  - CS Communications
- Shinawatra International (80)
  - Cambodia Shinawatra (70)
  - Lao Shinawatra (70)
  - Isla Communications (30)
  - Microwave Communications (40)

(Note: Bracketed figures are percent ownership.)

Since I have been in business, I've found that no business is better than telephones because the investments get cheaper all the time as a result of more advanced technology. . . . We will apply the concept of full integration into the telephone business. . . . Soon our telephone business will be as successful as the poultry business or better. (Sakkarin 2000, 188)

Thaksin claimed to have helped CP secure its 3-million-landline contract in 1990, but was then angered when CP failed to buy the AT&T equipment for which Shinawatra was agent. When the 3-

million-line contract was trisected by the Anand government, Thaksin bid for one of the portions against CP. He failed, but had clearly announced a rivalry (Thaksin 1999, 132; Sorakon 1993, 86).

By entering into the business of telecom concessions, Thaksin had also entered into the world of politics because the grant of the concessions and the details of their benefits were decided by political processes. In the 1980s, such politics were mostly a matter of relationships and money transfers with the civilian and military bureaucracy. But over the 1988–92 transition, the military was largely removed from the picture, and politicians rose greatly in importance. Thaksin kept up his bureaucratic connections. He hired Paibun Limpaphayom after Anand removed him from TOT under a cloud, and poached the electrical engineer, Boonklee Plangsiri, from CAT (Ariwat 2003, 207–8). But he and other telecom players moved decisively towards the new world of parliamentary politics. And politics moved towards telecoms. The 1992 Chuan Leekpai Cabinet had no fewer than five ministers (one full, four deputies) in the Ministry of Communications. So did the two following Cabinets of Banharn Silpa-archa and Chavalit Yongchaiyudh. No party wanted to be left out.

The telecom companies became roughly aligned with political parties. Efforts by the companies to improve existing concessions or gain new ones became one element of political competition. CP TelecomAsia was close to the New Aspiration Party; Ucom aligned to the Democrat Party; and the Loxley group floated between the Democrats and Chat Thai Party. These relationships were located in the shady background of the political world. But Thaksin was emerging as both the biggest player in the telecom segment, and the most ambitious exponent of the sector's relationship with politics. He stepped across the line dividing business and politics.

In November 1994, Thaksin joined the Cabinet as foreign minister under the ministerial quota of the Phalang Tham (moral force) Party. On first sight, this party was a strange choice. Its leader, Chamlong Srimuang, was a former soldier who had become a lay Buddhist ascetic. In 1985, he won election as Bangkok mayor on an anti-corruption platform, and gained reelection by a landslide in 1990. In 1992, Chamlong opposed the military junta in parliamentary elections and led the street demonstrations that brought the junta down. Thaksin was hardly in tune with Chamlong's anti-military crusade. Moreover, while Thaksin's career to date had been single-mindedly dedicated to the pursuit of wealth, Chamlong and the adherents of the fringe Buddhist Santi Asoke sect, who formed a "temple wing" inside the party, adopted an aggressively frugal lifestyle. Besides, the party was already in a state of decay because of Chamlong's fading luster and revealed lack of administrative skill (McCargo 1997).

But Thaksin along with several other rich new-generation Bangkok businessmen were attracted to Chamlong because of his repudiation of old-style politics and his stance against bureaucratic corruption. It was probably also no coincidence that the Ministry of Communications came under the Phalang Tham's quota of Cabinet posts. At the same time as Thaksin joined the Cabinet, his friend, the banker Vichit Suraphongchai, became minister of communications under Phalang Tham. According to press analyses of the time (*Phuchatkan*, 25 November 1995), Thaksin hoped to use this connection to extend the scope of his concessions—particularly by gaining more numbers for his mobile phone network.

But Thaksin's entry into Phalang Tham increased the party's internal division. A large group opposed the appointment of outsiders to Cabinet posts. A powerful party figure, Prasong Soonsiri, charged that Thaksin should be constitutionally debarred from the Cabinet because his companies were state concessions.[13] Largely as a result of this internal turmoil, only six months later the Phalang Tham Party withdrew from the coalition and forfeited its hold on the Communications Ministry (McCargo 1997, 296–7; Thaksin 1999, 166). Chamlong partially retired from politics, handing the leadership of Phalang Tham to Thaksin.

At elections in July 1995, Thaksin stood in a central Bangkok constituency, projecting himself as a modern high-tech business-man. He easily topped the polls (table 2.3).

The Chat Thai Party of Banharn Silpa-archa headed the coalition formed after the election. Phalang Tham was deeply divided over whether it should join a Cabinet headed by such a figure. Thaksin strongly backed joining the Cabinet and prevailed over the "temple

Table 2.3. July 1995 Election, Bangkok Constituency 2*, 3 MPs

1.	Thaksin Shinawatra	Phalang Tham	68,831
2.	Supachai Panitchapakdi	Democrat	48,796
3.	Orathai Kanchanachusak	Phalang Tham	45,542

*Including Phranakhon, Pomphrap, Satruphai, Pathumwan, Sampanthawong and Bangrak districts. Among the losers were: Marut Bunnag (Democrat), Suranand Vejjajiva (Phalang Tham), Ong-art Klampaiboon (Democrat), Sukhumbhand Paribatra (Nam Thai)

wing" (Thaksin 1999, 177). He became deputy prime minister (a conventional post for leaders of minor parties in a coalition) with a special assignment to solve Bangkok's traffic problems. Shinawatra managed to get its mobile phone concession extended from twenty to twenty-five years, and its revenue sharing with government marginally reduced (Ucom gained parallel improvements). But the New Aspiration Party (NAP) controlled the Communications Ministry, put its placemen in TOT, and seemed to favor Shina-watra's rival, TelecomAsia.

After NAP rose to head a new Cabinet coalition in 1996, TelecomAsia and TT&T both won concessions to launch new mobile phone services in direct competition with Shinawatra.[14] NAP's leader, General Chavalit Yongchaiyudh, floated plans for the army to launch a satellite and for the Veterans Organization to run yet another mobile phone network.[15] Two executives of Thaksin's direct rival, Ucom, were drafted into Chavalit's Cabinet.[16] The enormous profits from telecom concessions had attracted both business and political entrepreneurs who threatened Shinawatra's dominance.

Thaksin did not stand for reelection at the polls in November 1996 "because the political atmosphere is not good" (*TN*, 30 September 1996). He tried to resign the Phalang Tham leadership but was dissuaded. At the polls, the party was reduced to a single MP (Sudarat Keyuraphan). Even so, Thaksin was drafted back as deputy prime minister in 1997, but only for the last three confused months before the Chavalit government fell in November. His political achievements to date—three brief spells as a minister, and the destruction of a political party—were not promising.

In the Bangkok Post 1995 election special, cartoonist Nop puts Thaksin in a satellite.

Besides this rising competition, the threats of liberalization and regulation also loomed closer. Earlier, the Thai government had agreed to join the international Negotiating Group on Basic Telecommunications, which in February 1997 concluded an agreement to open up national telecom markets to free competition. Thailand also signed the GATS and WTO agreements, committing the country to liberalization of service industries including telecoms by 2006. In late 1997, the Cabinet finally agreed on a telecommunications master plan that had been drafted and redrafted several times over the past three Cabinets. The master plan proposed the privatization of TOT and CAT, establishment of an independent regulatory authority (mandated by the 1997 constitution), consumer protection, and liberalization of the industry in line with international commitments. All this was to begin in October 1999 (Sakkarin 2000, 107, 126). To add to these troubles, the stock market, whose rise had multiplied Thaksin's worth, had begun to plummet.

Thaksin's concession-based business empire, built on political foundations, was under increasing political threat. Thaksin was saved by the nation's worst ever economic crisis.

CRISIS

> But I dare to state that Shinawatra was hurt much less by this crisis
> when compared to rival companies in the same field. (Autobiography,
> 1998–9)

On 2 July 1997, the Thai government unpegged the baht from its fixed exchange rate around 25 baht to a US dollar. This followed a series of attacks on the baht by international speculators, spurred by signs that the Thai economy had become badly distorted and the currency vulnerable. The Bank of Thailand's attempts to defend the baht against these speculative attacks had sacrificed most of the country's currency reserves, forcing the government to seek help from the IMF. As a condition of its help in raising a US$17.2 billion loan, the IMF insisted that the Thai government unpeg the currency and reveal the state of the reserves. Short-term capital stampeded out of the country, and the baht plummeted to a low of 53 baht to the dollar in early 1998.

Any company that had borrowed loans in foreign currency and failed to protect them by hedging now found that its indebtedness more than doubled. As foreign loans had been available at much lower rates than baht loans over the previous five years, most companies had acquired some foreign debt. Many companies were technically bankrupt. As the creditors also demanded quick repayment, many became illiquid too. And as the shock sent the whole economy into a nosedive, business revenue and profits also declined away.

All the telecom companies had raised funds through the stock market, but like other corporations, they had also been seduced by low interest foreign loans, and were badly hit by the baht fall. But the Shinawatra group lost much less than its rivals. According to the group's own figures, the exchange losses in 1997 were 26.1 billion baht for CP TelecomAsia, 11.1 billion for Jasmine, 17.7 billion for Ucom, and only 1.1 billion for Shinawatra (Ariwat 2003, 159). The liabilities of Shinawatra companies increased in 1997, but much less than those of the two major rivals, TelecomAsia and Ucom (see table 2.4). Thaksin claimed that the Shinawatra companies suffered less than competitors because they had hedged their foreign loans six months before the baht was floated (Ariwat 2003, 159). But some have suspected that other reasons came into play. At the time of the float, Thanong Bidaya was finance minister.[17] Thanong had arranged Thaksin's first loans from Thai Military Bank (TMB) in 1986, and joined Shinawatra as financial overseer for 1989–92, before returning to TMB as president. He was Thaksin's foremost financial adviser and had been a director of Shinawatra companies. He was part of the decision made to float the baht, a week before it was announced. In a parliamentary no-confidence debate a few months later, Bokhin Polakun, who also

Table 2.4. Total liabilities of telecom companies (million baht), 1996–2002

	1996	1997	1998	1999	2000	2001	2002
AIS	10,974	23,373	26,751	18,339	31,045	72,517	74,844
Shinawatra Satellite	8,270	12,927	8,692	6,860	7,594	8,581	13,103
Shinawatra Corporation	27,117	50,800	46,607	11,006	17,775	17,398	20,191
TelecomAsia	62,304	94,415	85,346	86,020	79,757	81,577	86,049
TT&T	30,595	48,453	44,878	44,339	47,726	34,357	32,681
Jasmine	12,784	19,871	20,440	21,743	19,382	17,009	16,129
Ucom	48,740	101,787	79,455	68,178	15,070	13,108	13,130

Source: Ukrist (2004) using company reports.

attended the meeting as an adviser, was accused of leaking the news to Thaksin. He denied it. In 2004, Thaksin made him minister of interior (*TN*, 2 July 2001; *KT*, 27 September 1997).[18]

Some Shinawatra companies made large losses in 1997 and 1998 because of the general economic downturn (table 2.2). But the group was much more lightly affected than its rivals, and indeed than most other major Thai corporations. Most business groups were obliged to sell off some assets to survive, and some were reduced to a fraction of their former worth and size. But Shinawatra disposed of only a few minor projects. It reduced its share in the directories business, delayed the fourth Thaicom satellite, and sold off its overseas ventures in India and the Philippines. Its major adjustment was to sell a stake of around 20 percent in AIS to Singapore Telecom, but this amounted to a strategic partnership as much as a cash generating maneuver.[19]

Rivals fared much worse. Ucom and TelecomAsia floundered. Two new rival mobile phone systems that were close to launching when the crisis struck disappeared. A rival satellite project went the same way. For other reasons, the Iridium global satellite network, in which CP TelecomAsia had taken a share in the hope of gaining some technological advantage, was aborted.

The three listed Shinawatra companies still made a narrow profit in 1998, and then a substantial profit in 1999 (see table 7.1). Armed with such figures, they were able to raise funds from the stock market by offering new shares at a time when few other companies could hope to succeed in such a tactic. The group even had enough cash to take over a digital phone project from Samart, and consider a bid for some of TT&T's business.

Because of its limited damage from the baht devaluation, the Shinawatra group emerged from the crisis much stronger than its rivals in the telecom sector, and much stronger than most Thai business groups. In June 2001, Thaksin made his first appearance on the Forbes list of the world's richest people, ranked 421st with an estimated worth of US$1.2 billion (*Forbes*, 9 June 2001).

CONCLUSION

> I believe politics is a huge burden. Every Thai should make the
> sacrifice to participate. And someone like me should make the
> greatest sacrifice to participate in politics since I have the knowledge,
> the economic standing, and the management experience.
> (Autobiography, 1998–9)

Thaksin has mythologized his life story as poor boy made good with
shades of the "pillow and mat" tales of a migrant who arrives with
nothing and succeeds by hard work, sacrifice, and daring. Certainly
his family went through some bad patches because of his father's
wayward business career. But, in truth the Shinawatra family saga
over four generations is more interesting as part of the transformation of Thailand's urban society and culture over a century.

The Sae Khu/Shinawatra clan accumulated through three stages,
which reflected the changing economy and society over a century:
first, through tax farming under the old royal state; second, by
developing the silk business to supply the tastes of the new national
bureaucrats; and third, by adding finance, construction, and property
in the era of urban development. By the inter-war years, the family
was dispatching children to France, Germany, and Japan to get new
skills and technology. As the family became more established, it
spread out from commerce into the professions with status and
power, especially the army. By the time of Thaksin's birth, the
Shinawatra were a relatively long-settled, highly successful, very
well-connected, politically prominent family in Chiang Mai's new
commercial elite. Thaksin's progress through the best local schools,
the military academies, political apprenticeship, and marriage to a
powerful general's daughter belongs not to the "pillow and mat"
legend but to a more universal theme about the arrival of a new
bourgeoisie.

Thaksin entered the police, but in fact his career from the start
was in the twin fields of politics and business. His success arose from
his ability to synergize the two. His first success came from an
exclusive contract secured through personal connections. The

legendary version of his business success stresses his persistence and his flare for risk taking. To these should be added his understanding that political regulation of business is the source of abnormal rates of profit. Since he secured a computer contract from his own department in the police, he has understood what works.

The fortune Thaksin made over five years beginning in 1990 was quite extraordinary. The booming economy, and the state's abysmal failure to expand either landline or mobile networks had created enormous unfulfilled demand. The monopolistic concession structure allowed the new mobile suppliers to charge high prices with enormous profit margins. The TOT constructed a built-in market advantage for Thaksin because it suited them in their competition with CAT. Finally, the stock market, pumped up by financial liberalization and a worldwide enthusiasm for "emerging markets," translated the high profits into even higher net worth.

His enormous success inevitably inspired rivalry. Competitors understood that Thaksin's success was grounded on political links, and hence competition was as much political as commercial. Thaksin—and his rivals—were pulled deeper into politics by the nature of their business and by the logic of intensifying competition.

3

POLITICAL RISE

In late 1997, Thaksin was a very rich businessman whose foray into politics seemed to be going nowhere. Just over three years later he became prime minister with greater electoral support than any previous incumbent. His party was new, and his electoral campaign had been innovative. He also faced the possibility of being the first prime minister removed from office by legal process for corruption.

Thaksin's rise to power was framed by the 1997 economic crisis and by the new 1997 constitution. In different ways, these two factors rang down the curtain on the political system that had developed over the prior two decades. The crisis wrecked the Democrat Party, the most successful political party of the 1990s, and thus created a vacuum that Thaksin was able to fill. The crisis also stirred a greater interest in politics by many groups in society; Thaksin and his advisers were able to channel this interest into support for their party. The constitution changed the electoral system in ways that favored a business-based party. Above all, the constitution and the crisis created an expectation for something novel that Thaksin could promise to fulfill. Even a prominent radical welcomed him as "a breath of fresh air" (Kasian 2002, 339).

FROM MORAL FORCE TO LOVING THAIS

All this thinking has a single purpose: to lead Thailand to survive amid globalization and world capitalism by being able to compete. (Autobiography, 1998–9)

Thaksin's forays into the political arena between 1994 and 1997 had not achieved much success in the public eye. His three spells as a minister had each been too short to make much impression. As deputy prime minister in the Banharn Cabinet, he carelessly gave the impression that he had vowed to solve Bangkok's traffic problems within six months—and was constantly taunted for failing in this impossible task. His decision to enter the Phalang Tham Party resulted in the party's destruction. Under Chamlong's original leadership, Phalang Tham had stood for a cleaner and more principled politics. But in the public mind, Thaksin was a concession hunter associated with some of the most flagrant "money politicians" (Montri, Chaloem), and with the corrupt and discredited 1991–2 coup junta. His leadership widened the division and public bickering in the party. In 1996 many party members left, and the Bangkok electorate punished the party by denying Chamlong a third term as Bangkok mayor, and reducing the party to a single MP at the parliamentary elections. "In effect," concludes Duncan McCargo (1997, 299), "Thaksin had—in the space of twelve months—destroyed the bulk of the political 'credit' built up by Chamlong and Phalang Tham over eleven years of hard work in the capital."

Thaksin describes it a little differently. He expresses his admiration for Phalang Tham's "ideology" (which he does not attempt to define), but claims he found the party disorganized and backward looking. It could not "adjust its thinking to keep up with the modern world" (Thaksin 1999, 186). After leaving the party in the wake of the 1996 election defeat, Thaksin relates that he spent the following months traveling throughout the country, consulting academics and local leaders, and applying "scientific thinking" to the search for a new political paradigm.

His conclusions from this search are set out in the two final chapters of his autobiography. These chapters amount to his "first political testament." His ideas at this stage were strongly influenced by the experience of the 1997 economic crisis.

The world, Thaksin argued, was changing rapidly because of technology, free trade, the trend towards regionalism, environmentalism, and the coming of the information society. Thailand's politics needed to change "to prepare ourselves to cope with globalization and the international political system which is increasingly ruthless with developing countries" (Thaksin 1999, 230). But Thailand was bedeviled by "professional politicians" that needed to make an income from their jobs and hence defended their positions by attacking enemies with slander and other dirty methods. This system favored people that were good at dirty politics rather than management.

The old "destructive politics" of competition had to give way to a new "creative politics" in which factionalism is replaced by cooperation, and good people are not discouraged from entering politics by exposure to dirty political infighting. Then political leaders would be able to manage the country efficiently to achieve the goal of competitiveness in the world. In addition, "Because one weakness of the nation is a tendency to prioritize law as a way to solve problems, management principles should be used instead and law treated as only one supporting element" (Thaksin 1999, 231).

What is striking in retrospect about this initial political testament is what is missing. There is no social analysis except for a passing mention of Thailand's wide social division in half a line. There is no social agenda except for one brief general commitment "to bring happiness to the majority of the country." Instead, the single-minded focus is on "enabling Thailand to keep up and be competitive with other countries" so it can "face the next century with strength" (Thaksin 1999, 211).

Thaksin launched the Thai Rak Thai Party on 14 July 1998. The party had twenty-three founding members (table 3.1). Five were former members of Phalang Tham. Two were big property developers (Phanloet and Wirachai). The rest were mostly academics, officials, and retired officials. Thaksin initially set the party's ambitions rather low. He expected little change in the political environment after the next election, and described the party's main goal as overcoming the crisis: "Although the Thai Rak Thai Party has no chance to run the country, I'll consider the party successful if it can push the present government to adopt its proposals…. It is more important to tackle woes than to compete for state power" (*TN*, 25 July 1998). Thaksin was also not at this stage opposed to the IMF-mandated strategy for managing the crisis. Two weeks after the party foundation he said the Democrat government was on the right track in tackling the economy (*BP*, 27 July 1998).

Three of the party founders were of special significance for the evolution of the party's stance. They also trace Thaksin's expanding political network over past years.

Table 3.1 Founding members of the Thai Rak Thai Party

	Background	Later role in TRT
Dr Karun Jantharangsu	Bangkok municipality	
Dr Kitti Limskul	academic economist, Chulalongkorn	adviser
Dr Kantathi Suphamongkhon	bureaucrat, MP, Phalang Tham	MP
Dr Kanit na Nakhon	lawyer, ex-Attorney General	
Narong Patthamasewi	financier	
Police Lt Col Dr Thaksin Shinawatra	police, business, Phalang Tham	
Gen. Thammarak Issarangkura na Ayutthaya	career army	MP, minister
Dr Tiraphat Serirangsan	academic (politics)	
Prachuap Ungphakorn	Bangkok municipality	MP
Dr Pracha Gunakasem	bureaucrat (foreign service)	
Prasit Mahamat	lawyer, Bangkok municipality	
Purachai Piumsombun	police, NIDA, Phalang Tham	MP, minister
Paphasara Trangkininak	student	
Pansak Vinyaratn	journalist	adviser
Phanloet Baiyok	real estate, Phalang Tham sponsor	
Phuwanida Khunpalin	insurance, women's business association	MP
Dr Wiriya Namsiphongphan	academic lawyer, Thammasat	
Dr Wirachai Wiramethikun	real estate, CP in-law	MP
Dr Somkid Jatusripitak	academic, NIDA	MP, minister
Dr Sirikorn (Linutaphong) Manirin	academic, auto business	minister
Dr Suwan Valaisathian	tax lawyer	minister
Sutham Saengpathum	activist, MP, Phalang Tham	MP, minister
Dr Samran Phu-anantanan	businessman (Samsung)	

Source: Founder list from www.thairakthai.or.th

Purachai Piumsombun met Thaksin at the Police Academy. In parallel with Thaksin, he went to the US on police scholarships to get an M.A. from Michigan State University and Ph.D. in criminal justice from Florida State University in 1979 with a thesis on "A theory of job attitudes in policing: its empirical test in Thailand." He resigned from the police two years later and went to teach at the National Institute of Development Administration (NIDA), a graduate university, where he eventually rose to become rector. In a 1983 article, he described how the police systematically collected money from bribes and protection fees, and how these funds were distributed for both private gain and to supplement inadequate police budgets (Purachai 1983). He met up with Thaksin again as an admirer of Chamlong and a part-time helper in the Phalang Tham Party.

Phalang Tham and NIDA were two of the secondary nodes of Thaksin's network. Phalang Tham brought together military and police figures, especially those clustered around Chamlong and his Class Seven from the military academy, along with several rising Bangkok entrepreneurs, including the property developers, Anant Asvabhokin and Phanloet Baiyok. Many of these followed Thaksin from PDP to TRT. Meanwhile both Purachai and Thaksin's financial adviser, Thanong Bidaya, were prominent figures at NIDA. Through them Thaksin met Somkid Jatusripitak, a rising lecturer in business and marketing.

Somkid came from a very modest Chinese-origin family, and studied in a Chinese primary school and a Bangkok commercial college. He was a brilliant student and made his way to a doctorate from the Kellogg Institute at Northwestern University. He returned to teach in business and marketing at Thammasat and NIDA, and write on marketing topics, often published by Sondhi Limthongkun's Manager group. He also became adviser to the stock exchange and to several firms, including the Sahapat consumer goods empire (Ariwat 2004, 10–12). In the mid 1990s, he served as secretary to Thaksin during two of his spells as minister, and also to Thanong Bidaya and his own elder brother Som (head of Siam City Bank) when they held ministerial posts. His academic work focused on competitiveness. While at Northwestern, he worked with Philip Kotler on *The New Competitiveness* (1985) about Japanese company strategy. Later he adapted Michael Porter's study of *Competitive Strategy: Techniques for Analyzing Industries and Competitors* (1998) into Thai, and collaborated again with Kotler on *The Marketing of Nations* (1997). The latter book advocated applying business school techniques of corporate management to national economies:

> If the focus here was a business firm instead of a nation, we would call this methodology strategic market management. We wish to take the view that a nation can be thought of as running a business and, as such, can benefit from adopting a strategic market management approach. This is not to ignore the much greater cultural and political complexity of running a nation. . . . Strategic market management is a continuous self-correcting process that consistently considers where a nation is heading, where it wants to be heading, and how best it can get there. (Kotler et al. 1997: ix)

Somkid's own articles were collected under the title *Borisat prathet thai* meaning "Thailand Company." Through Somkid and his association with the Manager group, Thaksin developed a link to Pansak Vinyaratn and another network node among political activists.

Pansak Vinyaratn had been head of the "Ban Phitsanulok" policy advisory team during the Chatichai Cabinet of 1988–91. His father, starting from poor Bangkok origins, had made a brilliant bureaucratic career, before being drafted into the Bangkok Bank group and making the family fortune. Pansak was educated at the London School of Economics, then became famous as a journalist in the 1970s period. He was arrested in 1976, but escaped to the US through connections. On return to Thailand in 1981, he briefly revived the *Chaturat* magazine, and started dabbling in computers. He became head of the Chatichai policy team through friendship with Chatichai's son, Kraisak. After the NPKC coup, he fled over-seas again for a time, and returned to run computer-related busi-nesses before being recruited by the expansive media entrepreneur,

Sondhi Limthongkun. He worked for Sondhi's Manager group, particularly as editor of *Asia Times*, Sondhi's ambitious attempt to found a regional English-language newspaper. Sondhi was toying with the idea of a satellite venture when his financially overextended group was wrecked by the 1997 economic crisis. The *Asia Times* disappeared, and soon after Pansak fell in with Thaksin. Several other members of the Ban Phitsanulok team subsequently came to work with Thaksin.

Purachai became secretary general of the party and oversaw management of the election campaign. Pansak supervised development of the party's platform and the marketing of the new party. Somkid helped craft the party's economic policies, and also used Kotler's ideas on "political marketing" to orchestrate the campaign.[1]

Another node of the network developed among participants in the student radicalism of the 1970s who had fled to the communist bases in the jungles after the Thammasat massacre in October 1976. These were not a group as such, but were recruited by Thaksin individually by very different routes. The key figure was Phumtham Vejjayachai, a former Chulalongkorn University activist, who had met Thaksin when Thaksin was working as a ministerial aide in 1975–6. Phumtham returned from the jungle to work in NGOs, before switching to a Japanese garment business. He remained interested in politics and worked for several politicians before attaching himself to Thaksin at Phalang Tham. Thaksin hired him into the Shinawatra companies in 1996. He arranged the 1999 autobiography of Thaksin, worked on party publicity, and became the party's deputy secretary general. Praphat Panyachatrak, another student radical in the 1970s, had become an orchard farmer, and was recruited to help formulate rural policies (see below). Surapong Seubwonglee was one of several medical students from Mahidol University swept up in the 1976 events. On return from the jungle, he completed his medical education and worked in hospital administration before being attracted away to business and taking an MBA degree. Phrommin Lertsuridej followed a similar route, returning from the jungle in 1980 to finish at Mahidol, spending several years as a government doctor and health ministry official, before being recruited into the Shinawatra companies by Pojaman in 1993 (*TN*, 4 and 14 October 2002). Kriengkamon Laohapairot, another former student activist, also helped TRT contact activist groups.

These ex-radicals helped to articulate TRT's social agenda. They gave Thaksin a tinge of legitimacy with journalists and activists from the same generation. According to some, this shows that "Thai politics may not be a matter of left and right, but statist and anti-statist. . . . These are people who believe all along that state power can solve all problems" (Kasian 2004).

THAKSIN AND BIG BUSINESS

We have just come out of the Cold War between communism and the free world. From here onwards it will be an economic war, and no less brutal. In the past, countries were seized as colonies by using gunboats and troops. . . . Nowadays the mode of warfare has changed. It is about the movement of capital and the use of technology for economic competition. It is not territory that is seized but the economy. . . . And from 2000 onwards, this war will be more violent. (Speech, 23 August 1998)

Over the two years following its foundation, the TRT Party became a magnet for some major business leaders who had suffered greatly from the crisis and yet survived (Ukrist 2002). As a result of the crisis, leading businessmen saw the need to participate more actively in politics to avoid being "globalized into bankruptcy" (Kasian 2002, 327).

In the telecoms sector, the sharpening rivalries of recent years were at least temporarily restrained by the need to survive the crisis. In February 1998, Shinawatra and CP announced they were merging their cable TV companies. Cable TV was small compared to their other businesses, but the two companies had been engaged in a fierce marketing war, and hence the merger had great symbolic significance. Shortly after, Thaksin sold his share in the merged company to CP.

Dhanin, the head of CP, later endorsed Thaksin for premier by emphasizing the need for Thailand's businessmen, in the wake of the crisis, to draw on the power and protection of the state: "This is an age of economic war. It's crucial that we have a prime minister who understands business and the economy" (*BP*, 31 October 2000). One of the TRT founding members (Wirachai) was Dhanin's son-in-law. A CP executive (Viraphon Sarasin) was also expected to be on the list but withdrew at the last moment. Pitak Intarawitayanunt, who served as a political ambassador of the CP group, joined the TRT Party and later became a Cabinet member. Wattana Muang-suk, a son-in-law of Dhanin's brother, also became a TRT MP and a Cabinet minister in 2003. Adisai Bodharamik, head of another of the "Big Four" telecom companies, Jasmine, also joined TRT.

Bankers were also drawn to the new party. The Thai Military Bank and its leading executive, Thanong Bidaya, were by now very closely associated with Thaksin. Chatri Sophonpanich, head of Bangkok Bank (the largest bank), explained that he supported Thaksin as prime minister "because as a businessman, he understands business" (*TN*, 28 November 2000).

Next came property developers and construction companies whose businesses were among the worst hit by the crisis. M. Thai was connected through founding member, Wirachai. Anant Asvabhokin, head of the Land and Houses group, one of the largest housing developers, was a long-standing friend of Thaksin. Along with Phanloet Baiyok, builder of Bangkok's tallest building, and Sudarat Keyaruphan, another property developer, Anant was a former supporter of Phalang Tham. The Srivikorn family, whose property empire was badly savaged by the crisis, also moved into the orbit of the new party. Italthai, one of the two largest Thai construction companies, was drawn to the new party, perhaps in reaction to the fact that its rival (Ch. Karnchang) had been more successful in getting major public sector contracts from the last two or three Cabinets.

Another sector that became associated with Thai Rak Thai was media and entertainment. Pracha Maleenont belonged to the family that ran TV Channel 3 on a concession from the government. Paiboon Damrongchaitham was head of the Grammy group, which had begun as a music company but branched out into other forms of entertainment (e.g., TV program production) as well as education-related ventures such as textbook publishing. Sondhi Limthongkun, whose expansive Manager group had crashed badly in the crisis, also became a fervent supporter of Thaksin.

Few manufacturing businessmen counted among the Thai Rak Thai supporters. One major exception was Suriya Jungrungruang-kit, whose family had the largest auto parts business (Summit), and a special association with Toyota. Another was Prayuth Mahakitsiri, who had interests in steel, mining, and food products. The liquor tycoon, Charoen Siriwattanapakdi, was associated with the party but remained in the background.

There had not been such a concentration of leading Bangkok businessmen involved directly and openly in party politics (and later in the Cabinet) since the early 1980s. Partly they had been squeezed out over the 1980s when provincial bosses learned how to manipulate elections. Partly they had not seen the necessity of taking a direct role in politics. Their return was motivated by the economic crisis. It was made possible by the party list system introduced by the 1997 constitution as a way to increase the representation of "national" (i.e., Bangkok) interests against the provinces. An extra one hundred seats were added to parliament, elected on a vote by party, with seats distributed proportional to the vote to parties that secured at least 5 percent of votes cast. Candidates did not have to campaign, just get listed on the party's slate. Adisai, Sudarat, Pitak, Pracha, Suriya, Prayuth, and Wirachai all entered parliament in 2001 through the TRT party list where they were positioned 5, 6, 8, 10, 12, 27, and 48.

The companies they headed were among the survivors of the crisis. Often they had come through the experience with considerable difficulty. CP had sold off many ancillary businesses, both in Thailand and China. Bangkok Bank had increased foreign ownership from 25 to 49 percent, and downsized. But in the aftermath, the survivors were in some ways strengthened (Hewison 2000). Many of their competitors had disappeared. Many dominant conglomerates of the pre-crisis period had been crippled, making space for new leaders. The Maleenont family had not earlier been placed in the front rank of conglomerates, yet in 2000 it had the largest family holding of shares on the stock exchange (*MR*, 19 December 2000; Hewison 2001). When the property market revived in 2002, Land and Houses became a much more dominant market leader than before.

Many of these firms were in service industries. Several domestic conglomerates based in manufacturing had either been squeezed out by the influx of foreign capital in the late 1980s, or bought out in the crisis. But some service industries still enjoyed state protection in various ways. The telecoms sector was parceled out by concessions and licensing arrangements. Media ventures were barred to foreign companies under the alien business law on grounds of national security. The real estate sector was protected by a ban on foreign ownership of land. Banking was protected by licensing arrangements that severely restricted foreign participation before the crisis. These service sectors represented the future source of profit and growth for Thai domestic capital.

Not surprisingly given these protective conditions, several of these business leaders had a history of tapping political power for business benefit. Bangkok Bank's preeminence was created by its association with military dictators in the 1950s, and sustained by persistent lobbying to maintain the protected banking cartel up to the crisis. The Maleenont family won their television concession from bureaucrats. The telecoms companies depended on government concessions. The auto parts industry was protected by local content rules until the mid 1990s, and still depended greatly on investment promotion policies. Major construction companies depended on public sector contracts.

By early 1999, the Thai Rak Thai Party was accused of being simply a logical extension of the political connections which enabled

Table 3.2 TRT "Shadow Cabinet," August 1999

Ministry	Name	Background	Future in party
PM's Office	Phongthep Thepkanchana	legal bureaucrat	MP, minister
	Police Gen Chumphon Atthasat	Dep Police Commissioner	
	Phanloet Baiyok	property developer	
	Thamnun Prachuapmoh	ex-head, Tourism Authority	
	Hamdos Alim Minsar	Pattani Muslim leader	
Defence	Gen Thawan Sawaengphan	ex-Dep Army Commander	
	Gen. Aphiwan Wiriyachai		
Finance	Pol Lt-Col Thaksin Shinawatra		MP, PM
	Dr Kitti Limsakun	Chula economist	adviser
	Suvarn Valaisathian	tax lawyer	minister
Foreign	Dr Pracha Gunakasem	ex-Under Sec, Foreign	
	Dr Kanthati Sukmongkhon	ex-foreign service	MP
Agriculture	Praphat Panyachatrak	activist, orchard farmer	minister
	Rungruang Julachat	ex-head of Irrigation Dept	
	Wirat Sakjiraphaphong	CP executive	
Transport	Dr Sarit Santimetanidon	Khon Kaen MP, Dep Min	MP
	Phongsak Raktaphongpaisan		minister
	Rungrot Siprasoetsuk	ex-head, commercial aviation	
	Phatarasak Osothanukroh	ex-MP	MP
Commerce	Somkid Jatusripitak	NIDA academic	minister
	Suthep Laohawatthana	business executive	
	Dr Wirachai Wiramethikun	property business	MP
Interior	Gen Jarat Kullawanit	National Security Council	
	Dr Tiraphat Serisangsan	Thammasat academic	
	Gen Thammarak Issarangkura na Ayutthaya		minister
	Udomdet Rattanasathian	ex-MP	MP
Justice	Prof Dr Kanit na Nakhon	ex-Attorney General	
	Assoc Prof Chusak Sirinin	Ramkhamhaeng law academic	
Labor	Sutham Saengpathum	ex-MP	minister
	Sunee Chaiyoros	women's activist	
	Chanon Suwasin		
Labor	Assoc Prof Dr Prasaeng Mongkhonsi	environment bureaucrat	
	Thinnawat Marukhaphitak	ex-MP and Dep Minister	
	Wuthiphong Phongsawan	computer academic, AIT	
Education	Prof Dr Kasem Wattanachai	academic	minister
	Prof Dr Purachai Piumsombun	NIDA academic	minister
	Dr Sirikorn Manirin	ex-academic, auto executive	minister
Health	Prof Dr Arun Phaosawat	medical academic, Siriat	
	Dr Surapong Seubwonglee	medical academic, Mahidon	minister
	Dr Prachuap Ungphakorn	medic, Bangkok municipality	MP
	Dr Pruetthichai Damrongrat	business executive	MP
Industry	Pansak Vinyaratn	journalist	adviser
	Dr Samran Phu-anantanan	business executive, Samsung	
	Suranan Vejjajiva	ex-technocrat	MP

Source: (Phak thai rak thai 1999)

businessmen to gain government favors, and, in particular, of being the political agency of the Shinawatra group. As a result, Thaksin moved the party's offices out of the Shinawatra building, and renamed the group's holding company from Shinawatra Corporation to Shin Corporation (Ariwat 2003, 185; Nichapha 2003, 54).

In sum, Thaksin's venture into the political world over the mid and late 1990s was the logical extension of his business success based on state concessions. His main agenda, expressed in his first political testament in 1998, was to protect Thailand's "competitiveness" in the face of globalization and transnational capital. His new party attracted other big business families that had survived the crisis, knew the value of state protection, and were convinced by the experience that they needed closer control over state power. Although at its July 1998 launch, most of the founding members had been academics and intellectuals, within a year the complexion of the party changed. Twelve of the founding members remained to become part of Thaksin's government (as MPs, ministers, or party workers), but the rest faded away (table 3.1). When in August 1999 the party announced a sort of shadow cabinet to monitor the government (table 3.2), more of the members were representatives of business families, or former bureaucrats who had been their sympathetic connections inside government.

Over the next eighteen months, however, the party changed yet again. Only nine of the forty-three members listed in this shadow cabinet were appointed ministers in Thaksin's cabinet in February 2001. The party was changed by the realities of electoral politics, but also by other social forces intruding on the political system in the context of the financial crisis.

THAKSIN AND SMALL BUSINESSMEN

A lot of my brothers and sisters are still enduring great suffering and my business friends still cannot find money from banks. . . . Don't worry for me but for the country. (Press, 27 December 2000)

Over 1998–9, Thaksin appealed to small businessmen with proposals to stimulate entrepreneurship as a route to recovery from the economic crisis.

The IMF, which arrived in July 1997 to dictate crisis policies, blamed the crisis on Thai companies for excessive borrowing and poor investments. This interpretation was corroborated by the international media and academic analysis that attributed the crisis to an "Asian model" of development marked by "crony capitalism." The IMF strategy assumed that debtor companies (including financial intermediaries) would have to go bankrupt in large numbers, and the economy would regenerate through a "fire sale" of cheap distressed assets to foreign buyers. Financial firms were closed down, restrictions on foreign ownership removed, and asset sales orchestrated to favor foreign bidders (Pasuk and Baker 2000, ch. 9).

Most local businessmen interpreted the crisis quite differently. The typical urban Thai enterprise had been developed by an immigrant family over two to four generations by hard work, thrift, mutual cooperation, and investment in education. A few became sprawling conglomerates. Most were small businesses relying on family labor, or medium enterprises with ten to twenty employees. All but a handful were family concerns. Less than four hundred out of several hundred thousand registered businesses had entered the stock market. Most businessmen, big or small, did not see themselves as proponents of any "Asian model" or as "crony capitalists." Rather, they felt they had made two mistakes which brought about their downfall: they had followed market forces by seeking credit from the lowest-cost supplier (foreign loans), and they had believed their government when it promised the baht would remain pegged to the dollar. They did not feel inclined to take both the blame and the pain for the crisis. As one leading businessman explained in 1998, "our priority is survival" (*BP*, 28 November 1998). Many reacted to the crisis by refusing to repay their creditors—a dramatic change in the business culture since formerly debtors repaid religiously in order to maintain their creditworthiness. One businessman described this reaction as "a scheme to counter the threat of extinction" (Suthep 1999, 24).

Many businessmen perceived the IMF-inspired policies towards the crisis as an abdication of the government's usual relationship to domestic capital. New organizations appeared to oppose the IMF and Democrat government including the Alliance for National Salvation, National Salvation Community, and United Thai for National Liberation Club (Kasian 2002). But these groups were small and their efforts gained only a narrow base of support. An attempt to hold an anti-IMF rally, in cooperation with other protest groups, drew only fifteen hundred people. The formal business associations gave no endorsement. One of the most prominent leaders of this business protest failed to get reelected to a post in the Chamber of Commerce because of his activism. The press was lukewarm. The attempt by the largest bad debtor, Prachai Liao-phairat of TPI, to portray his own plight as a nationalist cause, gained precious little support from press, colleagues, or politicians. From mid 1998, these activities declined. The indebted business-men failed to persuade a broader public that their decline was a public cause.

Mass reaction to the crisis developed more slowly. Over 1998–9, the hopes for a rapid and moderately painless recovery were abandoned. International criticism of the IMF handling of the crisis rose. A sense of resentment against outside forces (globalization, the IMF) developed but faced difficulties finding clear expression. Thailand had no mass nationalist movement in its history. The elite had fended off colonialism, the nation had been formed top-down, and national symbols had remained "official property," not easily appropriated for mass action. Attempts to express mass concern over the crisis in 1998 adopted metaphorical symbols such as the elephants which had migrated to work in the city and which suffered in this unnatural, modern environment (Pasuk and Baker 2000, ch. 7). In 1999–2000, television dramas began to reflect this resentment, but struggled because of the lack of a local nationalist tradition. The first drama to adopt a defend-the-homeland theme, *Khon khong phaendin* (People of the country), was set in a mythical pan-Asian country with foreign rulers modeled on a Latin American junta and nationalist heroes drawn from Indian models, including obvious representations of Gandhi and Nehru.[2] The homeland was rather far from home.

These expressions moved closer to classic nationalism by borrowing stories from schoolbook national history. The shorthand for the fall of the old capital of Ayutthaya to the Burmese in 1767 (*sia krung*, the fall of the capital) transferred easily to the modern crisis. In 1999, *Bang Rachan*, a film based on one of the most popular stories from this history, enjoyed unprecedented popular success. In 2001, the film of *Suriyothai*, a sixteenth-century queen who died fighting the Burmese, extended this theme with speeches calling on countrymen to "save the country" punctuating the battle scenes.

In 1999, the business critique of crisis management reemerged. The parliamentary opposition launched a no-confidence debate that criticized the Democrat government for being subservient to the IMF, biased in favor of foreign capital, and negligent in its duty to foster Thailand's "real economy." The opposition New Aspiration Party (NAP) took this message on a stump tour. Compared to a year earlier, the message about the government's duty to protect domestic capital was more acceptable now that the crisis had become worse, and now that the message was delivered by politicians rather than indebted businessmen.

Against this background, Thaksin began to present himself and his party as the savior of the small and medium entrepreneur. In June 1999, he stated his difference from the Democrats' finance-led strategy with the remark, "I wouldn't solve this crisis just from a commercial banker's point of view" (*FEER*, 17 June 1999). In September, he described the Democrat leader Chuan Leekpai[3] as a bureaucrat-like "salary man who cannot even buy a house of his own" in contrast to Thaksin's own status as a self-made businessman of great wealth. He went on: "If I'm the government, I will open things up for people who have the leaning and ability to be entrepreneurs to have that choice so that people who earn salaries now will have the opportunity to quit and become entrepreneurs without facing excess risk" (*MS*, 11 September 1998).

This public bickering with Chuan defined the difference between Thaksin and the Democrats as entrepreneur vs. bureaucrat. Thaksin now promoted recovery from the crisis through growth in small and medium enterprises (SMEs) on an Italian or Tuscan model achieved by the marriage of traditional craft skills and high technology. The party staged an SME exhibition that showcased examples of successful small Thai businesses. The idea appealed so successfully to the entrepreneurial aspirations, local pride, and sense of abandonment among small businessmen, that the government and other parties rushed to form their own SME policies (*TN*, 6 November 2000). Shortly before the spat with Chuan, Thaksin was talking about coming "third or fourth" in any future election (*TN*, 24 March 1999). Shortly after, he was talking about becoming premier.

In March 2000, the TRT Party announced its plan for economic recovery. It dropped the "Italian" inspiration of the concept, but retained the emphasis on SMEs, and the combination of local skills and inputs with high technology in production and marketing. It added a business school model that divided sectors into rising stars, cash cows, and sunset industries, and promised capital injections and other government aid to boost the stars. It emphasized the need to revive the banking system (*BP*, 20 March 2000).

The party's name and symbol expressed the theme of national defense. Thaksin claimed fifteen thousand people responded to an invitation to suggest party names and then to vote on a short list. He insisted only that the final choice must contain the word "Thai." The runner-up option was Ruksa Thai, meaning "looking after Thai/Thailand" (Nichapha 2003, 21). "Thai Rak Thai" clearly echoed *Thai chuai Thai* (Thais helping Thais), a radio station which mobilized listeners to fight crime and help people in distress that had become highly popular over the crisis. The party's slogan, "Think new, act new, for every Thai," combined a promise of change with an inclusive nationalism. The party symbol used the red-white-blue of the Thai flag, and combined the number "1" with the letter ท, which is the initial of both Thaksin and Thai/Thailand.[4] Two other newly founded parties also adopted clearly nationalistic titles—Thin Thai or the Thai Motherland Party, and Thai Maharat or the Great Thai Nation Party.

TRT Party symbol

By mid 2000, a "new nationalist" group had formed within the TRT Party. It held seminars that attracted businessmen, cultural nationalists, and ginger groups from other political parties. Leaders of the movement argued that "new" nationalism was not based on the imagined ethnic identity that had led earlier nationalisms towards race hatred, fascism, and wars of nationalist expansion. States like Thailand contained a variety of different peoples bundled together within the territorial boundaries by historical fate. New nationalism's enemy was international capital, which had taken advantage of the crisis to invade Thailand on an unprecedented scale. Thai politicians were "soft-headedly" following foreign advice and allowing multinational capital to "dominate the country." The key principle, argued the new nationalists, was that the interests of the people bundled together in this nation must be paramount. This new nationalism was not aggressive and expansionist like the old kind, but defensive. Nor was it anti-globalist in the long term. Less advanced countries needed to integrate with the world at their own pace so that they could participate "on fair and equal terms" and retain their cultural identity. The priority was to restore the national government's duty to manage the economy. The TRT "new nationalists" hoped to "plant the love of country in every person in every corner of the country" so that "the power to rescue economic sovereignty will grow of its own accord" (Narong 2000, especially 13–29).

In sum, the initial attempt by wrecked businessmen to rally domestic capital against the IMF program was a failure. But over 1998–2000, the crisis impact deepened, debates on self-strengthening proliferated, and a diffuse resentment of external forces spread. Thaksin responded to these trends by giving his new party a nationalist aura, and crafting a political platform that made government support for small businesses a route for recovery from the crisis.

THAKSIN AND RURAL DISCONTENTS

> Nothing will stand in my way. I am determined to devote myself to politics in order to lead the Thai people out of poverty. . . . I think the people want Thai Rak Thai to take the government's reins and solve the country's problems. (Press, 23 December 2000)

Business support was not enough. The majority of the Thai electorate still lived in the villages (the 2000 census classified 69 percent of the population as non-municipal, and 51 percent as agricultural). In his electoral campaign, Thaksin made a direct appeal to the rural voter with a policy platform. No previous political leader had done anything similar.

The financial crisis increased the intensity of the rural protests that had been building through the 1990s. Initially farmers did well after July 1997 because agricultural prices rose in local currency. But from mid 1998 onwards, the impact of the crisis spread through rural society. The international price of rice dropped sharply. The cost of imported inputs rose. Remittances from family members working in the city shrank. Rural migrants lost their jobs and were thrown back on the support of the rural family. The number in poverty rose by 3 million, virtually all rural (World Bank 2001).

In early 1998, when government wanted to implement IMF measures for the financial sector, farmers' groups demanded that government help the poor rather than the rich through agrarian debt relief. This protest was repeated in 1999 and 2000. Farmer groups also protested for price support. Paddy growers invaded Bangkok's northern suburbs and blocked roads. Cattle raisers started marching on the capital with herds of cows. Cassava farmers threatened to build a bonfire in the city center. During an UNCTAD conference in late 1999, the police had to block radial roads to prevent sugar trucks invading the city. Displaced villagers and unemployed workers occupied empty land in forests, and unused land held by speculators. The Assembly of the Poor revived the protests against the Pak Mun dam and other big infrastructure projects. The Democrat-led government branded such protests as illegitimate and usually refused to negotiate.

At the launch of TRT, Thaksin espoused the principle of rural uplift, but initially had no rural program at all. His early recruitment efforts focused on urban groups. Praphat Panyachatrak, a prominent student activist from the 1970s, now turned orchard farmer, faxed him a three-page rural program but received no response. In early 1999, however, the rural protests for debt relief, price support, and land reached a peak. Thaksin's team now began to consult with rural leaders and NGO workers. They took up Praphat's three-page plan and did research to test and refine it (*TN*, 23 March 2001). Some NGO activists who advocated a localist opposition to the crisis contributed ideas. Thaksin adopted some of their vocabulary about strengthening communities and building recovery from the grassroots. In March 2000, Thaksin announced that the main feature of his rural platform would be a moratorium on rural debts (*TN*, 28 March 2000). On 26 June, the party announced a "National Agenda" with eleven points directed at both urban and rural audiences:

1. Develop the financial market and capital market
2. Restructure the economy and debt
3. Generate income and solve the unemployment problem
4. Revive Thai farmers
5. Education: build people to build the nation
6. Eradicate drugs
7. Declare war on corruption

8. Transform health care
9. Build strong families and increase the political role of women
10. Privatize state enterprises
11. Pursue a new regional policy (Nichapha 2003, 63–4)

In August, TRT fine-tuned the rural program into three points: agrarian debt moratorium; revolving fund of 1 million baht for every village; and a 30 baht-per-visit scheme of health care (*BP*, 17 August 2000). In December 2000, farmer groups in the Northeast resolved to "drive the Democrats to extinction" at the polls in revenge for the party's antagonism to rural protest (*BP*, 11 December 2000). The following week, Thaksin held a meeting with the leaders of the Assembly of the Poor (*BP*, 19 December 2000). Several NGO leaders and advisors publicly supported Thaksin.

Thaksin had distanced himself from the Democrats who collaborated with the IMF's destructive strategy, abandoned the government's duty to protect domestic business, and treated rural protest with contempt. Thaksin bid for support of small business-men and farmers by adopting these groups' own demands.

THE 2001 ELECTIONS: CAMPAIGN AND RESULT

I hope to be the link between the old generation of politicians and the new generation. (Autobiography, 1998–9)

The election of January 2001 was a complex mix of the old and the new. Thaksin campaigned in a totally new style and secured a dramatically different result—a simple majority in the house after a little bit of juggling (see below). But at the same time, the deployment of money and influence was similar to previous polls, and about half of Thaksin's victorious party consisted of old-fashioned elements in Thai politics.

The January 2001 polls had a prologue. In March 2000, elections were held for the Senate. Although the rules differed from those for the lower house,[5] the Senate elections served as a test run for the 1997 constitution, and for the mood and preferences of the electorate. The results were instructive. In Bangkok and some other urban areas, the electorate returned social activists and media figures of a new style in Thai parliamentary politics. However, these were a minority of around thirty to forty senators within the overall complement of two hundred. The rest were ex-bureaucrats or local businessmen connected to local political bosses, often by marriage or kinship. Money and influence were as much in evidence as ever. The new Election Commission canceled seventy-eight of the victories for malpractice, and eventually held seven polling rounds totaling 306 contests before every victor was approved (Gothom 2001). The old politics was still alive.

Around this time, Thaksin agreed to admit Snoh Thienthong and his faction into the TRT Party. Snoh was a trucking magnate from the eastern border who had proved the most enduring of the political godfathers of the 1990s. He led a faction of provincial MPs into the junta's Samakkhitham Party in 1992, then to Chat Thai in 1995, and to New Aspiration in 1996. In both 1995 and 1996, his support helped to decide who became premier. After Chavalit's fall from the premiership in November 1997, Snoh eased away and formally entered TRT in mid 2000. Thaksin's decision to admit Snoh appears to have been taken shortly after the Senate election results emphasized the surviving importance of the old politics. Snoh's shift started the process of logrolling which had preceded all recent elections. By August 2000, it was estimated that around 100 sitting MPs from other parties would run under TRT at the coming election, including 58 from NAP, 16 from Chat Phatthana, 11 from Social Action, 9 from Chat Thai, and 6 from the Democrats (*TN*, 30 August 2000). The Democrats accused Thaksin of "sucking" in MPs with money.

The TRT electoral campaign was also emphatically new in several ways. The party spent two years setting up a local network, and used the principles of pyramid selling in an attempt to sign up enough party members in each constituency for electoral victory. By the election it claimed 8 million members (*TN*, 18 December 2000).

The party established awareness of its name, image, and message using standard marketing methods and a considerable budget over the two and a half years between its foundation and the election.[6] From mid 2000, the party highlighted its three-point rural platform (debt moratorium, village funds, 30-baht health care) on election posters throughout the country. The impact of the TRT rural program and particularly of the three-point posters was so strong that other parties scrambled to produce their own rural platforms (*TN*, 14 October 2000; *BP*, 6 October 2000).[7]

The TRT campaign focused heavily on the party leader. From two years ahead of the poll, TRT erected large posters all over Thailand showing Thaksin with the party motto, "Think new, act new, for every Thai." During the run-up to the polls, TRT posters in every constituency were produced in a uniform format showing Thaksin with the constituency candidate. Thaksin's autobiography was serialized in *Matichon Sutsapda* weekly news magazine from August 1998 to February 1999 and then assembled as a book. As described in the previous chapter, this autobiography portrayed Thaksin rising from modest origins to outstanding commercial success through hard work, persistence, and daring (Thaksin 1999). As the climax of the TRT election campaign, the essence of the book was distilled into a press ad and posters headlined: "Let me use my life's knowledge and experience to solve the problems of the people." In the full text of the press ad which ran a month before the polls, the policies of TRT emerged from the life of its leader.

Respected Thai brothers and sisters

The nation still has many problems of many kinds that need a rapid solution. Today I believe that you have entrusted me and the Thai Rak Thai Party to take responsibility for the people's suffering and the future of the nation.

Our lives have both their dark and bright sides. We come up against things that are difficult and things that are easy. Sometimes life is difficult, sometimes smooth sailing. Sometimes we are smart and sometimes stupid. Some are born poor and others wealthy. I believe these experiences are great teachers and good lessons for the future. As Buddhadasa said: stupidity is like fire; if you don't know how to use it, your hand will be burnt; but if you do, you can cook food. All of us must use these lessons in life as a warning, as a light to illuminate the route by which our lives can become brighter.

Brothers and sisters, I come from the countryside. I studied primary at the public school in Sankamphaeng. I gained admission to the Police Academy by examination, and received government scholarships to acquire a Ph.D. from the US.

As a rural kid, the son of a coffee shop owner, I helped my father with his orchards, newspaper delivery, and mobile cinema, until I began a computer business. I married a police officer's daughter who had grown up in a police hostel. We started together from zero, facing troubles and triumphs together, helping one another to raise three children from the womb until they are now in their youth.

On my own I started out managing a company of seven people. Now it has over six thousand employees and a turnover in billions. I put satellites up in the sky. I invested overseas. I had to chase after customers to collect checks. I became a bad loan at the banks, known as an NPL [non-performing loan]. I almost went bankrupt three times but now I have more wealth and property than I could ever have imagined. Even today, my friends range from hired motorcycle drivers to the presidents of great countries.

Today I'm fifty-one years old. The experience and knowledge I've acquired throughout my life is not something I want to keep to myself. Let me devote the remaining span of my life to this country that has given me more than I should have received. I want to combine my knowledge with modern technology to solve the problems of the country.

Brothers and sisters, as someone born in the countryside, I'd like farmers to have a life that can be self-reliant, without debt, and with enough money to educate their children. I'd like them to get medical care when they are sick, sell their produce at a price which is not exploitative, and have supplementary work if they are seasonally unemployed.

As someone who passed through education at many different

"Let me use my life's knowledge . . ." press ad

levels, and who constantly follows the changes in the world, I'd like our children to understand Thai wisdom, be good at the English language, be good at technology, not have to study by rote, not have to go through special classes so they have no time for other pursuits like sport, music, art, and culture, and lack closeness with their parents because everyone is too busy.

As someone who was once an NPL bad debtor, I'd like to see all bad loans cleared from the banks, and loans restructured, to give an opportunity for those Thai who suffered during the crisis to recover and be a major force in the country, and enable the presently troubled Thai banks to escape from the crisis, increase their capital, and rapidly extend loans.

As someone who once had companies in the stock market, I'd like to see the stock market recover as before, have more good companies and state enterprises listed on the stock market, and, when the market expands, have more foreign investment come in, both medium and long term, while speculative short-term investment is reduced. I'd like to see a revival of the property market so wealth can recover rapidly.

As a father of children, I'd like to see our children grow up in warm families, in a good environment, with good health, free of temptations, with the ability to choose the studies they like, the ability to think and act, employment when their studies are over, and good ideas to start their own businesses.

Finally, as a Thai, I'd like to see my country have a modern bureaucracy which serves the people and gives them access to data and information rather than administering and controlling them. I'd like to see a rapid reduction in corruption through good systems of prevention. I'd like officials to have good and fitting welfare provision. I'd like politicians to love their fellow citizens, be compassionate and unselfish, and not be so protective of their political careers and positions that they forget the overriding importance of the nation and people.

Brothers and sisters, the country awaits the solution of its problems. Most Thai are still in great difficulty. I and the Thai Rak Thai Party have the target of not just leading the nation out of the crisis into a situation of strength and security, but also enabling all levels from the grassroots upwards to be able to compete on a world scale with pride. I believe that every Thai wants to see our country improve, be a country of opportunity, so we can all pass through the crisis and create the best possible society for our children in the future.

Today let me volunteer to serve all of you, my brothers and sisters, by shouldering the duty to help create a new life and future along with your cooperation. Let me commit myself to use the knowledge and experience I have gained throughout my life to solve the problems of our country in totality. I know that the tasks ahead are difficult and heavy, but I am ready.[8]

At the polls themselves, the deployment of money and influence appeared little different from previous elections. Indeed, the uncertainty of this election may have tempted some candidates to invest more than usual, and to experiment with new tactics. Policemen and military officers were allegedly hired to threaten voters (*BP*, 13 December 2000). Two campaign cars were discovered with trunks full of small denomination notes and campaign materials (*TN*, 19 December 2000, 6 January 2001). In a tapped telephone conversation, an ex-minister instructed campaign managers how to direct their "ammunition" (meaning money) in the final stages of the campaign. In many constituencies, the vote counting developed into a secondary battle, with officials and election monitors accused of malpractice. The Election Commission canceled some candidatures before the polls (*BP*, 5 January 2001), refused to register 62 of the 400 victors in the first round, and eventually conducted a total of 486 contests over six polling rounds (Gothom 2001).

The results reflected the mix of old politics and new. Local influence still counted, but party affiliation was more important than before. Almost two-thirds of voters chose one of two parties (TRT or Democrats). Many candidates from influential local families that failed to enter TRT were massacred at the polls;[9] those that did enter TRT had a high chance of victory.[10]

Table 3.3 Election results by party and region, January 2001

	North	Northeast	South	Center	Bangkok	Total	Party List	Grand Total
Thai Rak Thai	54	69	1	47	29	200	48	248
Democrat	16	6	48	19	8	97	31	128
Chat Thai	3	11	–	21	–	35	6	41
New Aspiration	1	19	5	3	–	28	8	36
Chat Phatthana	2	16	–	4	–	22	7	29
Seritham	–	14	–	–	–	14	–	14
Ratsadon	–	1	–	1	–	2	–	2
Social Action	–	1	–	–	–	1	–	1
Thin Thai	–	1	–	–	–	1	–	1
Total	76	138	54	95	37	400	100	500

Note: Results as announced by the Election Commission on 2 February 2001 to inaugurate the parliament.

Table 3.4 Voting by party and region, January 2001

	North	Northeast	South	Center	Bangkok	Total	Party List
Turnout	71.9	67.9	74.8	69.7	66.7	69.9	69.9
Thai Rak Thai	47.2	38.0	11.7	39.7	43.9	37.1	40.6
Democrat	28.8	8.5	60.3	26.4	32.4	25.9	26.6
Chat Thai	6.1	9.2	2.9	15.8	1.2	8.6	5.3
Chat Phatthana	3.8	16.7	11.1	4.5	3.2	9.4	6.1
New Aspiration	8.1	12.9	4.1	7.7	6.0	8.9	7.0
Seritham	1.5	9.8	1.9	0.2	0.2	4.0	2.8
Ratsadon	2.6	2.8	7.2	3.2	0.7	3.3	1.3
Social Action	0.0	0.0	0.6	0.0	-	0.1	0.2
Thin Thai	0.8	0.4	0.3	1.1	5.3	1.1	2.1
Other	1.1	1.7	0.1	1.5	7.1	1.8	8.0

Note: Voting on 6 January 2001. Figures are percent of all valid votes.

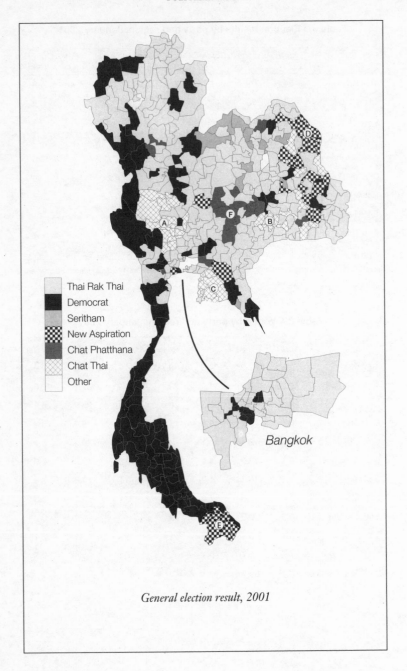

General election result, 2001

In some cases, the failure of influential people was directly linked to tighter election controls. In Samut Prakan, the Asavahame clan had dominated politics for two decades. But in 2001, the patriarch Wattana Asavaheme's two sons, brother, and daughter-in-law (a popular singer) all lost at the polls, while Wattana himself failed on the party list. After the previous polls in 1996, a judge ruled that Wattana and his two allies had stuffed 20,000 votes into the ballot boxes, but had to acquit them on a technicality. When Wattana's son contested election for mayor, television cameras had filmed ballot stuffing. Without these tactics and without the TRT stamp, the clan lost.

The result redrew the political map (see tables 3.3, 3.4, and map). The 1997 constitution had deliberately changed the electoral system with the objective of reducing the fragmentation of parliament into many small and medium-sized parties.[11] This constitutional engineering worked. Several parties disappeared. The Solidarity and Muanchon parties retired before the contest. The Prachakon Thai, Ratsadon, and Social Action parties were obliterated at the polls. The Seritham Party secured fourteen constituency MPs, but its leaders lost on the party list, and Seritham agreed to merge into TRT in February 2001. Three of the largest parties of the 1990s were reduced to a few isolated clusters of seats that represented the local networks of their leaders. The Chat Thai Party won three such "islands" representing the networks of the Silpa-archa family around Suphanburi (A on the map), Chidchob family around Buriram (B), and Khunpleum (Kamnan Po) clan around Chonburi (C). The New Aspiration Party won two areas corresponding to the bases of Chavalit around Nakhon Phanom (D) and Wan Muhammed Noor in the far south (E). Chat Phatthana won just one (F) around the Khorat base of its late founder-leader, Chatichai Choonhavan.

Outside these islands and Bangkok (which for the first time voted close to the national pattern), the electoral map was divided by an arc drawn east-west through the capital. South of this line, in the region that had long been the party's heartland, the Democrats won 61 seats and lost only 7. North of this line, TRT won 166 and lost 75.

Back in 1998 Thaksin had said: "I hope to be the link between the old generation of politicians and the new generation" (Thaksin 1999, 97). This hope now came true. The TRT parliamentary party consisted of two groups of roughly equal size. Among the 200 TRT MPs from territorial constituencies, 110 were new MPs with an average age of 42, while 90 were former MPs—defectors from other political parties including the Snoh Thienthong group—with an average age of 51. Thaksin mixed the old and new still further by forming a coalition with the Chat Thai Party of Banharn and New Aspiration Party of Chavalit—the prime leaders of the "old politics" he had rejected in his "first political testament" two years earlier.

THAKSIN IN POWER

> We dream of making big changes, but in reality it is not the way things are. Half the MPs are old-timers, so it takes time to replace them with fresh faces. . . . I don't know what they [Cabinet ministers] did in the past, but I will give them all a chance. . . . If any of them are found to be corrupt while working for me, I will get rid of them. (Press, 18 February 2001)

Thaksin's first Cabinet (see appendix 3) reflected the various groups that had become aligned to the party over the past three years. First, there was an inner circle including close associates (Purachai, Somkid), two founding members (Sudarat, Thammarak), and two professionals (Thaksin's tax adviser, Suwan Valaisathian, and corporate lawyer, Phongthep Thepkanchana). They took charge of the main portfolios of interior, finance, and justice—posts which were important for economic policy but which also might have some bearing on Thaksin's pending assets case.

Second, five ministries went to key business supporters, especially from the telecoms sector. Apart from Thaksin himself, the Cabinet included Adisai Bodaramik, head of Jasmine; Pitak Intarawitaya-nunt, CP's political ambassador; Sombat Uthaisang, a former TOT official who had become closely associated with CP;[12] Pracha

Maleenont of the family running TV Channel 3; and Suriya Jungrungruangkit from the Summit auto parts empire.

Third, several portfolios critical for implementation of the party's electoral program were allotted to committed technocrats and civil society activists including former 1970s student activists, Praphat and Surapong. Finally, ten portfolios went to old politicians who had been logrolled into the party, and another eight to coalition partners. Snoh Thienthong pushed for a Cabinet post but was persuaded to accept instead the posts of chief whip and chief adviser, along with the right to attend Cabinet meetings.

Thaksin rapidly implemented his electoral agenda for the rural mass (Hewison 2003). The agrarian debt relief scheme allowed the 2.3 million existing debtors of the government's agrarian bank either to choose a three-year moratorium on repayment of past debt, or a reduction of interest payment with the chance to increase their loan. About half took each option (*BP*, 18 October 2001). The village fund scheme provided one million baht to each village as a revolving fund, managed by a village-level committee that could normally make loans of up to 20,000 baht per debtor. Some 71,102 villages and 2,339 urban communities qualified to enter the scheme, and 5.3 million loans were made by September, mostly for agricultural production or local commerce (Worawan 2003).

The 30-baht-a-visit health care scheme began rolling out province by province before mid year. To qualify, people had to register with a hospital and be issued with a card that entitled them to pay 30 baht for each visit. By May 2003, 45.6 million people had registered at one thousand hospitals (TDRI 2003, 87). Hospitals received a per capita subsidy based on the number of people registered. If patients had to be referred on to another hospital for more specialized treatment, there was a system of transfer charges. To a large extent this was simply an innovative approach to distributing the government's health budget. In practice, the distribution of money and workload was much more difficult than at first envisioned. The cheap price increased the demand for health care. Many local hospitals with limited staff became overloaded. The estimation of the per capita subsidy and transfer payments was too simple, with the result that the financial impact was very uneven—some hospitals prospered, others went virtually bankrupt. Several doctors resigned due to overwork and frustration. Some hospital chief administrators publicly condemned the project. The government struggled to fine-tune the system, but it undoubtedly made basic health care much more accessible to a large number of people, and was highly popular. Polls regularly rated it as the government's best scheme.

Finally, the government negotiated directly with rural organizations. Thaksin spent his first lunch in office at the Assembly of the Poor's protest encampment outside Government House. After agreement to set up committees to negotiate the Assembly's demands, the encampment dissolved some weeks later (*BP*, 4 April 2001).

PARLIAMENTARY POWER

We used to have so many political parties that we could not remember all their names. We used to set up parties only to see them collapse later. We are now sending a message to the world that there will be continuity in politics and we can run the country for the next ten years. (Press, 28 January 2002)

After the favorable conclusion of the asset declaration case in August 2001, Thaksin found himself in a more powerful position than any previous elected Thai premier. Three main factors contributed to this position: new features of the 1997 constitution; the scale of his electoral victory; and his personal popularity.

The drafters of the new constitution aimed to create more stable governments (Connors 1999; Klein 1998; Hicken 2001). Through the 1990s, Cabinets had been fractious coalitions of several small parties, reshuffled on a roughly annual basis. No Cabinet lasted its full four-year term, and most were brought down amid corruption scandals aired by the press. The 1997 constitution attempted to overcome this situation in several ways. It changed the electoral rules with the aim of engineering a two-party system. It strengthened the prime minister by requiring 40 percent of MPs to demand a no-confidence debate against him (but only 20 percent for other ministers). It introduced a range of new institutional checks and balances in the hope of preventing malpractice without recourse to the messy public business of press allegations and televised no-confidence debates.

The constitution also inadvertently increased the premier's power in other ways. First, on the principle of separating executive and legislature, those appointed to Cabinet posts had to forfeit their parliamentary seats. As a result, a minister who lost his post in a Cabinet reshuffle was out of politics. This made ministers reluctant to oppose the premier and risk such an exit. Second, the premier could call a general election at forty-five days' notice, but electoral candidates had to have been members of their party for at least ninety days. This made it more difficult to bargain against the prime minister through threats of defection.

The consolidation of the party system continued. Chavalit's New Aspiration Party dissolved itself into TRT in early 2002.[13] Chavalit confessed he no longer commanded the funds required for party leadership after Thaksin's entry into the political market had changed the price levels. Thaksin assured the public that Chavalit had "done it for the sake of the country and the people," and that the merger "would assure the world of uninterrupted political and economic developments in Thailand" (BP, 24 April 2002). After this merger TRT had 296 seats. Two other parties with reputations for joining any government were also drafted into the coalition—Chat Thai immediately and Chat Phatthana in March 2002. This created a dominant coalition of 364 out of 500 seats, reduced to 340 after Chat Phatthana was ejected from the coalition in November 2003 (the numbers of seats by party fluctuated slightly because of by-elections).

Parliamentary opposition was ineffectual. Only the Democrat Party was left out of the coalition. Under the new rules, it had too few seats to launch a no-confidence debate against the prime minister. As a result of its identification with the IMF-nominated crisis policies, it had lost widespread public support. "Talking about the Opposition," Thaksin noted, "I can only laugh" (*TN*, 27 September 2001). In May 2002, the Democrats launched a no-confidence debate targeting fifteen ministers with charges of corruption and mismanagement. Given the government's solid majority, the house votes on these motions were a foregone conclusion. But the Democrats also used a new provision of the constitution to forward the charges against eight of the ministers to the National Counter Corruption Commission for impeachment. But the commission ultimately rejected every case. The importance of parliament declined. Government ruled through Cabinet decisions and executive decrees. Parliamentary sessions were repeatedly aborted for lack of a quorum—by early 2004, around once a week (*BP*, 27 April 2004).

Thaksin also increased his popular support *after* the election. In part, this reflected popular optimism that the new prime minister would be able to revive the crisis-hit economy. In part, it was because Thaksin communicated with people in a more open and intimate manner than his predecessors. He started giving weekly live radio broadcasts in which he talked about his activities and the issues of the day. As the asset declaration case approached, he adopted a more presidential style, and began to promise that he would "end poverty" in Thailand. The ABAC opinion poll showed preference for Thaksin against other potential leaders rose from around 30 percent in December 2000 before the election to a peak of 70 percent in May as the asset case decision approached (*TN*, 7 January 2002).

After the decision, Thaksin immediately predicted he would govern for two four-year terms. Over the next year, this estimate swelled to twelve, sixteen, and then twenty years in power for Thaksin and his successors in the TRT leadership. "If I'm still alive then," he told a party assembly, "I will appeal to the people to choose other parties out of sympathy with them for having waited so long, and out of sympathy with journalists for having no political news" (Thaksin 2003b).

CONCLUSION

The government's actions have no hidden agenda. Everything is about the people who are the focus. The government is ready to listen to the opinions of the opposition, but doesn't pay them much attention, because the opposition finds fault with the government as a matter of course. If the government truly acts for the people, it will be popular, just like my government at present is becoming more and more popular, and I'm confident the next election will be a landslide victory. (Press, 11 September 2003)

In early 2001, Thaksin Shinawatra led a group of the major domestic capitalists who had survived the financial crisis to capture state power with the explicit aim of using it to protect and promote domestic capital. This group was mobilized in reaction to the damage inflicted by the 1997 Asian crisis. Thaksin's rise was a logical extension of Thailand's business-dominated "money politics," but also a dramatic change of scale. It brought some of the wealthiest elements of domestic capital into the seat of power. It superseded "money politics" with "big money politics."

The extent of Thaksin's electoral success in January 2001 can be partly attributed to the constitution, which changed the electoral system with the aim of reducing the fragmentation of political parties and the instability of coalitions. But Thaksin magnified this trend by logrolling old politicians, by constructing a party platform that appealed to social forces stirred up by the crisis, and by investing in a much more professional and expensive campaign than any previous example in Thailand.

Until 1999, there was no sign that Thaksin would attempt to change the style of Thai politics. Until then he projected himself as a modernizer focused on economic growth and cleaner politics. This had been the appeal of the Democrats, and the initial incarnation of Thai Rak Thai seemed like an updated version to supplant the crisis-stricken Democrats. The founding members of the TRT Party, and its first "shadow cabinet," were a conventional mix of businessmen, bureaucrats, and intellectuals. The party's policies, and Thaksin's rhetoric, changed over 1998–2000 as the social and political responses to the crisis became better defined.

The 1997 crisis affected everybody. Business and the urban middle class at first trusted the Democrats to handle it. But as the crisis deepened and lengthened, the Democrats were seen as ineffectual, too subservient to the IMF, and leaning too far towards globalization. TRT seized the resulting opportunity. The party focused on two of the largest segments of Thai society—small family businessmen and the rural mass. It asked these two groups what they wanted from the state, turned the results into an electoral platform, and campaigned on this platform in a way that partially circumvented old structures of local influence. Once in power, it delivered probably more of its promises than its supporters expected; polls after the election showed that many voters believed the TRT platform was "too good to be true" (*BP*, 12 February 2001). Thaksin's popularity ratings increased steeply *after* the elections, partly because of his attempts to court popularity before the verdict on his asset case, and partly because the government seemed much more effective than its predecessors. Many businessmen hoped that Thaksin's own business success meant he would be able to revive the boom economy of the early 1990s. Although Thaksin's asset case directly challenged the spirit of the constitution, an overwhelming majority, including many respected senior citizens and a majority of the Constitutional Court judges, were quite prepared to overlook the legal issues on grounds of pragmatic politics. Thaksin simply seemed the best alternative at a moment of national crisis.

The new constitution's efforts to engineer a more "stable" politics, the eclipse of the Democrats, the size of the TRT's electoral victory, the rapid delivery on its election promises, Thaksin's courting of popularity, and the symbolic significance of the verdict on the assets case, combined to put Thaksin in a more powerful position than any previous elected Thai leader. From this vantage point, he set out to change Thailand's economy and politics.

4

THAKSINOMICS

In mid 2001, the Bangkok press began to refer to the TRT's economic policies as "Thaksinomics." By early 2002, the term had been legitimized in articles by prominent academics (e.g. Nidhi 2002; Ammar 2002). In a speech delivered in Manila in September 2003, Thaksin himself embraced the term on grounds that President Gloria Arroyo, who has an economics doctorate, was already using it (Thaksin 2003f).

But what is Thaksinomics? When the new government came to power in early 2001, some predicted a relaxation of the banking standards imposed by the IMF, introduction of capital controls, restrictions on expanding foreign businesses such as retail, and a repeal of the "eleven bills" passed at the height of the crisis.[1] Certainly some of the government's supporters wanted these measures. None of them came about. After a few months when the government showed it was serious about implementing its electoral program, some predicted a rapid rise in government debt and a "second crisis" on the pattern of Latin American populism. That too did not happen. In 2003, as the growth rate lifted and stock market soared, foreign analysts enthused about a new "super cycle"; a TRT adviser described the TRT government's strategy as a "major paradigm shift" in the practice of economics with global implications (Olarn 2003); and even the IMF hosted a seminar which discussed Thaksinomics as a new development model for Asia (IMF 2004, 30). Possibly those assessments are wrong too.

This chapter argues that Thaksinomics represents a sharp shift away from the neoliberal model that the IMF tried to introduce during the crisis. That model imagines that growth comes from well operating markets, that markets work well when left alone in their "natural state," and that government's role is to create the laws and institutions that enable that to happen. Thaksinomics is a shift towards the "developmentalist" view that in catch-up economies, government has to play a positive role in protecting and promoting firms and sectors to overcome the disadvantages of competing against more advanced economies. "If I want to play [golf] with Tiger Woods," said Thaksin, "Tiger must give me enough handicap" (Thaksin 2003e).

GROWING TO THE FIRST WORLD

And we don't even have to wait until 2020 like Malaysia to realise the goal of becoming a developed country. We can do it faster. (Press, 30 September 2003)

The primary aim of Thaksinomics is GDP growth. Of course this was true of past governments in Thailand and governments in most other countries. But it needs to be emphasized, because other aspects of Thaksinomics were subordinate to this overriding objective. Indeed, the TRT government made even more of a fetish of GDP figures than its predecessors had. At first, the aim was to find a route out of the worst economic crisis in the country's modern history. In Thaksin's telling,

the big question in the minds of all Thais was how long would the country recover from the deepest economic plunge in our history? Ten years? Fifteen? Or twenty? To all walks of life, it was the time of darkness. It was the time of despair to business communities, large and small. It was a nightmare for many who had just started business and were yet to taste the sweet smell of success. To everyone, it was simply disaster. (Thaksin 2003f)

But overcoming the crisis was only a first stage. The larger aim was to leapfrog the Thai economy into the first world. In the US in December 2001, Thaksin said: "Wait for my government's second term, Thailand will apply for OECD membership. I have the right to dream. . . . A proper degree of ambition gives us encouragement . . . [rather than] remaining an international beggar. " (Pran 2004, 322)

Once some momentum was attained in 2002, Thaksin constantly talked up the growth rate by ambitious predictions. By early 2003, he promised that the GDP rate would move into double figures in his second four-year term. Somkid announced that 2004 would be a "golden year for Thailand to step forward as part of the First World like Singapore, South Korea and Taiwan" (*TN*, 27 December 2003).

COUNTRY=COMPANY

> I want to see how we can earn more income from agriculture, manufacturing and the service sectors using our existing strengths. (Press, 28 April 2001)

Thaksin's economic policy team approached this task, not with the tools of conventional economics, but from the perspective of corporate management and business school thinking. The core team (Thaksin, Pansak, Somkid) came from this background. Somkid had written extensively on this approach for fifteen years. Thaksin adopted the phrase "Thailand Company" which Somkid had used for the title of his collected articles. In a speech in Khorat in 1997, Thaksin said:

> A company is a country. A country is a company. They are the same. The management is the same. It is management by economics. From now onwards this is the era of management by economics, not management by any other means. Economics is the deciding factor. (Chumphon 2002, 105)

In his "first political testament," he showed how, from this perspective, national resources are conceived like the inputs available to a business manager engaged in making a profit:

> Thailand can be compared to a large-scale company that has to seek profits in order to provide for its large number of employees by producing goods to sell in competition with other countries. If we don't push our way up, both in terms of respect, and in terms of our capability to negotiate with other countries, create alliances, and seize opportunities, where will we find the money to pay our own company employees—in other words, where will we get the money to support the country's population? . . . The proper role of an MP is to manage the nation's biggest organization, Thailand Company. Politics are just the outer surface. Management is the substance for moving Thailand ahead as an organization. (Thaksin 1999, 233, 228–9)

Once in power, he presented himself as a "CEO prime minister." He claimed the methods of business management were superior to the traditional practice of bureaucracy or government. He lectured the Cabinet on the latest management theory. He launched schemes to convert diplomats and provincial governors into "CEO diplomats" and "CEO governors," meaning they were to prioritize their role in assisting economic growth.

No conventional economists were allowed into the front rank of policymaking where they might interfere with this approach. But many, including Virabhongsa Ramangkura and Kosit Panpiemras, were recruited as advisers so they could monitor matters in the background. For this task, the government rehabilitated several of the technocrats and financiers whose careers and fortunes had been devastated by their role in the 1997 crisis. Vijit Supinit's performance as governor of the Bank of Thailand had been singled out for special criticism in the 1997 Nukul Report on the origins of the crisis. He became a government adviser, and later chairman of the stock exchange. Chaiyawat Wibulsawasdi had also been removed from head of the central bank. He became an adviser and chairman of the Shinawatra property company. Olarn Chaiprawat had been removed as head of the Siam Commercial Bank. He also became an adviser and chairman of Shinawatra University. Narongchai Akrasanee was one of several financiers accused of fraud and malpractice in connection with the crisis. The central bank cancelled most of such cases (including one against Somkid's brother) and Narongchai also became a government adviser (*TN*, 1, 15 and 17 August 2001). These figures were presumably chastened and educated by the experience of the crisis and could be expected to be vigilant. They were also presumably grateful for their rehabilitation.

Approaching the government of the country like the management of a company meant treating the national economy like a business, and looking for ways to mobilize any dormant, hidden, or underexploited assets including unused natural resources and neglected human resources. In 2002, Thaksin said: "We are in a state of economic war . . . the poor are like wounded soldiers. If we don't cure their injuries, where shall we find the soldiers to fight the war?" (Pran 2004, 93). It also meant mobilizing every arm of government, even unlikely ones; Thaksin said: "I will change the police, make it a tool of the state, to help increase the national income" (Pran 2004a, 229). Most of all, it meant reviving the entrepreneurs who had been devastated by the crisis, and mobilizing the stocks of capital which were lying unused after the collapse of the financial system. Under this approach, government assumed a more active role than before.

In earlier developmentalist states (Japan, Korea, Taiwan), the government took a more active part in protecting and promoting domestic capital in order to achieve catch-up economic growth. The two main policies were directed credit, meaning government control of capital funds, and industrial policy, meaning packages of protective and promotional measures for selected sectors or firms. Thaksin's version had its own distinctive character because of time and place. But it shifted in the same direction.

STIMULATING DEMAND

Such policies have mistakenly been branded as "populist" by some critics. (Speech, 24 August 2001)

Thaksin and Somkid laid out their thinking on the economy in several speeches during 2001. Their aim was to move away from an "East Asian Economic Model" that was "overly dependent upon exports produced by foreign technology brought in by foreign investors with low value-added content and relying mainly on cheap labor. As a result, Thailand's economy was extremely vulnerable to the fluctuations in the global economy" (Thaksin 2001d). In the longer term, this old economic model condemned Thailand to competing in the world economy by offering cheap labor with the result that incomes and domestic demand was low. Their alternative was to stimulate a mutually reinforcing process of rising internal demand, and expanding domestic entrepreneurship. In the short term, this would drag Thailand out of the lingering crisis. In the longer term it would make more productive use of local labor skills, capital reserves, and other assets (including cultural assets) and thus allow Thailand "to move further up the value chain and achieve the level of prosperity attained by the industrialised countries of the west" (Thaksin 2001b).

The previous Democrat government had begun a Keynesian-style budget stimulus from mid 1998, and boosted it in 1999 with help from the Japanese government under the Miyazawa Initiative. The Thaksin government marginally increased the budget deficit in 2001, but faced constraints on continuing this policy due to the high level of public debt (57.6 percent of GDP in 2001). It planned to continue budget deficits through to 2003, but in fact the deficit as a percentage of GDP declined in 2002 and was converted into a surplus in 2003 (fig. 4.1). The Thaksin government's innovation was to intensify the stimulus by using credit.

Banks were swamped with deposits but reluctant to lend, with the result that increasing amounts of their surpluses were being invested abroad (fig. 4.3). Several of the schemes promised in the TRT electoral platform (and others added after the party came to power) were financed by tapping unused reserves of credit in the state banking system.

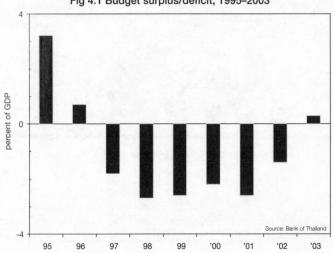

Fig 4.1 Budget surplus/deficit, 1995–2003

Source: Bank of Thailand

Funds from the Government Savings Bank were mobilized for the one million baht village fund. In addition, a People's Bank for small loans was set up by creating another window into the Government Savings Bank. Government also adopted the Japanese campaign of "One Village, One Product," offering another source of credit for community enterprise; 6,340 villages applied to join the scheme (*BP*, 9 November 2001). Several state financial institutions were required to provide the loans.

The government's agricultural bank (BAAC) financed the agrarian debt moratorium. In addition, government widened the scope of BAAC to provide credits for village communities, local administrative organizations, and cooperatives. As a result, the total loans of the agrarian bank increased by around one-fifth over 2001–3.

Thaksin by the Bangkok Post's *cartoonist, Wallop, 28 August 2002*

The Government Housing Bank and the Government Savings Bank provided credit for real estate companies and their clients under schemes to boost the real estate market. Several government banks were directed to provide credit for small and medium enterprises.

Government also sought ways to mobilize dormant funds in the commercial banking system for this credit-driven stimulus. In 1999, interest rates had fallen to historically low levels as a result of excess liquidity both locally and worldwide. After a slight hump in 2001, engineered to deter capital exit, rates declined still further in 2002 (fig. 4.2). Several commercial banks looked to consumer lending and other forms of private credit as a way to deploy their excess deposits. From early 2002, such loans increased rapidly (see consumer and financial in fig. 4.3). Foreign firms like GE Capital opened specialty consumer loan businesses. Government eased credit card regulations resulting in the launch of several low-end cards, and an increase in the total number of cards from three to six million (*TN*, 20 January 2004). Consumer debt increased for housing, automobiles, other durables, and credit card usage.

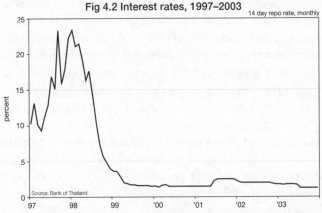

Fig 4.2 Interest rates, 1997–2003

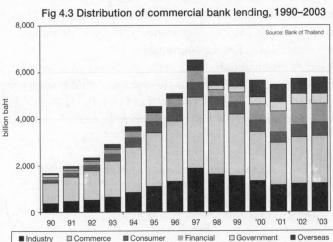

Fig 4.3 Distribution of commercial bank lending, 1990–2003

Government also hoped to intensify the impact of the stimulus by lowering some household expenses and thus increasing the surplus available for other forms of consumption. The prime example was the 30-baht health scheme. In similar vein, the government later added a cheap form of life insurance (one baht a day), a scheme of low-cost housing, supplies of cheap computers and televisions, subsidized credit for buying taxis, and loans of bicycles for children to get to school.

In the Thaksin government's thinking, these schemes would deliver a stimulus by three principles, namely "1. reducing the people's expenses; 2. increasing the people's incomes; and 3. expanding the people's opportunities" (Pran 2004, 69). By targeting funds mainly to the rural grassroots, the government hoped for a strong multiplier on grounds villagers would immediately spend any extra income rather than saving it, and would spend a high proportion on goods produced domestically. The government pushed out the village fund as quickly as possible, without seeming to care how the funds were spent and whether they could be recouped. Evaluation of the scheme was difficult because of politicization. Government claimed that default had been very low, and that a large percentage of loans from the village funds were used for "productive" expenditure. Independent surveys showed that many loans were used to defray other debt. More circumstantial observation suggested many loans were used to finance consumption.[2]

Average consumption expenditure per head had fallen by a fifth in the crisis (fig. 4.4). Driven by these stimuli, consumption climbed steadily to surpass the pre-crisis level in late 2002. Household debts also climbed. In 1994, the average household debt had been 31,079

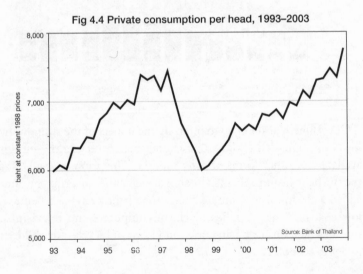

Fig 4.4 Private consumption per head, 1993–2003

baht, equivalent to 3.7 months of household income. The figure rose to 84,603 baht in 2002, and then leapt to 130,881 baht or around nine months of income in 2003 (Somchai 2003; *TN*, 3 February 2004).

DIRECTING CREDIT

> I ask banks to forget the past and support the future. Because if you look at the past, no one would get loans. (Press, 26 July 2001)

One major innovation of Thaksinomics was the increased role of government in the allocation of credit.

In early 2001, untangling the collapsed banking system was an immediate priority. Commercial banks had been shrinking their loan portfolios for three years, and had resisted the previous government's entreaties and threats for them to provide more credit to get business moving. Bad loans had come down from the 1998 peak of almost half the total credit in the financial system, but were still cluttering the banks' balance sheets. Thaksin devoted the first weekend of his prime ministership to a brainstorming session with all the major bankers and financial officials. But he failed to reach a deal with the bankers. Over the next year, they repeatedly rebuffed his calls for them to add to the stimulus by expanding lending.[3] Thaksin seemed to lose interest in revival of what he began to call "the old banking system" (*BP*, 26 July 2001). The era of "bank capitalism," in which the commercial banks had dominated the capital market, slipped into the past.

Thaksin hoped to increase the role of the stock market to replace the banks. But the stock market was also mired in the doldrums. In mid 2001 and again in early 2002, the government tried to revive it by providing tax incentives, investing some of the state pension fund, and by floating a "Thai Opportunity Fund" (*TN*, 23 May 2001). It also proposed to privatize sixteen state agencies to attract more funds to the market and boost total capitalization to 100 percent of GDP. But the market remained dull until early 2003 when foreign funds began to return. Over 2003, the market rose a spectacular 117 percent. Thaksin and Somkid continually talked the index upwards. When in late 2003, the regulators wanted to impose controls on speculative trading and some obvious ramping of stocks, Thaksin said such controls were "distorted" and had them watered down (*TN*, 19 November 2003). When the overbought exchange began to slide again in early 2004, Thaksin had the controls loosened yet further, and ridiculed investors who were selling out. The government planned to invest 100 billion baht from pension and social security funds, and the Vayupak Fund (see below), to revive the market (*TN*, 19 April 2004).

In practice, the stock market played only a minor and wayward role in the capital market. Changing this would take time. Instead, the retreat of the commercial banks made way for a rising role for state-owned banks. By taking over many collapsed banks and finance companies in the crisis, the state banks (especially Krung Thai Bank) had become a major part of the financial system. In early 2001, Thaksin moved quickly on his election promise to establish a Thailand Asset Management Corporation (TAMC) to take bad loans away from the banks, but failed to make the conditions attractive enough to persuade the commercial banks to transfer more than a small fraction of their loans. As a result the TAMC became principally an agency for removing bad loans from the state banks.

Some 781 billion baht of bad loans were transferred from state banks to the TAMC (*BP*, 13 January 2004). With their balance sheets cleaned up, the state banks were in a better position to loan than the commercial banks. At Krung Thai, Thaksin removed the old management and installed Viroj Nualkhair, one of the most prominent and aggressive financiers of the boom era. Krung Thai and other state banks were told to be more expansive in their lending policy to compensate for the commercial banks' nervousness. The volume of banking credit pulled out of its nosedive in 2002, and the major portion of new loans came from state banks working under political direction. The state banks' share of total credit increased from 27 percent at the end of 2000 to 35 percent three years later. More importantly, the state banks accounted for 112 percent of the net increase in credit in 2002, and 96 percent in 2003 (table 4.1). Other banks complained of unfair competition (*TN*, 31 January and 10 October 2003).

Table 4.1 Total banking credit, 2000–2004

	2000	2001	2002	2003
Total credit (baht billion)	5,962	5,687	5,892	6,145
Percent of total credit				
State institutions	15	17	18	19
Krung Thai Bank	12	12	14	16
Other commercial banks	65	63	64	60
Other	8	7	4	5
Percent of net change				
State institutions		38	39	38
Krung Thai Bank		-4	73	58
Other commercial banks		-101	75	-19
Other		-33	-88	23

Source: Bank of Thailand, table 28; Krung Thai Bank website

Note: "State institutions" includes GSB, GHB, BAAC, EXIM, IFCT, SIFC. "Other" includes finance, securities, credit foncier, and life insurance companies.

Special credit schemes were devised for the real estate sector, which was highly credit dependent, which had collapsed specially heavily in the crisis, and which was one of the focuses of the Thai domestic capital clustered around the TRT government. Preferential interest rates were provided to both developers and home buyers. Taxes on property transactions were also temporarily reduced. By late 2003, this had helped to create a miniature property boom, and an anxious debate whether this was a reinflated bubble.

In 2003, the government tried another method to circumvent the commercial banks. It launched the Vayupak Fund, named after a mythical bird that lays golden eggs. The aim was to raise funds directly from the public by offering a better return than currently low bank interest rates. The first fund hoped to raise 100 billion baht for buying out the Finance Ministry's shares in state enterprises and private companies (mostly finance firms which the ministry had had to bail out during the crisis). However, the public response was below expectations. Plans for more Vayupak funds were quietly forgotten.

The state banks were urged to lend to SMEs and to priority sectors. The TAMC was also directed to concentrate on firms in these sectors (*BP*, 17 September 2002). But the state banks, the TAMC, and other state financial institutions also had great powers to favor specific businesses. A few examples give some of the flavor. Prayuth Mahakitsiri, an industrialist and property developer who was 27th on TRT's party list slate at the 2001 elections, received a 15 billion baht haircut from TAMC for a copper smelting project whose development had stalled because of bad debts. He did not need this haircut because he was short of money: a few months later he bought a golf course for 1 billion baht cash (*TN*, 31 October 2002; *BP*, 10 February 2003). For one company owned by Sondhi Limthongkun, head of the badly indebted Manager group and supporter of Thaksin, the TAMC and other creditors wrote off 75 percent of a loan, while Krung Thai Bank also wrote off a quarter of Sondhi's 1.65 billion baht debt (*TN*, 9 and 11 April 2002, 20 August 2002, 8 February 2004; *BP*, 23 May 2002). Foreign creditors complained bitterly of government pressure to forgive a large amount of the bad debts of the Jasmine group (*TN*, 20 May 2003). A real estate developer associated with Chavalit was given a 50 percent haircut on a 2 billion baht loan (*TN*, 26 December 2002). A respected former judge resigned from the chairmanship of TAMC saying discreetly he was "heavy-hearted" (*BP*, 3 October 2003).

NURTURING COMPETITIVENESS

We are going to free Thais who are the slaves of capitalism. . . . We cannot run away from capitalism. But we can increase our competitiveness. (Press, 2 October 2003)

In his first major speech on economics as prime minister in April 2001, Thaksin described Japan, the US, and the "former Asian Tiger economies" as failed development models given their low current rates of growth. He announced:

> We are going back to basics in every sense of the word and especially in light of the new and less than friendly world environment. . . . We are looking inwards to our original strengths, our unique local know-how, and matching them with new marketing and communications technology. . . . We must look inward to new products and SME industries that are unique, crafted from domestic inputs, traditional or local know how with special appeals into the new market. . . . The process of development is an unending quest to produce competitively. . . . Our hope is to develop a balanced way to attain such growth with grace, style and harmony. (Thaksin 2001a)

A month later, he elaborated the theme. The aim was to create "a new class of entrepreneurs" who could marry local skills and products with international technology and hence move "up the value chain." This strategy, Thaksin claimed, was appropriate not just for Thailand but for Asia:

> Asian capabilities, aesthetic skills, unique local know-how, knowledge and dedication, when combined with world-class modern design, cutting-edge technology, appropriate cost-effective engineering, modern packaging, advanced marketing and Internet capabilities, will be the key to the new Silk Road and the new spicy life styles. (Thaksin 2001b)

While the TRT rhetoric tended to highlight the efforts on behalf of SMEs and grassroots enterprises, in fact the policy extended across the size range, and was especially focused on some of the big enterprise groups associated with TRT.

Somkid led a project to enhance Thailand's "competitiveness." The international consultant, Michael Porter, was hired for US$1 million to identify sectors in which Thailand could find a competitive niche (Pran 2004, 366). By mid 2002, five sectors had been identified: tourism; fashion, especially for tropical regions; food; computer graphics; and automobiles (*TN*, 21 May and 4 July 2002). Subsequently the list was widened a little to include agri-processing, more computer-based segments, and more service sectors including medical care and logistics. This longer list was a compromise between the strict results of the competitiveness study, and the business interests of the groups clustered around the Cabinet.

Porter's presentation in May 2003 provided only limited guidance on how to increase Thailand's competitiveness (Porter 2003). Its analysis of Thailand's problems rehearsed some familiar factors: low skills, weak technology, obstructive government. More surprisingly given his audience, Porter also criticized Thai firms for their "connections with government" and "protected market positions." While emphasizing the need for "clusters" to synergize innovation and growth in the target sectors, he tended to look outwards rather than inwards for sources of change. He recommended a larger role for transnational companies, more foreign investment, and free trade zones. Among priorities, he suggested opening the telecoms market, and concluding a free trade agreement with the US. Perhaps more to the liking of the audience of local entrepreneurs, Porter stressed the need to overhaul government, increase business-government collaboration, and strengthen micro policies (meaning assistance to specific sectors or firms). He also supported a larger role for local authorities in promoting growth (consistent with the idea of CEO governors), and more emphasis on building synergies within the region.

The Board of Investment's operations were revised to target the new priority sectors, and to encourage cluster-based growth (*BP*, 21 December 2002; *TN*, 9 December 2003). The NESDB was relieved of its old role as a planning agency and commissioned to oversee the new sectoral strategy. Government put together packages for each priority sector. An institute was established for the textile sector as an experiment for the new approach. Government staged a flashy public event to inaugurate the scheme to make Bangkok a fashion capital.

In parallel with this high-level approach to national competitiveness, the government also pursued the idea of creating a new structure of production at the grassroots. In place of the reliance on foreign investment and technology, Thailand should create industries which combined "local ingenuity and wisdom" with the country's "rich natural assets" to produce goods with "high touch and high tech," appealing to the jaded markets of the advanced world (Pansak 2003). The "One Tambon, One Product" (OTOP) scheme was based on the idea that localities would have better chances to compete in national or international markets if they specialized in a single product (or type of products). Government provided loans for OTOP projects along with some help in technology and marketing, as well as promotion through retail events and awareness raising.

DEEPENING CAPITALISM

Capitalism needs capital, without which there is no capitalism. We need to push capital into the rural areas. (Speech, 21 August 2003)

One objective of the government's several schemes was to deepen and extend capitalism. Thaksin repeatedly emphasized that the various loan schemes were attempts "to encourage Thais to be more entrepreneurial and to harness their innovative and creative capacities" (Thaksin 2001d). Rather than delivering a stimulus by enlisting peasants on employment generation schemes, this government handed them loans in the hope they would start a business. Thaksin said: "I will make more Thai be *thaokae*,[4] because business creates growth, employment, and circulation of spending" (Thaksin 2003b). Pansak (2003) claimed: "For the first time in the history of Thailand, we have moved capital closer to the people." Thaksin often expressed amazement that critics branded these schemes as "populist" when their intention was firmly capitalist.

This approach started from the idea that large numbers of Thai rural people were imperfectly integrated into the market economy.

Some practiced farming primarily for subsistence, and only secondarily for market sale. They used limited technology. They spent a lot of time on hunting and gathering. Thaksin believed the way to bring them further into the market economy was to provide them with capital. Integrating them further into the market would both overcome poverty and contribute to GDP growth. He said: "under the capitalist system, if villagers have no access to capital, they have no opportunity to get something going for themselves (*luem ta aa pak*). And who will say it is debt? I will. If I had not been in debt before, I would not be where I am today" (Pran 2004, 68).

By a similar logic, many illegal and underground businesses were imperfectly integrated into the formal economy. Bringing them above ground would contribute to both growth and government revenue. Thaksin estimated this could boost economic growth by 2 percent (*BP*, 22 February 2003). From 2002 onwards, the government took special interest in the gambling industry, most of which was technically illegal. Estimates suggested its value added might be around 7–8 percent of GDP (Sangsit et al, 2003). Most of this leaked away because punters preferred the underground lottery to the government's version; because they visited the twenty-three casinos located only a few hundred yards across the borders in neighboring Laos, Cambodia, and Burma; or because they went on junket tours farther afield. In 2003, government began to annex the underground lottery to the government's own lottery system, with some success. It also floated proposals to legalize casinos but met opposition on social and moral grounds, which made the issue not worth pursuing in the run-up to an election. In similar vein, government contemplated making the sex industry more legitimate and taxable, but faced opposition from the moral lobby (and possibly also from the police which benefited from levying its own informal taxes on the sex trade).

During a visit in mid 2002, Bill Clinton told Thaksin about the ideas of the Peruvian economist, Hernando de Soto, on deepening and extending the capitalist economy (*Nayok Thaksin lem 3*, 57). In *The Mystery of Capital*, De Soto argued that Western economies were more advanced than all others because their states established a uniform system of property rights that allowed everyone to use their assets to raise capital. De Soto was invited to Bangkok in November 2002 and feted. Pansak said: "Mr de Soto has given us the intellectual and practical groundwork for the direction we are taking" (*TN*, 11 November 2002). Soon after, the government announced a grand scheme to "turn assets into capital," meaning increasing the forms of property which could be used as collateral for loans from banks. Partly this meant ensuring that all landowners had a full title deed rather than some more qualified document or no document at all. Partly it meant issuing new documents conferring some form of property right. The prime example was a vendor's right to occupy a certain location in a market or on a pavement. In reality, this was a considerable distortion of De Soto, who was scathing about such changes in documentation. He focused much more on: eliminating rules and regulations which raise the cost of starting a business; creating a judicial system which is accessible, efficient, and fair; and politically defeating the predatory instincts of carpetbaggers such as the corporate elite and the state itself. These tasks would be much more difficult to achieve in Thaksin's Thailand than extending documentation. The commercial banks listened to the government's proposals to expand forms of collateral with a distinct lack of enthusiasm. Thus again the state banks had to play the lead role, while government sought ways to allay the commercial banks' reluctance to lend to small farmers and traders.

In late 2003, government launched the "war on poverty" which had been part of its election promises. It began by inviting all those who felt poor or disadvantaged to register themselves by filling out a form stating their difficulty. Some 7.2 million responded. Analysis of the forms showed that the two major problems were lack of agricultural land and heavy indebtedness. Government promised to find unused land for distribution, and to restructure debts through the state banking network. An initial part of the "war on poverty" was thus another scheme to extend government-directed credit at the grassroots.

In Thaksin's view, the promotion of national capital on the one hand, and the populist schemes on the other, were part of a single strategy for deepening and expanding capitalism: "We are fully committed to making economic prosperity and social development mutual and reinforcing components of each other" (Thaksin 2003f). Distributing some of the gains of growth more equitably was necessary to achieve the peaceful society in which capitalism could flourish. Thaksin talked of a "social contract" (see chapter 5), the "coexistence between social objectives and capital management," "social capitalism," and the "coexistence of socialism and capitalism." Both were necessary, he explained, because "Capitalism has targets but no ideals, while socialism has ideals but no targets. . . . We need to combine the best of each. . . . I'm applying socialism in the lower economy, and capitalism in the upper economy."[5] In his grandstand speech in Manila, Thaksin claimed: "This successful partnership between the Government and the poor is virtually the first partnership in Thai history that actually works" (Thaksin 2003f).

FINANCING THAKSINOMICS

I once went to Las Vegas and lost US$5,000. For me, that was a big thing. I stopped playing immediately. Too risky. But on a business investment of a billion baht, I can make the decision in 10 minutes. No problem. That's me. (Speech, 12 February 2003)

To finance its ambitious plans, the Thaksin government used methods known in other countries but novel for Thailand. Because of growing debt servicing costs and inflexible current expenditure (mainly salaries), the capital budget's share of the total budget declined from 40 percent in 1997 to 20 percent in 2003 (fig. 4.5). Although the economic recovery and aggressive tax collection raised tax returns by 13.7 percent in 2003, this only slightly improved the budget position. The government (like its predecessors) talked of new methods to tax wealth, but did little.

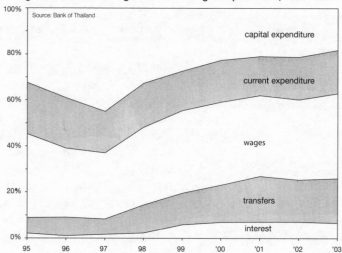

Fig 4.5 Distribution of government budget expenditure, 1995–2003

Source: Bank of Thailand

capital expenditure

current expenditure

wages

transfers

interest

Many of the new schemes were financed using funds from state financial institutions. This "quasi-fiscal" technique has been common in other countries that faced budget constraint and a high public debt burden. Japan began using the technique after the Second World War, and the amounts involved rose to be roughly equivalent to the regular budget. The Thaksin government's usage was more modest. Preliminary estimates suggested the amount of quasi-fiscal financing in 2002 and 2003 was in the range of 2–3 percent of GDP, or 10–17 percent of the regular budget (table 4.2).

The Thaksin government also became interested in selling off shares in state enterprises, in part, as a way to raise funds. This involved political risks. The economic nationalism that Thaksin tapped at the 2001 election had been directed, among other things, against the IMF's proposals for privatization. In its policy statement, the TRT Party had said: "Privatization must be consistent with long term development perspective, and the process must not be rushed into" (Brown and Hewison 2004, fn. 14). Thaksin hoped to lull the nationalistic opposition by selling only a limited proportion of any

Table 4.2 Quasi-fiscal financing 2002–3 (million baht)

Project	Financial Institutions	2002	2003 (June)
1. SME Loan		57,098.2	58,012.0
	BOT	4,130.0	26,986.5
	SMED	15,410.0	9,552.6
	IFCT	15,078.6	8,601.9
	EXIM	7,283.2	3,379.4
	GSB	2,144.9	1,498.0
	BAAC	8,935.0	6,053.7
	SICGC	4,116.6	1,939.9
2. Graduated Payment Mortgage Loan	GHB	26,748.3	0.0
3. People's Bank	GSB	10,294.7	1,861.3
4. National Village Fund	GSB	80,000.0	0.0
5. Community Enterprise Loan	BAAC	8,319.0	6,725.0
6. Matching Fund		1,208.7	86.5
Thailand Equity Fund	GSB + IFCT	8.7	86.5
Thailand Opportunity Fund	KTB	1,200.0	0.0
Total (1–6)		183,668.9	66,684.8
7. Homes for the Poor 1, 2 & 3	GSB + GHB	0.0	57,704.0
8. Vayupak Fund 1		0.0	30,000.0
Total (7–9)		0.0	87,704.0
Grand Total		183,668.9	154,388.8

Source : Preliminary estimates by the Fiscal Risk Management Group, Ministry of Finance, as of December, 2003.

enterprise's shares through the stock market, and waiting until domestic investors had recovered from the crisis enough to be in the market. The pioneer case of this "corporatization" approach involved sale of around 30 percent of the government petroleum company, PTT, in late 2001. The press suspected the sale had been discreetly managed since ministers' relatives and known friends of the government acquired large holdings.[6] Moreover, the initial sale price was modest (the shares sold out in two minutes), and the value of the shares inflated fivefold over two years, helped by some obvious ramping. Five other smaller corporatization projects followed the same pattern. In short, corporatization looked like a means to turn state assets into crony capital.

For 2004–6, government proposed twelve corporatization projects including electricity, water, ports, airports, and expressways. When government started with the electricity generating authority, EGAT, in early 2004, the proposal was strongly opposed by the union, by former governors of the authority, and by activist groups. Thaksin's attempt to calm this opposition by, among other things, promising to ensure a fair and transparent sale of the shares, seemed like a tacit admission of what had happened with PTT. Selling off state enterprises was not going to be a problem-free way of financing Thaksinomics.

GOING DUAL TRACK

By investing in Thailand, you are effectively taking multiple bites from the same apple. You can produce for the 62 million people in Thailand and, at the same time, target the 500 million people in Asean . . . and in the near term you can also increase production for the 1.3 billion Chinese. (Speech, 20 November, 2001)

Thaksin's April 2001 speech about "looking inwards to our original strengths" provoked a minor panic among foreign journalists and businessmen who imagined the government planned some more seriously nationalist policy. From mid 2001, the government began to explain that its domestic measures were only one half of a "dual track policy,"[7] and that the other half was stimulus of the external economy (exports, tourism, and foreign investment). Given the relatively open nature of the Thai economy, this was simple realism. Thaksin recanted his rejection of the "East Asian Economic Model" by explaining: "we are not looking to abandon the East Asian Economic Model. Rather we are seeking to improve and build on it" (Thaksin 2001e). Thaksin also made a point of emphasizing that he was a believer in free trade: "Thailand, and in particular my administration, is firmly committed to maintaining an open, free enterprise economy. Our welcome to investors, old and new, continues. We shall honour our international commitments. There is no backtracking" (Thaksin 2001b). For emphasis, he noted that his own business empire stretched beyond Thailand's borders: "I'm very international . . . and my business is very international, even though it's a domestic business" (*BP*, 26 July 2001).

The plan to pass a law restricting the roles of foreign retailers—initially a highly symbolic part of plans to stimulate domestic enterprise—was suddenly abandoned in late 2002. The expansion of large-scale international retail chains had been a major effect of the crisis. Small retailers protested against this powerful competition. Thaksin had initially supported the drafting of a bill to impose some regulation. This policy was suddenly reversed, a minister explained, "simply because we don't want to send a wrong signal to the foreign community." Thaksin added: "External trade is important to the Thai economy since it generates new investment and increases our productivity" (*TN*, 17, 18, and 20 November 2002).[8] Plans to modify the IMF-imposed legislation which domestic business opposed (the "eleven bills") were quietly dropped.

In the second half of 2001, Thaksin and other members of the government traveled overseas to solicit investment, using the "dual track" tag as their theme. They stressed Thailand's attractions, its central position in Southeast Asia, and its proximity to China. Somkid especially emphasized that the TRT's "inward" policies would benefit foreign investors just as much as domestic ones. Speaking to businessmen in New York in December, he insisted that the help for SMEs would build "supporting industries for your investments"; the domestic demand stimulus would "expand the buying power of 62 million Thais" for the benefit of investors targeting the domestic market; and the cheap health care scheme would "ensure a strong and healthy workforce" so that "production need never be put on hold by disruptions in supply of utilities, or by sick-leave" (Somkid 2001).

At the same time, the Thaksin government put considerable efforts into promotion of the export of goods and services. An ambitious plan was drawn up to double tourist arrivals within a decade. Thaksin led trade missions to China and South Asia where the large populations and liberalizing economies offered prospects for growth. The baht exchange rate was depressed to help exports.[9]

PROMOTING REGIONALISM

For me, I see this time as the opening of a new era of the Asian phoenix flanked by all our crouching tigers and no longer invisible dragons. (Speech, 10 May 2001)

One major part of Thaksin's economic policies was a call for closer regional cooperation and synergies. As with many other parts of his programs, this was not new. The sentiment had been shared by others in the wake of the 1997 crisis. But Thaksin seized control of the rhetoric more impressively than others.

This enthusiasm was underpinned by some strong economic logic. First, growth rates in the Western economies were modest, while China was racing ahead. Largely because of China's pull, trade within Asia was growing faster than Asia's trade with other areas. Second, by virtue of its location and its history, Thailand had an opportunity to act as a bridge between China and other countries in the region. Thailand had no history of conflict with China. The population of Chinese origin had integrated and indeed come to dominate both the economy and politics. In other countries of ASEAN, historical memories and ethnic frictions between the Chinese and "host" communities continued to complicate relations with China.

Third, closer cooperation within Asia was important for the ambition to "move up the value chain" and produce more value-added goods in at least two ways. On the one hand, products that incorporated Thailand's "local ingenuity and wisdom" were more likely to find a market in countries with cultural and climatic affinities. On the other hand, the integration of ASEAN or similar groupings as a single market was important to attract large-scale foreign investment. Thaksin urged neighboring countries to follow their own "dual track" policies so rising domestic consumption would stimulate intraregional trade. He strongly supported the development of a free trade agreement within Asean, and new projects for agreements linking ASEAN to South Asia (BMIST) and East Asia (ASEAN+3).

Fourth, the neighboring countries of Laos, Cambodia, and Burma had great potential as markets and sources of labor and raw materials, but also great risks because of histories of conflict. The latter point was punctuated by an anti-Thai riot in the Cambodian capital of Phnom Penh in January 2003. Thaksin proposed to offer aid funds to these neighbors, and began a practice of joint Cabinet meetings.

In mid 2002, Thaksin invented a new forum, the Asian Co-operation Dialogue, as a vehicle for promoting regional integration. The first meeting was sparsely attended, but the follow-up in Chiang Mai in June 2003 was more convincing. The main substantive issue was some progress towards financial integration in the wake of the crisis. Thaksin pointed out that Asia generated over half the world's foreign exchange reserves, but invested these in the West.

> In turn these reserves—our own reserves—were used to create and add more wealth to the western hemisphere. Sometimes they became loans given to us by the West, even though they derived from our own money. . . . So the problem with Asia is not the fact that we do not possess enough capital to create wealth—indeed, we do—but rather that we do not possess the instruments through which we can utilize our capital to create enough of our own wealth. (Thaksin 2003c)

The previous Democrat government had already helped to pioneer a network of reserve swap arrangements designed to provide some insurance against financial volatility. In the same vein Thaksin promoted the concept of an Asian bond market that would "enable the surplus capital from one Asian country to be used to create wealth in another" (Thaksin 2003c). A symbolic start was made with twelve countries agreeing to contribute to an Asian Bond Fund of US$1 billion.

FACING REALITIES

> The Asian miracle and success was predicated on the principle that economies can achieve rapid sustained growth as long as their exports will increase exponentially without end. . . . That good feeling era came to an end in 1997, and that development model has become obsolete. (Speech, 23 April 2001)

The Thaksin government's economic agenda had a strong internal logic. Thaksin's team believed that external dependence constrained growth and made the country vulnerable to crisis. Policies to stimulate entrepreneurship and competitiveness would bring growth, a better balance between external and domestic sectors, and a cure for poverty. Integration and synergistic development within Asia would speed the process.

But these ambitions had to confront the long-run realities of the Thai economy, and the specific legacies of the 1997 crisis. Over the boom and over the bust the economy had become much more externally exposed. Since 1995, foreign trade had grown from 85 to 125 percent of GDP. Since 1990, foreign debt had multiplied over ten times. Many critical sectors of the economy—including export manufacturing, finance, and large-scale retail—had moved substantially into foreign hands. Tourist arrivals, capital inflows, and foreign participation in the stock market had all increased sharply. Despite the rhetoric about reducing this form of dependence, the short-term imperative forced the government to chase after exports, tourists, portfolio inflows, and foreign investment.

The stimulus programs had boosted consumption (fig. 4.4), but the multiplier effect was less than expected. NESDB calculated the stimulus contributed no more than 0.7 percent to growth in 2002 (*BP*, 21 June 2003). Investment failed to respond to the increase in demand. As widely recognized, such stimulus programs are less effective in open economies, because the impact can leak away through imports and capital outflows. In Thailand's post-crisis situation, with large excess capacity in many sectors, and a collapse of the bank-based financial system that traditionally had converted savings into investment, this leakage was magnified. Imports increased. Savings piled up in banks that invested an increasing portion of them overseas (fig. 4.3).

The government's attempts to solicit foreign investment were also unsuccessful because of Thailand's excess capacity and recent financial history, and because China in particular offered a more attractive alternative. Private investment, which had run around 33 percent of GDP before the crisis, dropped to 10 percent in 1998 and only crawled back to 15 percent in 2003.

Table 4.3 Contributions to GDP growth, 1999–2003 (percent)

	1999	2000	2001	2002	2003
private consumption	2.3	2.7	2.1	2.7	3.5
government consumption	0.3	0.2	0.3	0.2	0.1
private investment	-0.4	1.9	0.6	1.7	2.5
public investment	-0.3	-0.8	-0.4	-0.4	-0.1
exports	5.0	10.1	-2.6	7.3	4.2
imports	-4.1	-11.2	2.7	-6.3	-3.7
change in inventories	2.3	1.1	0.3	0.1	0.2
statistical discrepancy	-0.7	0.8	-0.9	0.0	0.1
GDP	4.4	4.8	2.1	5.4	6.7

Source: Warr (2004).

Fig 4.6 GDP growth and export growth, 1994–2003

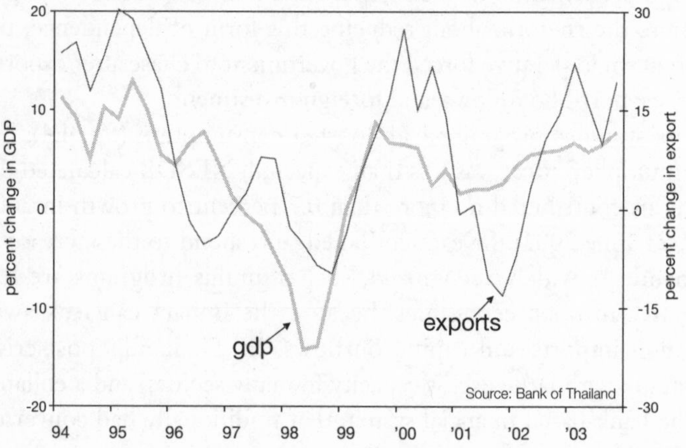

Source: Bank of Thailand

As a result, the trajectory of the post-crisis economy was largely determined by exports of goods and services (especially tourism), which had much more impact on GDP than consumption or investment (table 4.3). Exports spurted in 1999–2000, largely because of the devaluation of the baht, bringing four consecutive quarters of GDP growth above 6 percent year-on-year (fig. 4.6). But this export growth ran out of steam in 2001 because of a trade slump worldwide. Thailand's GDP growth slumped in parallel. From early 2002, exports climbed back again and achieved a 16.5 percent increase in 2003. This export growth had three main components: a spurt in sales to China as a result of China's strong growth and some specific internal bottlenecks such as temporary shortages of cement and steel; more modest growth in exports to South Asia which was not traditionally much of a market for Thai goods; and a surge in agricultural exports—29 percent in 2003 in US dollar terms—driven largely by world trends in agricultural prices. These increases may be rather temporary. China is trying to restrain its economy. Agrarian prices are always fickle.

In 2003, government decided that the public sector would have to lead the expansion of investment, especially through major infrastructure projects. This made sense. Infrastructure spending had dwindled over the years since the crisis. In past decades, building good infrastructure had been effective in stimulating other productive investment (e.g., building provincial highways in the 1960s made possible the expansion of agrarian exports which drove the economy in the 1970s). Thailand's attraction as an investment site within transnational production chains depended in part on good infrastructure. In late 2003, the government announced a slew of major schemes amounting to investment of over 2.4 trillion baht in the next six years. The schemes included a new city, and upgrading transport systems in and around the capital (table 4.4). Other grand projects aimed to create new regional centers of economic activity, including 28 billion baht to make the northern city of Chiang Mai an international aviation hub, 100 billion baht for a science park in Phuket, and "unlimited" investment in ports, airports, and roads to make Thailand a regional transport hub for the Mekong subregion (*BP*, 4 March 2004). Another massive scheme proposed to spend 300 billion baht to construct a national "water grid," pumping irrigation water around a piping system similar to an electricity grid. The government also revived the age-old dream of shortening east-west shipping routes by creating a canal or, more likely, a land bridge (two harbors, monorail, pipeline, and highway) across the Kra Isthmus (Looney 2003).

CONCLUSION: REWARD AND RISK

The old Thailand tended to inhibit new thinking and entre-preneurship. . . . Taking risk is good and rewarding, if well-managed and if it occurs under a framework of good governance and good regulation. I see a whole generation of Thais with great concepts, great entrepreneurial spirit, and great determination—whose aspirations I fear may never see the light of day. (Speech, 4 June 2001)

Thaksinomics is a growth-oriented strategy to drag Thailand out of the 1997 crisis and to make a leap towards first-world status. On its

Table 4.4 Infrastructure projects

	Projects	Period	Budget (mil. Baht)
1	The new city project at Nakhon Nayok	2004–2012	100,000
2	Khlong Prapa elevated roadway	2005–	20,000
3	Laem Pak Bia Bridge across the Gulf of Thailand	2005–2008	56,000
4	Bangkok Transport master plan (skytrains, subways)	2004–2009	397,800
5	High speed railway expansion projects	2004–2009	400,000
6	Expressways, outer ring roads and connecting roads	2004–2009	44,728
7	New canal and river routes (11 projects)	2004–2005	7,899
8	Chao Phraya River bridges (4 projects)	2004–2005	11,060
9	Motorways (10 projects)	2006–2010	118,553
	Total		1,156,040

Source: Nation Breaking News, 20 November 2003, http://www.pantip.com; *BP*, 3 December 2003; Manager Online, 25 November 2003, http://www.manager.co.th; *Phuchatkan*, 16 February 2004.

own terms, it can claim considerable success in the short term. The recovery from the crisis, reaching 6.7 percent GDP growth in 2003, exceeded almost everyone's expectations. Most people had more money in their pockets. Thousands of businesses revived. The stock market soared.

Although Thaksin paid lip service to the ideas of sufficiency and self-reliance, his economic policies and his true feelings were clearly diametrically opposed:

> Today the world is very interconnected. We are one part of the world, and we cannot close the country and stand alone having nothing to do with anybody—just living off fishing and harvesting rice. No way. To have concrete buildings, to have anything, we had to grow through interconnection with the outside world. (Pran 2004a, 204)

Thaksinomics approaches the national economy as a bundle of resources to be "managed" to deliver a higher "profit." The keys to raising profit are better skills and better infrastructure but, especially, more entrepreneurship to exploit the potential of the resources available. Government has a "developmentalist" role to encourage and nurture entrepreneurship, from the biggest conglomerate to the grassroots. The main two developmentalist strategies are directing capital and providing packages of assistance to priority sectors, projects, and firms. Resources that are currently partially or fully outside the mainstream economy—including semi-subsistence peasants, the disabled poor, and the criminal underground—have to be brought within the system. More regional cooperation can help in two ways: first by breaking down barriers to widen the market and the scope of resources available; second, by providing more protection against international instability.

Thaksin's "dual track" is an attempt to apportion the spheres of capital. Thailand's manufacturing has become integrated into global production chains. It will grow only if Thailand is more attractive as a site for investment than alternatives. But service industries are still protected by legal barriers, and grassroots enterprises are beyond the horizons of global capital. These areas still offer opportunities for domestic capital.

Business is about taking risks to make a profit. Equally, managing a country like a business is about taking risks to accelerate growth. In his rise as a businessman, Thaksin claimed he loved taking large risks. Most business risks are about debt. The same is true of the risks of Thaksinomics, which involves three kinds of debt risk.

The first is household debt. Thailand was formerly a saving society. The rate of saving (GDS) was in the range of 30 to 40 percent, among the highest in the world and adequate to cover the investment needed for growth. The Thaksin government has encouraged people not to save but to consume, and to go into debt to consume. Household debt has roughly quadrupled. In international terms, the level of such debt is not spectacular. Thailand's level of household debt (measured in proportion to disposable income) is less than two-thirds that of Korea where a similar debt strategy prompted a minor bubble crisis in 2002 (*BP*, 21 January 2004). But it is larger than Thailand has experienced in the past, and thus difficult to predict what level is critical. The accumulation of household debt has primarily been incentivized by interest rates lower than anything in living memory. Such rates are a legacy of the crisis and the generally low rates prevailing in an over-liquid world. This situation will not last forever, and indeed is likely to change very fast in the near future. In its own way, this new form of debt is no more "hedged" than the corporate dollar loans that underlay the severity of the 1997 crisis. Thaksin shrugs off this risk by reference to his own history as a debtor. But not every corporate risk taker becomes a dollar billionaire because there are not enough oligopolies to go around.

The second debt risk comes from the large role of the government as the allocator of business credit. Countries that have made a success of directing credit in line with policy goals have had systems that ensure the recipients of such credit (and other government-granted benefits) deliver high levels of performance. There is no sign such systems are in place, or contemplated, in Thaksinomics.

The third debt risk arises from quasi-fiscal financing of

government projects. This form of financing has the advantage that it apparently costs the state nothing. But if losses occur, they fall on the government budget and may increase the public debt. At present this quasi-fiscal financing is on quite a modest scale, and devoted mostly to grassroots projects. Here it is rather efficient because the corruption leakage is less than in projects financed from the main budget, and because the recipients are traditionally good debtors with a low rate of default. But these conditions may not endure. The government has an ambitious list of expensive megaprojects. It cannot finance these from the conventional budget without massive changes to the tax structure. It is reluctant to finance them through foreign loans. Hence it will be highly tempted to extend the usage of quasi-fiscal financing. This was the pattern in Japan over the past half-century. There, the choice and allocation of construction projects became highly subject to political manipulation. Rates of return became less certain, and losses common. After Japan experienced its bubble crisis of the late 1980s, such losses multiplied and became a major problem over the subsequent decade. As a result this quasi-fiscal approach is now highly controversial and subject to review. In Japan at least the system has been regularized so that quasi-fiscal projects have to be presented to parliament for scrutiny in a formal "second budget." In Thailand, no such system is in place. In fact it is difficult to work out how much money is actually involved (Pasuk 2003).

Ministers, advisers, and boosters insist that these risks are manageable, and they have their eyes on the key indicators. But in such an externally exposed economy, risks come from the outside. The government boasts of surviving SARS, bird flu, and the ripples from 9/11, but these shocks were minor and indirect. Rising interest rates, soaring oil prices, and faltering growth in China will have a direct impact. Confidence alone will not be enough.

Along with these debt risks, there is another form of risk that can be called the cronyism risk. The country is being managed as a business by people who also have their own businesses. The scope for confusion is large. Thaksinomics increases the role of government in the economy, and hence also the role of the government in determining who gets how much profit—especially the super-profits from monopolies or other favors. The financial haircuts offered by TAMC, loans from state banks, share allocations under corporatization, and grant of concessions on government projects have all been subject to political manipulation. Companies in the TRT inner circle have received favors, while some outside the circle have suffered.[10] A worldwide comparative study of links between business and politics found two-fifths of firms listed in the Thai stock market have political links, placing Thailand second to Russia with no other country anywhere close (Faccio 2003).

This cronyism risk is especially high in two areas: property speculation and the stock market. The Thaksin government set out to boost property and stock prices because they matter to people associated with the government, and because the resulting rise in asset values has a multiplier effect on the expansion of credit. But the personal impact of changes in these asset values on people in the government and their friends means that decision making may not be optimal. The country sleepwalked into the crisis in 1997 in part because politicians resisted preventive measures that seemed against the interests of themselves and their friends. Nothing here has really changed. In early 2004, an MP with a reputation for land and financial speculation proposed to install an electronic real-time stock market display in the parliament lobby at a cost of 20 million baht (*TN*, 18 February 2004).

Another, longer-term kind of risk arises from the consequences of the ambitious economic transformation that is the goal of Thaksinomics. The post-1985 boom delivered a major shock to the natural environment, and to the society. Much of the protest and mass political mobilization of the 1990s was a consequence of these shocks. The transformation imagined by Thaksinomics is much greater. In De Soto's description, unlocking the "mystery of capital" has only benign consequences, but history tells us that the deepening of capitalism is profoundly divisive. More competition means more winners but a lot more losers.

This social risk is one that has been at least partially factored into the Thaksinomics strategy. Besides stimulating consumption and nurturing entrepreneurship, the grassroots projects are designed as a "cushion" against social disorder. In May 2001, Thaksin said: "Eradication of poverty is a major socio-economic policy objective to ensure social cohesion and political stability, which will enable economic recovery and growth" (Thaksin 2001b). In Japan in November, Thaksin explained why the government was concerned about the "basic inequalities in the economic structure."

The government, therefore, deemed it essential to close this socio-economic gap in order to create a stable social platform for investment. . . . Improving the quality of life at the grass-roots level will create a stable social platform—a cushion. This social harmony protects and enhances your investments from the volatility of the global economy. (Thaksin 2001e)

Managing a country like managing a company meant managing not only the national economy, but also the society, to achieve a "social harmony" under which Thailand Company would grow.

5

MANAGING SOCIETY

In the 1990s Thailand seemed to be moving away from the centralization and repressive controls of the old security state towards more participation, debate, and respect for rights and freedoms (see chapter 1). As Thaksin took power in early 2001, it was easy to imagine he formed part of this trend. He had canvassed opinions and recruited followers among a wide range of activist groups. He presented himself as a contrast to the bureaucrat-like style of the Democrats. In public, he was often disarmingly open and spontaneous. It was not unreasonable to hope he would be "a breath of fresh air."

The unraveling of this optimism was rapid. Under Thaksin, the media were subject to tighter controls and more aggressive manipulation than anything experienced since the famously reactionary government installed after the Thammasat massacre in 1976. Protesters were beaten by the police and castigated as "anarchists." NGOs were condemned as almost treasonous. Public intellectuals who ventured dissident opinions were publicly rebuked. Several new laws were floated to control dissent. The anti-drug campaign launched in early 2003 seemed a return to the brutal methods and contempt for human rights, which had been the hallmark of the old security state.

What lay behind this? In this chapter, we look first at Thaksin's political thinking on the role of the state and nation. We then review the Thaksin government's management of public space, and the 2003 anti-drug campaign. In the conclusion we offer an interpretation of this abrupt reversal in the trend of Thailand's public politics.

SOCIAL CONTRACT AND MORAL LEADERSHIP

> Such adversary politics may not be for the best interest of the people. On the contrary, it may be a betrayal of our social contract to the people. (Speech, 23 November 2002)

Between around 1999 and 2002, Thaksin returned repeatedly to three political ideas: statecraft as management; a social contract in which people surrendered their freedoms; and an ideal rule by disinterested persons of vision.

In Thaksin's view, in the post–Cold War era, politics was no longer a matter of ideology. Rather, it was simply about "management" to solve "the country's problems." In the first testament he wrote: "The weak point of the nation is that it lacks institutions and leaders who can manage the country strategically, and that is what led the country to fall into the economic crisis" (Thaksin 1999, 231).

In this period, the "people" do not figure in his political reasoning. With the transformation of the TRT Party over 1999–2001, "the people" came to have the active role in his political rhetoric, though the content remained rather similar: "What do the people want? They want good management" (Pran 2004, 287).

While "the people" began to appear in Thaksin's politics, they were given a totally passive role. In explaining his decision to enter formal politics, he introduced the idea of a social contract:

> I have decided to enter formal politics because I believe that only formal politics is the most correct form of politics according to the social contract theory which I studied. When the people unite together in a state, they must agree to sacrifice some parts of their freedom so that the state can make the rules by which people can live together in society with justice. This is the true core of the system of representation. (Thaksin 1999, 185)

Behind this lay a malign view of human nature. Thaksin argued that evil existed inside all humans in the same way that the body played host to many viruses. As long as the body remains strong, these viruses lie dormant, but can create disease if the body weakens.[1]

In perhaps his most complex political speech, opening a conference of Asian political parties in November 2002, he repeated that the main point of social contract theory was the sacrifice of individual freedom for a general good. He quoted the opening lines of Rousseau's *Social Contract* (Man is born free and everywhere he is in chains . . .) and went on:

> These immortal words refer to the fact that men and women around the world are initially born in freedom. However through the act of setting up a state, the people consent to give up their personal freedoms and become bound by the laws and norms of the government and the general will. This is for the sake of social order and majority rule.

Thaksin also tied together the social contract from the Western political tradition with ideas on politics from modern Buddhist thinking. In 1999, he was invited to give a speech about Buddhadasa (1906–93), a renowned thinker who had provided the philosophical underpinning for a more socially and politically engaged form of Buddhist practice. Buddhadasa had argued that it was the duty of good Buddhists to improve this world rather than storing up merit for the next. Against the background of Thailand's military dictatorship during the Cold War, he argued for "dhammic socialism," rule by those who had escaped attachment to self and material things, and hence could lead society towards both material and moral improvement (Buddhadasa 1986; Jackson 2003, especially ch. 9).

In his 1999 speech, Thaksin expressed his admiration for Buddhadasa's ideas, and interpreted them in a way which aligned with the concept of a social contract:

Buddhadasa saw that politics is *thamma*[2] and *thamma* is politics. Politics is a duty. Politics is organizing the mass of people in society to live together peacefully, without crime. It's the same as the social contract theory which old philosophers like Montesquieu, Rousseau, John Locke, and Thomas Hobbes talked about. This is really about organizing people to live together peacefully without hatred or taking advantage of one another. When politics is a duty, it accords with the third principle of the *thamma*, namely doing one's duty according to natural law. (Chumphon 2002, 117)

Buddhadasa had in fact said that politics was "arranging or acting so that the many, many people who live [in this world] truly live together in peace and happiness" (Jackson 2003, 239). He believed this could only come about through the moral vision of leaders who had escaped the clutches of self-interest through Buddhist detachment from ego and greed. In the 1970s, Buddhadasa preferred a morally guided dictatorship, but in the 1980s he came to the conclusion that "the idea of democracy exists in every person by the principles of nature" (Jackson 2003, 248–49). Thaksin continued:

Politics which has *thamma* is the politics of men of moral integrity (*satthaburut*). He (Buddhadasa) said that the parliament should be an assembly of men of moral integrity, or an assembly of politicians who have *thamma*. But if parliamentarians argue, exchange abuse, and attack one another, just protecting their own interests, it should not be called a parliament in Buddhadasa's sense. . . . We ourselves must understand that politics in our country at present has been influenced by British politics where they argue against one another like lawyers. This may conflict with what Buddhadasa wanted, namely the parliament as a gathering of men of moral integrity. (Chumphon 2002, 117–8)

By quiet implication, Thaksin was laying claim to be a leader capable of the sort of disinterested vision idealized by Buddhadasa. In the period before the 2001 election, he repeatedly claimed that he was more disinterested than other Thai politicians on grounds that he was wealthy already and had no need to treat politics as a source of profit. In his later rhetoric, the source of his moral standing derived from his commitment to work "for the people." He told the political parties conference that for two years before the election, "our party members roamed the countryside and villages to listen to the needs and desires of the people." Later he told a party meeting: "Every breath we take, we think of the people" (*BP*, 6 April 2003). In the 2002 speech to the conference of Asian political parties, he emphasized that the social contract imposed obligations on political leaders:

> Since the government derives its powers and authority directly from the people, it also has an obligation to serve its citizens and do everything to promote their interests. Such is the Social Contract between the people and the State. But the true meaning of this sacred bond has often become diluted and distorted. In many cases, the concept was used to serve the interests of those in power rather than their electorate. Governments have enacted laws to sustain their own power rather than to empower the people who put them in office. Many authorities are often under delusion that what is best for themselves is best for the country. Rather, it has to be the *vice versa* that is correct: *only what is best for the country will be best for themselves.*
> . . .
> The post-cold war political parties should no longer compete on the basis of ideology, but on the basis of winning the hearts and minds of the people through their actions. Political parties must undergo a learning process with the people and for the people in order to become a party of the people. (Thaksin 2002, emphasis in original)

In his interpretation of Buddhadasa, Thaksin was also claiming that opposition to good and disinterested political leaders was illegitimate. Because good leaders have only the general interest at heart, such opposition must be based on some private interest or evil purpose. At the political parties conference, he went on to argue that parliamentary opposition could be anti-people:

Upon coming to office, many ruling parties try to do all they can to hang on to power, while those in the opposition try their utmost to topple the government and assume power themselves. Virtually anything initiated by the government is resisted by such opposition without considering whether the government's actions are in the best interests of the people. *Such adversary politics may not be for the best interest of the people. On the contrary, it may be a betrayal of our social contract to the people.* (Thaksin 2002, emphasis in original)

Thai military ideologists in the 1980s had used Rousseau and the vocabulary of the social contract to justify military dictatorship (Connors 2003a, 107–8). Thai military dictators since the 1950s had argued that they were disinterested and thus had a right to rule. Thaksin seemed to marry the same thinking along with a Buddhist notion of moral leadership to delegitimize political debate.

Thaksin said he wanted *kan mueang ning*, quiet or calm politics. He spoke approvingly of the Singaporean parliament where the opposition legitimized the form of parliamentary democracy without having any chance of challenging the government. In his ideal political system, people surrendered their rights and freedoms to the state, which was managed, just like a corporation, by people with a disinterested vision.

NATIONALISM AND CAPITALISM

Nationalism means prioritizing the nation above the interests of the people in the nation. . . . Everyone should put the interests of the nation first. Having debates and so many different opinions is just selfishness. And it's on the increase. These things slow the society down. Everyone has to unite for the country to progress. (Radio, 19 January 2002)

In forming his party, Thaksin drew on the emotional nationalism of the post-crisis reaction. But around that time, Thaksin did not directly contribute to the debate on "new nationalism." In 2002–3, however, both Thaksin and Pansak (2003) made several public references to the argument of University of Boston professor, Liah Greenfeld, that nationalism is the "spirit of capitalism." Greenfeld argued that periods of rapid growth that convert backward into advanced economies are characterized by surges of nationalist feeling. Her *Spirit of Capitalism* (2001) is a revisit to the Weber thesis, arguing it was not Protestantism (as Weber thought) but nationalism that provided the mental spark for capitalist growth. She states that nationalism under certain circumstances leads very rapidly to an economic "take-off":

> Where nationalism embraces economic competitiveness, the "take-off into sustained growth" can be expected to take place within a generation: at least such is the record of the cases analyzed here. Having begun, economic growth should logically continue so long as the motivation which sustains it lasts. (Greenfeld 2001, 474)

Greenfeld's book is totally blank on how exactly nationalism sparks capitalism. But who could resist a message that promises, "Nationalism was like the magic wand that changed Cinderella's pumpkin and mice into a gilded coach-and-four" (Greenfeld 2001, 223). Greenfeld also argued that big historical changes, such as economic transformation, are not driven by large economic, social, or cultural forces, but rather by a few prophets and practitioners, whose "agency" is able to change history.

Thaksin and his entourage sought ways to cultivate the nationalist feeling that had emerged in the aftermath of the crisis. This was a delicate matter given the relative external orientation of the Thai economy, and the sort of reaction that Thaksin evoked with his first speech on "looking inward." The solution was to tilt at largely symbolic and harmless targets, particularly foreign journalists and UN agencies. Critical or careless commentaries by foreign journalists evoked an immediate and sometimes savage reaction. In early 2002, the government threatened to expel two *Far Eastern Economic Review* journalists because of an article that had mentioned the king. When Washington queried the action, Thaksin claimed it was an issue of "national security" and insisted "Thailand's sovereignty is our business" (*TN*, 27 February 2002). After a critical article in the *Asian Wall Street Journal*, he said: "The news standard of this particular foreign newspaper is very low . . . just nonsense . . . Thai newspapers should not quote from foreign publications which are hopeless" (*TN*, 6 May 2003). When Philip Bowring, an experienced Hong Kong commentator, questioned Thaksin's optimistic growth predictions, he was treated to an epithet for which the Bangkok English-language press struggled to find a translation printable in a family newspaper ("idiot scum," *TN*, 10 January 2004). Many domestic commentators had raised very similar doubts but drew no riposte at all. Thaksin was publicly putting the idiot foreigners in their place.

In early 2003 Thaksin declared Thailand would no longer take "hand outs," meaning foreign aid and loans (Pran 2004, 118). In August 2003, he lashed out against UNHCR for granting refugee status to Burmese exiles: "Nobody can violate our sovereignty. We are a UN member. We are not a UN lackey." The agency claimed it was simply continuing practices followed for two decades (*BP*, 28 August 2003). In response to UN criticisms about human rights, Thaksin said: "We are an independent country and I would never bow to anyone. Thai people should also unite. . . . The UN does not give us rice to eat" (*TN*, 29 May 2003). Similarly in reaction to the annual US government report on human rights in 2003, he exclaimed: "We are a friend [of the US], but we are nobody's lackey. . . . The US should stop acting like a big brother" (*BP*, 3 April 2003). On the next issue of the report in 2004, he called the US an "irritating" and "useless" friend (*TN* and *TR*, 28 February 2004). He told a local audience:

> Don't complain to foreigners about Thailand violating human rights. . . . If foreigners misunderstand, it will ultimately create barriers against Thai products and that would damage all of the poor and the farmers of the country. Developed countries are already looking for ways to block our agricultural products. (*TR*, 19 January 2003)

Most strikingly, the government repaid the IMF loan two years ahead of schedule, and staged a public celebration of this "independence day." His televised speech was prefixed by a song about Bang Rachan, the village whose resistance to the Burmese in 1767 had become a hit film at the height of the economic crisis (*BP* and *TN*, 1 August 2003).

This speech was delivered against the backdrop of a massive national flag. On return from an overseas trip in 2002, Thaksin had noted that the national flag was used differently in other countries, and could even appear on underwear without infringing law or custom. He amended the 1930s laws on the use of the national flag so that institutions and individuals had more freedom (*TN*, 1 August 2003). He then ordered government offices to display the flag at all times, and encouraged corporations to fly the flag on their buildings and display it on products. In his "independence day" speech he said:

> Countries that succeed in the capitalist system have one thing in common, that is upholding the national interest. This is different from nation-building. . . . In many countries, they use the flag as a symbol. Hence today I want to tell all the Thai people that government officials have already been told they should fly the flag on every government office. As for other people who love their country, you can fly the flag on every house. It's legal. Even put it on products. (Pran 2004, 61)

Another message of Liah Greenfeld's *Spirit of Capitalism* that seems to have struck a chord with Thaksin is that the economic-nationalist surge to economic take-off can sometimes get distracted and derailed by other social and political agendas. She argues that the industrial revolution in Britain was unusual because it was the pioneer case, and that the USA's experience was in many ways copied from Britain. In these two places, the individualist entrepreneur of Weber's theory had a key role. But in countries that came later, success came from a belief that the nation was engaged in an economic war with more advanced rivals. Greenfeld's starring examples are Germany, which felt threatened by Britain's economic might, and Japan, which resisted colonialism. In these two countries, nationalism was romantic, anti-rationalist, and illiberal. Patriots were urged to forget their individualist urges, and contribute their talents to the nation. It seems likely it was these ideas that Thaksin was reflecting when he said in March 2002:

> Let me repeat again that sometimes we think individualism is what makes us triumph, but it is only a short-term victory which brings defeat in the longer term. So we have to think and act in unison, by thinking of the common interest as the overriding principle. It may seem like a defeat in the short term, but it will be a longer victory. Nationalism is the heart of success under capitalism. . . . For capitalism to succeed, the people in the country must be nationalistic. Individualism is highly dangerous to capitalism. (Pran 2004, 318–9)

Greenfeld contrasted the rapid economic growth of Japan and Germany with the more moderate growth in France. In the early nineteenth century, France seemed motivated to catch up economically with Britain. But after a time, this enthusiasm waned. People discovered they valued other things—rights, freedoms, democracy, even the peasant way of life—more than pride in being an economically powerful nation. Greenfeld sums up:

> The only certain threat to economic growth is a change in motivation—a reorientation of the economy to other goals, or simply away from growth, as a result of waning nationalist enthusiasms. (Greenfeld 2001, 474–5)

Thaksin cited many books in his speeches and weekly radio broadcasts. But among these, only De Soto and Greenfeld address large themes of economy, society, and historical change. The other books were about management theory and futurism.[3] Both De Soto and Greenfeld offered keys which unlock the magic of economic growth. Greenfeld may also have hinted how the antagonism to the outside world sparked by the crisis might be channeled into a more sustained economic nationalism.[4] She argues that in countries like Germany and Japan, leaders were able to persuade people to sacrifice rights, freedoms, personal goals, and immediate needs for the goal of an economically powerful nation. But Greenfeld also warned that such economic nationalism could be derailed if people prioritized other agendas. The new civil society of 1990s Thailand had done just that.

CONTROLLING PROTEST AND NGOS

A handful of people should not block the development of the entire nation. (Press, 23 June 2003)

Over 1999–2000, Thaksin had given the impression he would be sympathetic to NGOs and rural protest groups. He had talked to them directly, adopted some of their ideas and vocabulary. Many cooperated and supported him at the 2001 election. On the day after his election victory, he visited the Assembly of the Poor's protest encampment on the pavement outside Government House and ate lunch with them for the benefit of the media. He agreed to set up committees to solve the protesters' problems. Once these mechanisms were established, the protest camp was dissolved. On the Assembly's major issue over the Pak Mun dam, Thaksin ordered a temporary opening of the dam's sluice gates and commissioned research to evaluate the dam's impact on the local ecology and fisheries.

But it soon emerged that Thaksin's apparent sympathy for rural protest was entirely tactical. His real agenda—just like that of previous governments—was to suppress rural protests and the organizations behind them. Once the resolution of the assets case made him and the government more secure, this background agenda emerged to the fore. In late 2001, while still maintaining an appearance of friendly negotiation with the Assembly, the government instructed the foreign ministry to "negotiate" with foreign sponsors of Thai NGOs to withdraw funding, specifically naming some NGOs which helped the Assembly. The ministry refused to cooperate (and probably later leaked details of this approach to the press) (*TN*, 9 May 2003). Shortly after, in early 2002, twenty leading Thai NGO workers and forty-four foreign assistants were found to be under investigation by the Anti Money Laundering Office (AMLO), which was empowered to fight organized crime.

Over 2002, the government had to confront four cases in which local communities protested against large development projects—a dam, two power stations, and a gas pipeline.

The power projects were located on the east coast of the peninsula, and designed to use imported Australian coal. Local protests had become concerted enough for the government agencies to become nervous about proceeding. Two attempts had been made to hold public hearings, which the protesters disrupted on grounds they were dishonest attempts to legitimize the projects, not opportunities for reconsideration. The issue had become a spearhead for pressure to introduce proper procedures for environmental and social assessments of projects, including public hearings. Thaksin first officially delayed the projects, and then negotiated with the contractors to shift to alternative sites. These shifts would raise the cost of the projects, but this solution evaded the larger issue of project assessments and public participation.

The Pak Mun dam, completed in 1994, had been the most high-profile object of protest throughout the 1990s. Protesters claimed the dam had wrecked fishing in an important stretch of the northeast's major river in order to generate enough electricity for a small department store. The project had been almost universally condemned. Fishing communities and environmental groups demanded the dam gates be opened permanently to allow the river to revive. The electricity authority had undertaken to abandon all similar projects in future, but was reluctant to write off its Pak Mun investment or be seen to bow to protest. Thaksin undertook personally to negotiate a solution. Despite the high profile of the dam over the previous decade, he showed scant understanding of the issues involved. He clearly believed that poor fishermen could be persuaded to abandon the protest if enough money were offered for them to change occupation. Thaksin's financial temptation of the Pak Mun fishing communities was broadcast on live TV on 20 December 2002. After they rejected all his offers on grounds they had only the knowledge and inclination to fish, Thaksin exclaimed in frustration: "Surely you can do something else. In my life I have done many things." The reply came back, "But we don't have education like you."

When the Mun River villagers spurned his cash, Thaksin summarily decided the issue in favor of the electricity authority, without even waiting for completion of several research projects commissioned by the government. Officials then dismantled the protesters' camp. The Pak Mun case demonstrated Thaksin's conviction that communities at or beyond the periphery of the market economy should be integrated by monetary temptation if possible and by stronger methods if necessary.

The plan to construct a pipeline to transport natural gas from the Gulf of Thailand across a few kilometers of Thai territory en route to Malaysia had been concluded many years earlier as part of a larger scheme of Thai-Malaysian cooperation. The local villagers were angered because they had never been consulted on the project, and because the government had continually concealed plans to develop an industrial area around the pipeline. Thaksin first shifted the route of the pipeline slightly, but otherwise insisted on going ahead. In December 2002, the villagers staged a protest in Hat Yai where Thaksin was meeting the Malaysian premier. After the protest ended in violence, the interior minister immediately went on TV to parade slingshots and bags of chili sauce as evidence of the weapons that the protesters had planned to use. He condemned them as "anarchists." Thaksin followed up this theme on his weekly radio broadcast:

> NGOs that use violence will be blacklisted and severely dealt with by law.... Some of these people live an easy life, and have no occupation but at times create confusion and trouble. I repeat we'll use the full force of the law with people who have bad intentions towards the

country and their fellow countrymen. . . . These are people who have no credit, no credibility, because they use violence. (*KT*, 22 December 2002)

A video shot at the scene showed that the demonstration had been nonviolent. Instead, several hundred police had attacked the nonresisting protesters with batons, beating several people brutally, and overturning a truck and other vehicles. The National Human Rights Commission and the Senate separately investigated the incident and both blamed the violence on the interior minister and police (NHRC 2003). The government maneuvered to prevent the commission's report from being submitted to parliament.

In mid 2002, NGOs marked a formal break with the government by accusing it of waging a "war on the poor" rather than a "war on poverty" (*TN*, 31 July 2002).

Thaksin repeatedly portrayed protest NGOs as dishonest recipients of foreign funding: "Some of them want to make their presence felt. They record their rallies on video and send the tapes overseas to get financial support" (*TN*, 31 July 2002). He explained the government would "cooperate with NGOs that have identical policies to ours in terms of serving the people," but implied others should not exist (*TN*, 21 May 2003). Such NGOs were no longer needed because the TRT government had a direct relationship with "the people." Civil society had become superfluous:

In the past Thailand never had a strong government that sincerely solved the problems of the poor. If there is no gap between the people and the government then the career-less people who work in these organizations and live off subsidies from overseas are out of a job. . . . Some people finish their education and do nothing but work for these organizations and collect these overseas subsidies. . . . This group of NGOs includes people who want to be famous, who want to enter politics and so stir up other people. There are an estimated one thousand of them. They command no confidence among the other 63 million. I maintain most people understand that the government does everything for the people. I have no interest in their absurd gatherings. It's just people looking to make a name for themselves with no purpose. (*TR*, 31 March 2003)

"When compassion has reached its limit," said Thaksin, "legal measures will then be taken" (*BP*, 27 March 2002). From early 2002, the government looked for stronger legal methods to prevent and control demonstrations. The police drafted legislation criminalizing any protest that did not get prior permission, but the measure was dropped in the face of criticism. On 23 April 2002, the Cabinet passed a resolution to use "harsh action against protesters who violate the law," but then backed away in face of protests and issued a circular recommending negotiation and "mercy" (*BP*, 27 March 2002; *TN*, 23 September 2002). It then proposed to amend the Highway Act to criminalize any protest on a public road (*TN*, 17 September 2002). Among the people targeted in a government campaign against "influence," the police chief included "those who have persuasive power, who can manipulate or misguide others to do illegal things, create turmoil—such as leaders of mobs, or forest encroachers" (*TN*, 21 May 2003). NGOs were subject to petty bureaucratic harassment. Rules requiring NGOs to make monthly reports of their activities and finance were more strictly enforced. Foreign advisers had more difficulty getting visas (UN 2004).

In 2001, government began drafting a security bill to replace the old anti-communist law that had lapsed. The initial draft, which gave authorities wide-ranging powers of search and arrest, was delayed after strong public disapproval (*BP*, 19 May 2001). In 2003, the government produced another Act on the Investigation Procedure of Special Cases, which again gave authorities wide powers of search and detention. It also drafted a new National Police Act that placed the police force directly under the prime minister (*BP*, 8 June 2003). In May 2003, the government instructed the army security services to restart monitoring political activities—reversing an order of the previous army commander limiting these agencies to issues concerning the border and external security (*BP*, 20 May 2003). In August 2003, it implemented an anti-terrorist law by executive decree. Critics questioned why the government had not used the normal course of legislation, and pointed out that the definition of terrorism was broad enough to cover most dissent—a device used in earlier anti-communist legislation.[5] In early 2004, government drafted a new law to register and control NGOs (*TN*, 19 January 2004).

MANAGING MEDIA

About this public criticism . . . I'd like everyone to view the country in a positive light so that society, business, and people have hope and determination to solve problems with optimism. . . . I don't care about myself. I don't care whether or not the government has a good image. But I do care that people should feel encouraged in their work. (Radio, 17 November 2001)

Over the previous decade, the most strident criticism of political leaders had come not from the parliament but from the press and public platforms. Thaksin deployed both old and new methods to bring this criticism under control.

The first TV channel independent of government (ITV) was launched in 1996 and rapidly set new standards for news reporting and investigative feature programs. But, founded on the eve of the financial crisis, the channel never made a profit. This gave an excuse for a shake-up in 2000. The Nation Group, which was responsible for the news content but had only a 1-percent stake, was ejected. A rule restricting any single shareholder to a maximum holding of 10 percent was removed. Thaksin's family company acquired a controlling interest that peaked at 55 percent before the company was listed on the stock market in 2002.

Just before the 2001 general election, journalists on the channel complained that Thaksin was interfering in its election reporting. Twenty-three were summarily sacked. They went to the labor tribunal, which ruled that their dismissals were illegal, but the company launched an appeal that bogged down in the courts (*TN*,

27 September 2002). In September 2003, several other ITV employees were sacked, reportedly for resisting political interference (*TN*, 11 September 2003). In February 2004, a reporter was removed after an interviewee had criticized the premier (*TN*, 27 February 2004). The channel's programing was changed to lighten the content, while the management petitioned government to remove the restrictions written into its original charter and allow it to broadcast more entertainment (see chapter 7).

The five other free-to-air channels were owned by the army or government. Yet over the 1990s, these channels had broadcast more programing, particularly on current affairs, provided by independent companies and allowing public debate on social and political issues. The TRT government set out to roll back this partial independence. Pracha Maleenont, head of the family running one of the most popular of these channels, became a minister in Thaksin's cabinet. In August 2001, a prominent current affairs program was abruptly taken off the air just before broadcasting a discussion of Thaksin's Constitutional Court ruling. Subsequently the Watchdog Company responsible for this and other programs on radio and TV had all its contracts revoked on grounds of having the wrong license (Narongchai 2002, 98–106). In 2003, a popular radio station on an army owned frequency suddenly went off the air due to "technical malfunction" after it had aired Purachai Piumsombun criticizing Thaksin for demoting him in a Cabinet reshuffle. A general announced the station's concession would be canceled for broadcasting "nonsensical" content, but had to back down in face of popular support for the station's programing (*BP*, 3 March 2003; *TN*, 4 March 2003). A critical radio program by the senator Somkiat Onwimon was also taken off the air, and another produced from the parliament was blacked out, supposedly by a "satellite blip," in the middle of a report on the government's interference in the media (*TN*, 24 August 2001). Several reporters and news presenters were suddenly transferred.

Thaksin demanded that TV channels "cut down on negative news and bring out more positive news to boost businessmen's morale" (*TN*, 6 May 2003). The army sent a memo to all its radio and TV stations instructing them to focus news coverage on the work of the government (*TN*, 13 July 2001). Other army memos specifically instructed stations to ignore news unfavorable to the government. One such memo stated: "opposition to privatisation of state enterprises is not allowed to be broadcast" (*TN*, 4 March 2004). Whereas current affairs programs had earlier carried lively debate and involved viewer participation by phone-in or phone-voting, by 2002 the only programs left were interviews with ministers or permanent secretaries explaining government policies. Across all channels, news programing was shortened, and focused on government actions, crime, and human interest stories. There was little space for the parliamentary opposition and none for protest or non-formal politics. Entertainment programs increased, especially game shows. In the drama serials, the most popular segment of TV viewing, the trend over the past decade to tackle more serious and controversial subjects (corruption, rights, environment) was reversed. Many serials were thinly disguised propaganda for the uniformed services, and particularly for the anti-drug campaign. In virtual Thaksinland, the unfortunate were nurtured by an efficient government, bad guys were always defeated by dashing men in uniform, and ordinary people were showered with prizes.

The 1997 constitution laid down the principle that broadcasting frequencies were "resources for public interest" which should be controlled by an "independent regulatory body" (Section 40). By early 2001, the procedure for selecting members of this National Broadcasting Commission was under way. However, the officials, generals, and concessionaires who currently controlled all radio and TV frequencies conspired to obstruct this change. They put up a slate of candidates for the commission, and maneuvered to pack the selection committee (which presented a short list to the Senate) (Ubolrat 2001). In early 2001, activists challenged this stratagem by petitioning the Administrative Court that some of those on the selection committee had close links with candidates on the short list in contravention of rules on conflict of interest. The court scrapped the selection process (*TN*, 23 January 2001, 22 February 2002). The Thaksin government made no effort to end this jam, which meant all electronic media remained under the control of the government, army, and Shinawatra family. Meanwhile the Council of State drafted a new broadcast bill, which activists protested was designed to allow government to maintain its dominant control of the airwaves. In particular it removed two of the government's stations from regulation under the National Broadcasting Commission (*TN*, 17 December 2002, 13 March 2003, 18 March 2004).

Management of the press required different methods. The press was independently owned. It had played a prominent role in the critique of military dictatorship, campaigned successfully to revoke dictatorial press laws in 1991, and enjoyed its reputation as one of the freest and liveliest presses in Asia. The TRT government used several strategies to quiet it down. It revived previous military governments' tactic of calling in editors for friendly but intimidating chats; provided journalists with facilities (snacks, internet hookups) that they would be loath to put at risk; demanded removal of reporters and columnists who were critical; and attempted to micromanage the news content. Special Branch fired off warning letters to two papers for "irresponsibly publishing" a Reuters article on Thaksin's assets case (*BP*, 9 August 2001). The owner of *Naew Na* newspaper said that Thaksin and his aides repeatedly asked him to cancel the critical column by Prasong Soonsiri, a former security official and politician (*TN*, 14 March 2002). Most effective was manipulation of the large advertising budget from government agencies and companies associated with the government. Critics estimated that this combined budget amounted to 60 percent of all press advertising. Many press owners had suffered financially during the crisis, and were especially vulnerable to this strategy. After a few ads had been pulled at the last moment, most newspapers fell into line. The Thai Journalists' Association issued a statement: "It has become well known among print journalists that advertising incomes from companies under powerful people in the administration, and from government agencies and state enterprises, have been used to bargain against publishing stories that could negatively affect the government's image" (*TN*, 29 December 2003). The head of the association commented:

With his abundant financial and staff resources, Thaksin can easily orchestrate the direction of news to his favour and curb media freedom in the most sophisticated ways. . . . He has effectively silenced media by restricting advertisement from state bodies and enterprises. . . . As a result, he can map out long-term strategies and set agendas for the media, which consequently will lead to the so-called "media apartheid"—only pro-Thaksin media outlets will prosper. (Kavi 2001)

In early 2003, some TRT MPs drafted a bill to establish a body, appointed by the prime minister, with powers to issue "ethical guidelines" to the media and punish infringements. After an outcry, Thaksin dropped the idea (*BP*, 21 February 2003; *TN*, 27 March 2003, 1 April 2003).

In early 2004, the editor of the *Bangkok Post* was suddenly kicked upstairs. The paper had come under increasing pressure since publishing an editorial referring to Thaksin's "arrogance." Insiders said that editors received midnight phone calls instructing them to kill or bury critical items. In attempts to comply, they had censored whole columns, but this was not enough. The ex-editor said: "In 30 years, there has been no political meddling as shocking as this.... What is happening now is worse than under military regimes" (*TN*, 27 February 2002). At the established weekly newsmagazine, *Siam Rath Sapda Wijan*, a whole issue was withdrawn and rewritten overnight on the proprietor's orders. The editor resigned, and several columnists quit saying they had been subject to increasing censorship (*TN*, 28 February 2004).[6]

The *Thai Post*, *Naew Na*, and Nation media group[7] were virtually alone in defying these pressures. Indeed, the Nation group recognized that the government's controls created an opportunity to launch a new Thai daily with a more defiant line in late 2001. Within three months, this title (*Khom chat luek*, Sharp Clear Deep) had the third highest readership (but attracted far less advertising than its readership merited). At exactly this time in March 2002, documents were leaked showing that the Anti Money Laundering Office (AMLO), a new agency established to combat drugs and organized crime, was investigating the bank accounts of key figures in the Nation group, other journalists from *Thai Post*, an opposition MP, a handful of businessmen and officials, and several prominent NGOs (*TN*, 7 to 16 March 2003). AMLO claimed to have launched the investigation on the strength of an anonymous letter alleging the Nation group was a "major economic crime syndicate." The Nation secured a court injunction to halt the investigation. The government denied it had initiated the probe, but also established a committee that eventually absolved AMLO officials of any wrongdoing.

The Nation group's current affairs programs on the government TV channels were canceled on grounds the company was in arrears on fee payment. Its radio programs were banned from the military's radio network. The Nation's own TV channel on the UBC cable network was blacked out while Prasong Soonsiri was speaking. The channel was subsequently instructed to halt political programing and then told to quit UBC. "Military leaders called me," explained UBC's chief executive, "and asked me if UBC 8 had enough of that coverage yet." Nation TV moved to another cable network, TTV, which soon after was subject to harassment about infringements of its contract (*BP*, 15 March 2002, 9 April 2003; *TN*, 27 March 2003, 5 September 2003). In late 2003, relatives of industry minister, Suriya Jungrungruangkit, bought a 20 percent stake in the Nation group's holding company, but claimed they were only seeking profits (*TN*, 13 November 2003).

From late 2002, obvious interference with the media tailed away if only because most media owners and journalists became compliant. The head of the Thai Journalists Association said: "State power . . . is applied to proprietors of publishing firms who subsequently put pressure on media operators who are their employees. . . . This has caused the media to impose self-censorship to avoid problems" (*BP*, May 4, 2003). The Democrat MP, Abhisit Vejjajiva, talked about a "culture of fear" in the media (*TN* 5 March 2003). In May 2003, Freedom House, a US-based non-profit organization, downgraded Thailand's media from "free" to "partly free," and noted that "journalists exercise an increasing level of self-censorship" (*TN*, May 2, 2003). In late 2003, Shin Corporation launched a defamation case against Supinya Klangnarong, head of an NGO specializing in media issues, for an article in *Thai Post* (16 July 2003) which suggested the corporation profited from its political connections (*BP* and *TN*, 2 December 2003).

Opinion pollsters were subject to similar pressure. After one of the two leading pollsters published a survey showing 45 percent were worried about conflict of interest in the government, and the same proportion thought General Chavalit should "improve his image," its office received "frequent and unnecessary visits" from soldiers, special branch policemen, and officials who seized property and issued threats (*BP*, 1 March 2002). Shortly before this, the poll had published survey results showing that support for Thaksin had begun to decline (*TN*, 7 January 2002). Subsequently, the findings published by pollsters were conspicuously lacking in any opinions critical of the government. Thaksin reminded them that their work should "avoid causing damage to society and the nation" (*TN*, 11 December 2002).

SILENCING PUBLIC INTELLECTUALS

I have a good knowledge of democratic philosophy, so anyone who knows less, please refrain from talking too much. . . . I'm not mad, and I'm not a power crazy man. (Press, 29 November 2002)

One feature of the new civil society of the 1990s had been the emergence of public intellectuals who provided a constant commentary on social and political events. In 1998–2000, several welcomed Thaksin's rise and promise of change. As some turned rapidly critical, Thaksin reacted heavily against them. He denigrated their "outdated theories" by arguing how the 9/11 event showed the world had changed:

The shock of this event happened because economies are inter-connected like never before, and becoming even more so. Attempts to predict the future using textbooks and data as in the past—taking the trend from past to present and projecting it into the future—no longer works. If you have time, read Bill Gates's first book and you will see. The connections from past to present, and from present to future, are a different formula. (*Nayok Thaksin lem 1*, 176)

He constantly questioned the credentials and motives of any critic: "People in other countries put national interests before everything but here people criticize only because they want to look cool" (*TN*, 14 August 2003).

Thaksin reacted especially fiercely against figures who had taken a prominent part in Thailand's democratic development such as Thirayuth Boonmi, a leader of the 1973 student uprising; Anand Panyarachun, reforming premier and head of the 1997 constitution drafting committee; and Prawase Wasi, prominent advocate of social reform and political participation. When Thirayuth drew attention to the government's authoritarianism, Thaksin snapped back that "these people feel proud to be accorded quasi-hero status when in fact they have done nothing useful to society." When Thirayuth criticized him again, Thaksin wondered, "I don't understand why he still lives on a public salary" (*TN*, 7 January 2003, 15 September 2003). In response to advice from Prawase, Thaksin said: "He doesn't understand and all he ever thinks is that he's a cut above the rest" (*BP*, 25 May 2003).[8] After former premier Anand Panyarachun chided him gently, Thaksin asked Anand to "be patient and stop talking" because it was "too easy if one says something only in order to be perceived as a hero" (*TN*, 12 November 2002). The prominent economist, Ammar Siamwalla, took a vow of public silence after Thaksin called him ignorant. In a more general reaction Thaksin argued that "Thai leaders and academics like to talk problems, not solutions," and that "a lot of people feel like heroes when having a go at someone with their outdated opinions" (*TN*, 4 December 2002). These aggressive reactions to people with status derived from age, experience, and learning were a dramatic shift in the political culture, asserting the prime position of the elected leader.

In response to a critique of his foreign policy, Thaksin suggested the university should "question" the young academic responsible (*TN*, 28 June 2003). In May 2003, Thaksin threatened to purge the universities:

> Some academics, for example, cannot teach and cannot make students analyse. Some researchers cannot research, but want to draft the constitution. These people will have to go and do not worry about them. We need to move our country ahead. (*TN*, 21 May 2003)

In this response and in several others, Thaksin portrayed attacks on himself or his government as attacks on the nation. He warned critical journalists: "You media people have to believe me. Today, serving the country is more important than sending your news dispatches daily to your editors. Think before you do anything that damages the country" (*TN*, 20 May 2003). Talking about the prime minister with a taxi driver, he said, was "not good for the country" (*TN*, 24 March 2002). Even the opposition's parliamentary scrutiny of government policy, Thaksin noted, was "not done for the country's interests" (*TN*, 28 May 2002). He assured people,

> As long as I am prime minister, the interests of the nation are paramount. The people have no need to worry. Sometimes I get attacked. This happens because either: one, they just have to attack me; two, they don't know what is going on; or three, they have good intentions towards the country but lack full information. (*Nayok Thaksin lem 2*, 98)

Alternative opinions, or fallibility, were not on the list. As in Thaksin's theoretical discussion of political leadership, opposition was by definition illegitimate and anti-national.

WAGING WAR ON DRUGS

> With the [drug] traders, you must use hammer and fist, that is, act decisively and without mercy. Police General Phao Sriyanon once said, "There is nothing under the sun that the Thai police cannot do." So I'm confident that drugs are something that the Thai police can deal with. (Speech, 14 January 2003)

In early 2003, the Thaksin government launched a "war on drugs," specifically against the booming trade in methamphetamines. The campaign responded to a real social concern. But the methods used raised questions about Thaksin's attitude to rights, freedoms, and the kinds of abuses that had characterized the dictatorial past.

Drug usage is long established in Thailand. Opium remained legal and a source of government income until the late 1950s. Marijuana is rather normal through much of rural society. Heroin usage rose after the Second World War when Thailand became the transit route for exports from the Golden Triangle to the West. Large numbers of people take cheap analgesics to relieve the stress of manual work. Methamphetamine was adopted in the 1960s by groups like truck and bus drivers who named it the "diligent drug" because it enabled them to work longer. It was dubbed *ya ma*, the "horse drug," because of the logo of the original (legal) importer, and because it allowed users to work like a horse.

In the mid 1990s, the production of heroin was disrupted after the Burmese government captured the famous trafficker, Khun Sa. Manufacturers turned to methamphetamines as a substitute business. Cheap and easy to make, they soon found a growing market inside Thailand. Against the background of the economic crisis, the market spurted. Some took the drug for relief from the personal impact of the crisis. Others took up trading the drug when other businesses evaporated. Reportedly, large numbers of police, officials, and politicians became involved. Dealers expanded the market by classic pyramid selling—finding a customer and then encouraging that person to develop his own customer base. By this method, the trading networks penetrated into the schools. Taking *ya ma* became fashionable for teenagers enjoying nightlife. Elite families became concerned when they found their own children—rather than the workers and slum residents usually identified with drugs—were taking them.

From 1996-7, government agencies began anti-methamphetamine campaigns. They plastered the country with slogans, and used presenters ranging from authority figures (General Prem) to role models (actors and rock stars). As these campaigns had little effect on the rising market, the approach became more desperate. Snoh Thienthong proposed renaming amphetamines in Thai from *ya ma* to *ya ba*, "mad drug." The PR campaigns focused on violent incidents involving users who had psychotic reactions from taking large amounts.

Some of the pills were manufactured in Thailand, but most were made in Laos, Cambodia, and especially Burma, where the press reported sixty to ninety factories in the hill areas beyond Thailand's northern border. The biggest producers were the Wa minority. They had earlier made their peace with Yangon, and the Thai military believed their methamphetamine business was condoned by the Burmese government. A new town, Mong Yawn, appeared in the Wa area in the late 1990s, apparently devoted to drug production and trade. The Thai army's revelations about this town, and attempts to clamp down on the border trade, led to exchanges of gunfire across the border just at the time TRT came to power in February 2001, and again in May (*BP*, 12 February 2001, 10 May 2001; *TN*, 3 May 2001).

TRT included a "war on drugs" in its policy platform assembled in 2000. Six weeks after assuming office, Thaksin convened a meeting of related agencies which resolved to increase the propaganda campaign against *ya ba*, step up border patrols, negotiate with governments of the countries housing drug factories, and begin treating small users as patients needing rehabilitation rather than as criminals (*BP*, 12 March 2001).

This program was not a success. While Thaksin visited neighboring countries and signed agreements, Yangon seemed unwilling or unable to restrain the Wa. The propaganda campaign exaggerating the psychotic effects of the "mad drug" backfired because young experimenters discovered the drug had no "mad" effect at all and promptly disbelieved all government propaganda. The rehab centers were too quickly and inexpertly organized with the result that some inmates progressed from light to more serious usage, and repeat attendance was common (Lewis 2003; Nualnoi et al. 2000). In his birthday speech in December 2002, the king chided the government for not being effective against the methamphetamine trade.

The statistics became infused with a growing sense of panic. The National Security Council estimated the annual import around 800 million pills. A minister talked about 3 million addicts. A survey reckoned half of secondary students had tried *ya ba* at least once. In fact, the scale was rather more modest. The Office of the Narcotics Control Board (ONCB) admitted that all data on imports were no more than guesswork, that around 2 million people probably had some experience of *ya ba*, and around 400,000 took it once a month or more (*TN* 24 June 2001, 10 June 2002). The Health Ministry reckoned similarly there were around 2 million very occasional users, and around 540,000 more regular users (Lewis 2003, 13, 93).

On 14 January 2003, Thaksin briefed a gathering of officials on the government's new campaign to eliminate drugs within a deadline of three months. He told them the methods had already been pretested in certain provinces:

> Sometimes people were shot dead and had their assets seized as well. I think we have to be equally ruthless. The drug sellers have been ruthless with the Thai people, with our children, so if we are ruthless with them it is not a big deal . . . . If drug traders are listening they must make up their minds whether to stop selling or carry on. If they don't stop, there is a chance they will be dealt with in every way, both life and limb . . .
>
> With the traders, you must use hammer and fist, that is, act decisively and without mercy. . . . If some drug traders die, it will be a common thing. We have to send a message that they have to quit. Traders will get no return except risk to their own lives, risk of being

arrested, and of being finished off because all their assets are seized. (Thaksin 2003a)

He made it clear he believed many major traders were officials, policemen, and other powerful figures. He threatened to remove officials who failed in this campaign (the full speech is translated in appendix 2).

Ten days later, the Interior Minister Wan Muhammed Nor Matha reiterated the seriousness of the campaign:

> Tell them [drug dealers] to stop selling drugs and leave the communities for good or they will be put behind bars or even "vanish without a trace..." Who cares? They are destroying our country. . . . In our war on drugs, the district chiefs are the knights and provincial governors the commanders. If the knights see the enemies but do not shoot them, they can be beheaded by their commanders. (*BP*, 25 January 2003)

He clarified later that the talk of "beheading" was a reference to sixteenth-century King Naresuan and urged governors who failed to achieve their targets to bear this king in mind: "They should check out history books about what King Naresuan did to his generals who failed to keep up with him on the battleground during his great fight against the prince of Burma. The King had all of them beheaded" (*TN*, 15 February 2003).

In each province, blacklists of those involved in drugs were separately drawn up by the police, by village heads, and by the ONCB. In total, 329,000 names were eventually listed (*BP*, 11 December 2003). Each province was then set targets for the number of arrests and seizures within the three-month deadline. Police were incentivized with bonuses for the number of arrests, and later rewards of up to 40 percent of the value for information leading to seizure of assets. Provincial governors and police chiefs were threatened with removal if targets were not met. Anyone involved with drugs was invited to turn themselves in and promise to quit or face retribution.

From 1 February onwards, the nightly television news opened with clip after clip of prone dead bodies. The newscasters announced that these were drug dealers who had been killed by other drug dealers to prevent them giving information to the authorities. This kind of killing was named *kha tat ton*, roughly "kill to cut and remove," often translated as preemptive or silencing killings. For two months, the cumulative death toll was announced daily, increasing at an average daily rate of thirty. At the close of the three months, some 2,637 had been killed, of which officially 68 had been shot by the police in "self defence" (*BP*, 11 December 2003).[9]

Within a few days, a pattern emerged. Almost all were shot by handguns. Many were killed by a gunman riding pillion on a motorcycle, the classic style of professional hits. The forensic expert, Dr. Pornthip Rojanasunan, noted that the bodies were often found with a small packet of *ya ba* pills (often not noticed at first), that police resisted forensic examinations, and that the authorities seemed to be able to turn the killings on or off at will (*BP*, 17 and 19 February 2003). Several were killed soon after having reported themselves to the police.

The true story behind the killings is not publicly known. The authorities insisted throughout that the police were not directly involved. But the line dividing police from professional gunmen is so thin as to be nonexistent. Some police (and military) moonlight as professional gunmen. Others retire to this profession. Some senior officers run gangs of gunmen.[10] The police sometimes hire outside help in cases which are difficult to manage by normal police methods, or which are simply unlikely to be monitored (e.g., car smuggling across the eastern border). The pattern of killing recalled the campaign to mop up communists and sympathizers in the rural areas in the early 1980s, as described by the anthropologist Andrew Turton:

> A more recent development is the appearance of "death squads" (also known in some localities as "hunter killer units," "ruthless hunter units," "death squad infernal units") set up by provincial police authorities to pursue criminals without due process of law. There are indications that these units have been responsible for a number of

deaths and disappearances. . . . Villagers in many areas recall innocent farmers being killed in fields and swiddens by government troops literally "headhunting" for bounty and preferment. . . . At the outset we must note the very widespread legal and illegal distribution and possession of firearms in Thailand, and the existence of a large number of people willing to act as "gun hands" (mue puen), that is to say, to carry out killings on behalf of others, often for a quite small fee which may vary according to the rank or importance of the victim. Also most of the killings are shootings, at close range, and by such a third party, and frequently with military weapons such as the Ml6 and AK47 automatic rifles. . . . Extra-judicial killings include those of persistent offenders carried out with the approval sometimes of whole communities, which are tolerated by the police; those carried out by the police themselves, other than with legal sanction. . . . In this case the victim is often someone who has been critical of local power interests, and whose death is passed off as being that of a communist suspect, or alternatively, as having been caused by communists. (Turton 1984, 56–8).

General Chavalit Yongchaiyudh was involved in planning this communist suppression campaign, and General Thammarak Issarangkura na Ayutthaya was involved in the implementation in southern Thailand. As deputy prime minister and defense minister, they were closely involved in the 2003 anti-drug campaign.[11]

Two years earlier during TRT's first anti-drug drive, the police chief of the lower northeast had revealed that a similar campaign was under way. He told a Nation reporter about the "Shortcut to Hell" campaign:

Our target is to send 1,000 traffickers to hell this year, to join some 350 before them. . . . We have applied legal means, political science and even Buddhism, but the [drug] problem seems to be getting worse. Now it's time to rely on [the] Death Angel. Of course, it's a legally delicate means, but it's the path we have to take to bring peace back to society. . . . This year we expect at least 1,000 traffickers to travel to hell. (TN, 25 July 2001)

This officer, Police Lt-Gen Pichai Sunthornsajjabul, was still chief of region 8 (mid south) during the 2003 drug war. He announced that ten thousand anti-drug volunteers backed "a plan to shorten the lives of drug dealers. . . . A normal person lives for 80 years. But a bad person should not live that long" (*BP*, 25 January 2003). Another police colonel told the press he had been instructed to extract information from suspects and then kill them. He asked: "Why should we spare the scum?" (*BP*, 23 February 2003).

As protests mounted through February, the government issued a highly ambiguous message. On the one hand, ministers continued to deny any direct official involvement in the killings. Wan Noor urged the press to report that the victims had "expired" without any agency at all (*BP*, 19 February 2003). On the other hand, the (government-controlled) television continued to show pictures of bodies and announce the rising body count, while ministers issued statements that implied that the deaths were legitimate on grounds that drug traders had forfeited the right to life. Wan Noor suggested: "I think human rights activists should not worry too much about these traffickers' lives" (*TN*, 4 February 2003). Thaksin said: "It [murder] is not an unusual fate for wicked people. The public should not be alarmed by their deaths," and "In this war drug dealers must die" (*TN*, 27 February 2003; *BP*, 27 February 2003).

Criticism from outside Thailand was met with sharp replies. When a UN official expressed concern, Thaksin snapped, "The UN is not my father." In reply to protests from Amnesty International and others, Thaksin said: "We are an independent country. We do not need to give away our independence to others." He urged others to "do away with the thinking of the foreigners" (*TN*, 13 February 2003; *BP*, 27 February 2003). Thammarak suggested all critics, including the *Far Eastern Economic Review*, were in the pay of the drug lords as "traffickers were rich enough to hire anyone to do anything" (*BP*, 11 March 2003). After Pradit Chareonthaithawee, a human rights commissioner, disclosed that he had talked about the drug war with UN officials overseas, Thaksin lambasted him as a "whistle-blower" and called his action "ugly . . . sickening." The TRT Party announced it was planning to have him impeached, and

Pradit's family was subject to abusive phone calls (*TN*, 7 March 2003; *BP*, 9 March 2003).

One month into the campaign, the protests mounted. A nine-year-old boy was shot dead, and then a sixteen-month-old girl in the arms of her mother. A TV cameraman took the opportunity to fall to his knees in front of Thaksin and plead for his father whose name appeared on a blacklist. The US ambassador asked for a meeting with Thaksin. The diplomatic corps as a whole expressed concern. The legal profession sent an open letter raising fears of a police state. A hundred senior academics signed a protest, and a group of senators came out in opposition. The national police chief temporarily broke ranks and expressed concern that the blacklists might include "people trying to smear one another" (*TN*, 26 February 2003). Pichit Kullavanija, a member of the king's Privy Council, advised that such a campaign should involve "bringing culprits to justice under due process and not to silence them by what has been called elimination killings" (*TN*, 15 March 2003).

In early March the government announced it would no longer release a daily body count. Television coverage diminished. The idea of eliminating all drugs within the three-month deadline was quietly dropped. In March, Thaksin announced there would be a second stage, extending to November 2003, in which authorities would use the information gathered so far to go after the major traders. A senior police figure announced they had collected one thousand names of major drug traders, including politicians (*BP*, 11 March 2003). Thaksin urged the police: "In the first three months, the police did very well. . . . The enemy are weakening. Kill them off. Don't leave a trace behind, because they are threat to society" (Pran 2004a, 232).

In fact, over this second phase only one major dealer was caught, Suphap Saedaeng, from Bangkok's Khlong Toei slum. Others had reportedly fled abroad. However, many more mid-level dealers and officials involved in the trade were mopped up. On 3 December 2003, Thaksin held a ceremony to celebrate victory in a blizzard of statistics: 52,374 had been arrested, 327,224 sent for rehab, 1,257 officials caught, and 3.7 billion baht of assets seized (*TN*, 3

December 2003). Independent surveys showed that the price of a *ya ba* pill had risen around four times and the usage dropped accordingly (Lewis 2003). Habitual drug users had turned to substitutes (marijuana, glue, alcohol, sleeping pills, *kathom* leaves), but the trade had disappeared from the schools. Thaksin later said government surveys showed the campaign had been "68 percent effective." He noted, "Many Thai people now have their sons and daughters back" (*BP*, 2 December 2003).

Despite the protests of activists, the campaign had been highly popular. At the height of the killing in late February, the Suan Dusit poll of a ten-thousand-person sample showed 90 percent in favor of the campaign (*TN*, 24 February 2003). In a smaller Rangsit Poll taken at the same time, over two-thirds explicitly urged government to continue with its violent approach. Even a survey of monks found 70 percent in favor (Jaran 2003). A tape was released of songs supporting the campaign, with lyrics like: "One thousand deaths of bad men is like one dead ant. . . . Bad men must not have land to live" (*TN*, 15 May 2003). The popular northeastern monk, Luang Pho Khun Parisuttho, praised Thaksin to his face:

> It's good you were born to become powerful and help the nation. If you did not exist, *ya ba* would never be got rid of for sure. . . . Since the time of Field Marshal Sarit Thanarat, now it's you who has appeared as someone important to save the nation at the right moment. . . . Don't bother putting drug traders in jail. . . . The sin from killing a *ya ba* trader is the same as from killing one mosquito. Nothing to be afraid of. (*MR*, 30 September 2003)

The monk clearly had few illusions about the agency behind the killings. His remarks recalled another monk's statement in 1975 that killing communists was no sin—another echo between the anti-communist and anti-drug campaigns.

In his birthday speech just the day following Thaksin's victory announcement, the king expressed some reservations:

> Although the authorities say many of the deaths were caused by

killings among drug gangs, scepticism remains. . . . I suggest that the national police chief disclose the details of how the 2,500 deaths happened. (*TN*, 6 December 2003)

Thaksin promised to comply, but in fact the authorities simply issued new figures that gave no new details and repeated the claim that only a small number had been killed by the police and always in self defense. Moreover, these new figures reduced the number of deaths, and were confusingly different. Thaksin said 1,600, while two police sources offered 1,329 and 1,177. The National Human Rights Commission took the opportunity to release a report showing that the blacklists had ensnared several innocent people; that sometimes evidence against them was compiled after the event; that the supposed killings of "bad guys by bad guys" were not being investigated; and the seizure of assets had often proceeded on limited evidence (*TN*, 2 December 2003). In March 2004, Thaksin announced a follow-up campaign, urging authorities to "go for the kill (*sam hai tai*)" against the drug networks (*TN*, 9 March 2004; *TR*, 11 March 2004).

The war on drugs was a response to a strong social demand. But its implementation signaled a return to the thinking and methods of the Cold War. The outcome was not only destruction of the methamphetamine trade, but also a reminder that government claimed a monopoly on violence and was prepared to use it. It sent a message to all forms of dissent that such old thinking and methods were back in vogue.

SOCIAL ORDER AND THAI CULTURE

The culture and lifestyle of today's teenagers is frightening. They superficially adopt Western culture about having freedom but don't understand that Western kids have freedom along with responsibility. . . . If they want something, they have to make the effort to get the money first. Thai kids just wait for their parents to give it to them. And they put too much importance on form, like the culture of using expensive goods. (Interview, 2002)

The government launched projects that showed a trust in the ability of the state to mold or dictate social and cultural practice. The most prominent of these was the *rabiap sangkhom* or social order campaign undertaken by the Interior Ministry. In practice this was an attempt to control the lives of urban youth who had run out of parental control in the rapidly changing and increasingly globalized city of Bangkok. But the titling of the campaign betrayed a more ambitious scope. The word *rabiap* means rules or regulations, particularly the codes and procedures observed by official bodies. More broadly it means order, orderliness, and a proper arrangement of things. It is often yoked with *winai* (the monastic word for the same general meaning) to mean discipline or conformity. Campaigns of social discipline had been a regular fixture of Thailand's dictatorial era (Connors 2003a).

At first the social order campaign mostly involved raids on entertainment venues to check the age and drug use of patrons. But part of the campaign revealed growing parental panic at the relaxed sexual practices of the young. Pracha Maleenont, who took over ministerial responsibility for the campaign in 2002, wrote a book relating his horrified discovery of the fashion for pubic hairstyling. After a highly publicized gang rape, the government contemplated imposing a 10 p.m. curfew on all under-eighteen minors, but thought twice about it (*TN*, 14 February 2004). Thaksin instructed the new Ministry of Social Development to draw up a program to encourage young people to marry earlier, probably as a device to keep them out of trouble (*TN*, 3 April 2004). Some TRT members suggested the same moral sensitivities should be applied to the party itself by excluding adulterous husbands from the party slate. But realism prevailed.

As part of its scheme of bureaucratic reorganization in October 2002, the government established a Ministry of Culture. Similar bodies had been set up by military governments in the 1930s and 1950s to plan and execute schemes of social and cultural engineering. The ministry proceeded to draw up a cultural master plan. This document went out of its way to acknowledge the ethnic and linguistic diversity of the country, and undertook to promote egalitarianism and local cultures. Yet the plan as a whole was framed as a campaign to counter the spread of consumerism and individualism by promoting supposedly Thai values including "belief in society, kinship, respect for elders, deference, empathy." The plan also proposed to nurture the "Thai language, Thai manners, Thai food and Thai dress."[12] Despite acknowledging diversity, the plan betrayed a strong belief in a unified cultural core.

One of the culture minister's first plans was to establish "language clinics" to help people who got pronunciation wrong or mixed too many English words into their speech (*BP*, 19 November 2002; *TN*, 19 July 2003). The ministry also ran a television ad criticizing youths who failed to adopt a suitably deferential stoop in the presence of their seniors.

Much of the ministry's work was engaged in plans to promote artistic activities. But the ministry also fell in with the puritanical streak of the social order campaign. In 2003, it banned eighteen songs from broadcast media because of sexual content. Most were long forgotten. Several were on themes of adultery, but one was simply titled "Big Flabby Buttocks" (*TN*, 22 August 2003). The ministry also objected to skimpy female clothing, especially during the celebration of the Songkran water festival. After photographers managed to capture an errant nipple during a catwalk show, the ministry threatened to station police at fashion shows and formed a committee to draw up rules and regulations defining the limits of exposure (*TN*, 10 January 2004). The ministry also targeted the production of cheap underground porn CDs, and temporarily blocked a popular internet game.

The social order campaign and activities of the Culture Ministry appealed to largely urban middle-class panic about changing social practices. They were also in many ways ironic and hypocritical. The biggest booster of the consumerism against which the Culture Ministry railed was the mobile phone industry, which outspent every other sector on advertising. The two most prominent public speakers that delighted in using as many English words as possible were Thaksin and Somkid. The latter also spoke Thai with a strong accent—bravely overcoming one of the old nationalist prejudices against the Chinese. Pracha Maleenont confessed that he used to attend massage parlors but swore that he stopped before he became the chief of the social order campaign. As with the desire to restrict political space, this government believed it could invade, restrict, and shape social space too.

CONCLUSION

I am confident that politics are quiet nowadays because people are happy with the work of the Thai Rak Thai Party. I check the feeling of the people all the time. (Speech, 28 December 2003)

The 1990s saw a significant widening of political space (see chapter 1). Protests multiplied. Media became freer. Debates proliferated. New organizations mushroomed. More varied demands entered the political arena.

For big business, this trend was a threat. At the simplest level, the rural protests challenged the right of the state to manage natural resources needed for promoting urban growth. More subtly, liberal and communitarian movements wanted to disassemble the centralized state so that government could become responsive to more varied social demands. In the late 1990s, the agendas of these movements started to be written into the policy documents of the state itself—the 1997 constitution, Eighth Five-Year Plan, education and health reforms, decentralization proposals, and even national security plans. Big capital wanted a powerful central state in order to command and concentrate resources. These movements wanted to do away with the powerful central state and prevent such concentrated control over resources. Thaksin's antagonism to free expression was not just the result of his police training and mentality. It reflected the ambitions and fears of the big business groups clustered around the government.

More than any previous government, the Thaksin administration recognized the need to buy public support by sharing the fruits of growth slightly more equitably than in the past. But the government also saw a need to deny space to alternative political agendas, especially the liberal and communitarian ideas that had been rising in the 1990s. The government closed down political space in a general way by controlling the media, delegitimizing NGOs, and attacking protests. But it also targeted public figures like Thirayuth, Anand, and Prawase, who were increasingly part of a democratic tradition that was becoming more established.

The main agenda of the Thaksin government was to promote economic growth. This agenda faced threats from both without and within, from both globalization and democratization. Seizing the state offered the means to deal with both kinds of threat, including that posed by alternative domestic agendas which valued rights and freedoms above sacrifice for economic growth. Thaksin constructed a mix of Western social contract theory and modernist Buddhism to argue that "good" disinterested leadership justified itself, and that all opposition was by definition illegitimate. His arguments followed closely a tradition within the Thai military in the dictatorial era. Thaksin said:

> Democracy is a good and beautiful thing, but it's not the ultimate goal as far as administering the country is concerned. . . . Democracy is just a tool, not our goal. The goal is to give people a good lifestyle, happiness and national progress. (*TN*, 11 December 2003)

6

REMAKING POLITICS

In his "first political testament" of 1998–9 (see chapter 2) and in speeches from the same era, Thaksin identified three main problems of Thai politics. First, too many politicians treated politics as a career, as a way to make money. They invested money in gaining election, and then looked for ways to profit through corruption. They used "dirty politics" to fight against rivals who threatened to dislodge their hold on power and their access to opportunities for profit. Politics of this nature sacrificed the interests of the majority of people.

Second, the Thai bureaucracy was too powerful, too torpid, and too ignorant of the business world. It lacked not only the will but also the capacity to help Thailand develop and progress. As a result, Thailand remained backward compared to many other countries.

Third, both politicians and bureaucrats were simply "not modern." They failed to keep up with the pace of change in the world, and with globalization. The crisis of 1997, he argued, resulted from this simple and wholesale failure to understand the world (Thaksin 1999, 227–34).

The reformers in the 1990s had tried to overcome the bureaucratic problem by increasing popular participation in decision making. The constitution of 1997 attacked "money politics" by setting up a range of new independent bodies to monitor and constrain the politicians. Thaksin and TRT set out to remake Thai politics in a strikingly different way. They neutralized the principal independent bodies established by the constitution. They revived the political role of the military to strengthen the power of the executive. They subjected the senior bureaucracy to greater political control, and began attempts to change its operating methods and culture. They moved towards a political system in which the dominant element was a large political party financed by business.

MANAGING THE CONSTITUTION

> Every organization, even if it's called "independent," is independent only in decision making, not in common thinking. . . . Every organization in the country is just a small subsidiary within the big organization. (Radio, 10 August 2002)

The most active and important of the "independent bodies" established under the 1997 constitution were the Election Commission (ECT), which had the power to invalidate elections on grounds of malpractice; the National Counter Corruption Commission (NCCC), which investigated corruption charges and oversaw ministers' declaration of assets; and the Constitutional Court, which ruled on any issue relating to the constitution including whether malpractice justified a ban from politics.

Many MPs were forced to rerun elections and were resentful of the ECT. After his confrontation with the NCCC and the Constitutional Court, Thaksin took a very antagonistic stand towards these bodies as a whole. He wondered aloud why institutions appointed by a handful of people should have jurisdiction over those elected by millions. He told these bodies they should not be too "independent" and threatened to cut their budgets: "Their attitude has to be a correct one. At present we're spending an annual Bt3 billion on independent bodies. If they become antagonistic, I think spending even one baht would be expensive" (*TN*, 27 September 2002).

From late 2001, the government maneuvered to bring these various bodies under control. Central to this project was the Senate.

The duty of the Senate itself was to act as a monitor on the executive. In addition, the Senate made the final selection of the members of most independent bodies.

Nominally, senators were supposed to be nonpolitical figures. In fact, many senators elected in 2000 were tied by kinship, marriage, business contacts, or other relationships to politicians. However, at first the Senate's political alignment was not clear. The speaker elected in early 2001 was associated with the Democrats. In the early months of the Thaksin government, some thirty to forty senators with academic and NGO backgrounds were able to lead the Senate in actively monitoring government actions. But once the Thaksin government consolidated its power in mid 2001, it gradually built an effective majority in the Senate, signaled by the election of Sahat Pintuseni as deputy speaker in August 2002. Sahat was reckoned one of the "least known" senators but a close associate of Snoh Thien-thong, the government's chief whip (*TN*, 13 August 2002). In March 2003, Suchon Chalikrua, another Snoh man who had earlier worked for the 1991–2 coup junta, was elected as the second deputy, confirming the Senate's coloring (*BP*, 26 February and 7 March 2003). In November, the pro-Democrat speaker was finally forced to resign after a long campaign of intimidation, and in February 2003 he was replaced by Suchon.

All members of the independent bodies were appointed on fixed terms of varying length. As these bodies' original members reached the end of their statutory terms, new appointments changed the bodies' political complexion.

When the first batch of ECT members reached the end of their term in May 2001, the two who stood for reselection were rejected. New candidates lobbied senators. The replacements selected included General Sirin Thoopklam whose own election to the Senate had been voided by the ECT in 2000, a judge whose promotion had failed to gain royal approval, a bureaucrat under investigation for corruption, and another Interior Ministry official who had earlier been accused of printing fake election ballots (*BP*, 23 June 2001, 2 October 2001). Sirin later became the ECT chairman. After a Thai daily announced this new ECT team with a headline,

"Political reform is over," Sirin took the ECT members and their fifty staff to swear an oath before the Emerald Buddha, the palladium of the kingdom (*BP*, 2 November 2001). In mid 2002, Sirin was removed from the ECT by the Constitutional Court on grounds his appointment had been technically incorrect. He was replaced by a general associated with Chavalit (*BP*, 5 July 2002; *TN*, 19 September 2002). Earlier, some MPs had demanded revision of the ECT's powers, and set up a committee to propose revisions to the constitution (*TN*, 21 September 2001). Such calls now faded. The ECT had ceased to be a threat.

The NCCC took a little longer. It continued to deliver firm and occasionally politically daring judgments through to 2003. A first round of reappointments completed in November 2003 brought onto the commission Pol Maj-Gen Wichienchote Sukchotrat, a friend of Thaksin since cadet school, whose previous boss had been Thaksin's brother-in-law (*BP*, 24 April and 4 November 2003). At a second round, Klanarong Chantik, the former NCCC secretary general who had prosecuted the assets case against Thaksin, was conspicuously rejected, and five of the seven new appointees had close links to the government including Wuthichai Srirattanawut, a former deputy police chief who had mentored Thaksin at the cadet school and overseen Thaksin's early computer contract with the police department. Wuthichai was subsequently chosen as the NCCC's chairman (*TN*, 11 and 21 November 2003, 19 February 2004, 11 March 2004). The NCCC had also ceased to be a threat.

The Constitutional Court gained a reputation for relative independence, except in the small number of cases involving prominent politicians (Klein 2003, 77). In the latter type of cases, five of the judges appeared to vote consistently with the government, though the other ten were less predictable. In March 2003, four of these ten ended their terms. The government put up a slate of three people with close ties to Thaksin: one had been a customs official who defended Shin Satellite against charges of tax evasion;[1] another was a police officer who had taken a post in the Prime Minister's Office and orchestrated one of the signature campaigns for Thaksin's acquittal from the asset case; and the third had been part of Thaksin's secretariat and a business partner. All three were selected, giving the government an apparent majority of eight of the fifteen judges. Shortly after, Kamol Thongthammachat, the judge who had leaked the result of Thaksin's asset case to the press in obvious delight, was selected as the court's president (*TN*, 1, 2 and 12 March 2003). The Constitutional Court was under control.

In response to growing concerns about the decline of checks and balances, Thaksin counseled the people not to worry:

> The person who cautions me all the time is my wife. No matter how grown up I am, I have to listen to my wife. She doesn't get dazzled by the bright lights. She cautions me all the time. The people have no need to worry. They have my wife as a warning system for me. (*KT*, 3 January 2004)

BRINGING BACK THE MILITARY

> Everyone has to respect the commanding officer, listen to those more senior without exception, and follow the military mentality that obeying the commanding officer is imperative, because under threat from the enemy, obedience has to be strict and total. (Autobiography, 1998–9)

Thaksin halted the decline in the political role of the military, and built a personal network into the military hierarchy.

A military officer had occupied the prime ministership for all but eight years over 1938–88. Over this half century, the senior officer cadre became like a ruling caste. They dominated senior positions in government agencies and state enterprises. In Bangkok, they were taken onto corporate boards. In the provinces, they were invited to protect and profit from all kinds of local enterprise. Generals became heads of sports associations and social clubs while their wives chaired charities. Businessmen prominently displayed photographs of themselves with powerful generals like a modern version of fetishes to warn off evil forces. The special status and power of the military officer elite was replicated in smaller ways down through the ranks.

The political dominance of the military was first challenged by the student uprising in 1973, and then declined swiftly from 1988 onwards. The coup of 1991 hoped to end this slide but led to the street demonstrations of May 1992 that drove the generals from power and provoked a wave of anti-military feeling. Generals were ejected from many fiefs in government-related agencies. They disappeared more gradually from corporate boards. Successive army heads ritually foreswore any political ambitions, and talked of modernizing the armed forces. In 1992, the Cabinet oversaw the draft of a National Preparedness Plan, breaking the military's monopoly on defense planning (Panitan 1998).

But such a long period of military prominence in politics and society was not easily erased. As the memory of May 1992 faded, the military regained prestige. For ambitious and talented youths, the military offered opportunities for social mobility. For peasant conscripts, it provided education and technical training that increased their earning power. Through its half-century of dominance, the military had continually broadcast the message of its special importance to the nation and its special relationship to the monarchy. On grounds of national security, the armed services claimed control of two of the four main TV stations and around 250 radio stations. Despite the decline of military power in the 1990s, the military held onto these valuable assets, and continued to use them for propaganda. Within the military, the culture of their special role was strongly embedded. They told themselves repeatedly that they had led the nation, saved it from communism, helped install democracy, and promoted development (Ockey 2001). A military writer in 1995 claimed that "the army is the only organization that can solve the national problems" (Surachart 2001, 79).

In the mid 1990s, the military staged a partial comeback. In 1993, the National Security Council issued a "Master Plan for Regional Cooperation" which argued that the military should play a role in the fashionable process of making Thailand the centerpiece of mainland Southeast Asia. The Defense Ministry issued a white paper, *The Defence of Thailand 1994*, compiled with inputs from an elite group outside the military, which began to replace the old idea of "national security" (which principally meant anti-communism) with a wider concept of economic, political, and social security (Panitan 1998, 433–4). The document argued Thailand's booming economy provided a new rationale for investment in military power:

> After the end of the Cold War, the political situation changed rapidly. Confrontation between superpowers with different ideologies ended, and economic competition took its place. The contest for markets and resources could, however, lead to the use of force in the future. The Armed Forces therefore must change its focus and concentrate more on protecting national economic interests, develop weapons systems and technology to improve capability, and to produce skilled personnel to operate these weapons. (McCargo 2002, 54)

The White Paper also highlighted the army's potential to aid development: "If sufficient budget is allocated these units will be able to contribute greatly to national development." Military leaders sought a new role for the military in drug suppression, forest preservation, disaster relief, economic development, and even tourism. After the crisis of 1997, the claim for a larger economic and political role grew louder. The National Security Council attempted another major redefinition of the military role to focus on problems of internal unrest caused by rapid change. The council proposed that the military work cooperatively with the civilian government and civil society to allay the sociopolitical tensions that had escalated in the 1990s (Connors 2003b). The council developed experts in "conflict resolution" to negotiate between government agencies and protest groups.

But through the 1990s, the military's sources of official and unofficial income were under attack. The military share of the national budget declined from 17–18 percent in the mid-1980s to 11–12 percent in the mid 1990s (Panitan 1998, 431). Trade liberalization removed opportunities for making money from border smuggling. New influential figures at the local and national levels, often made powerful by the new representative politics, took over the old rackets in drugs, girls, gambling, and protection (Ockey 2001). Other sources of income were under threat. The 1997 constitution lay down that broadcast frequencies should be placed under public management—meaning that they would have to be removed from the military's close control. The military's two TV channels and hundreds of radio stations were a source of considerable revenues that were entirely hidden from public accounting. Chuan asked the army to surrender some of the 5.3 million rai of land under its control (*TN*, 18 October 1998). A 2000 report on land problems reiterated that this land should be released for agricultural use (LIF 2000).

In the middle and lower ranks, some soldiers compensated for declines in unofficial income by privatizing their services (*BP*, 16 August 2002). In Bangkok and elsewhere, they contested against police and civilian gangsters to offer protection to the entertainment industry. Midnight standoffs between police and soldiers in nightclub car parks were a regular sideshow of Bangkok's nightlife (e.g., *BP*, 31 December 1997). Trained military marksmen were in high demand as professional gunmen, hired to settle business, personal, and political disputes. On a slightly more legitimate level, junior officers organized their subordinates to moonlight as providers of professional security services. The Tesco supermarket chain suffered a run of arson incidents that seemed to stem from competition between rival security firms, both from the military (*BP*, 22 January 1999, 7 July 2001). In a famous incident in January 2003, an area of pubs and bars on a disputed piece of land on Sukhumwit Road was razed to the ground in minutes by rival teams from the police and military.

By the mid 1990s, Chavalit Yongchaiyudh was the most prominent survivor of the old era of military politics. He had been army commander in 1987–89, before resigning to form the New Aspiration Party. When he became prime minister in 1996–7, he revived the role of internal security agencies, took generals on shopping trips for arms in China, and proposed new commercial schemes for the military including a telecom satellite, mobile phone network, and plans to exploit the army's large reserves of land. But his tenure was brief, and his successor, Chuan Leekpai, returned to the process of military reform and depoliticization. He appointed himself as defense minister—something no previous civilian premier had done.[2] He pushed a plan to completely overhaul the topmost chain of military command. Over the heads of more senior candidates, Chuan handpicked a military chief, Surayuth Chulanon, who promised to keep the army out of politics and implement a program of reform including downsizing the bloated officer cadre, inoculating arms purchases from private interests, and increasing military professionalism.

In practice, Chuan and Surayuth were able to achieve rather little. The generals supported reform plans to reduce the overall size of the army, as this was one way to free up budget for arms and equipment.[3] But they blocked Chuan's revision of the senior command, sabotaged the attempts to slim down the officer cadre, and sandbagged other reforms by the usual tactic of delaying until Surayuth's tenure was over.

By the late 1990s, the military had recovered somewhat from the 1992 backlash. Yet it still lacked a clear role, its official and unofficial incomes were in decline, and its remaining assets of land and broadcast frequencies were under threat.

Thaksin had a broad network of connections through officialdom. In the military cadet school and police academy, he became part of a "class" network. It was a tradition of these institutions for members of the same class to commit themselves to help one another in their future careers, and to meet in regular reunions to reinforce these ties. These class networks could be very tight. The NPKC coup group that seized power in 1991 was based on Class Five of the military academy.

In addition, Thaksin had kin connections stemming from the Shinawatra clan's interest in military careers over two generations. His father's brother, Sak, had risen to the rank of general, and put all four of his sons into the armed services. Two of these, Uthai and Chaisit, had by the late 1990s risen to the rank of general.

Uthai became deputy permanent secretary in the Defense Ministry.

Thaksin's marriage also brought another network in the police. Pojaman's paternal grandfather had entered the police and risen to captain. His son, Samoe Damaphong, rose to be deputy chief of police and one of the most powerful police figures of his generation. Two of Samoe's three sons, Phrieophan and Phirapong, entered the police. In addition, Thaksin's elder sister Yaowalak married an army general and a younger sister Yaowapha married into another prominent bureaucratic clan (Wongsawat).

Thaksin thus has a dense and extensive network of kin, in-laws, and classmates spread across the military, police, and senior ranks of the bureaucracy. After becoming prime minister, he strengthened this network. In the military promotions of 2001 and 2002, he promoted several members of his cadet school class so that by 2003 some were rising to key military positions. In March 2003, he elevated one classmate, Major General Songkitti Jakkabatr, to head the Fourth Army in the South, and another classmate, Major General Manat Paorik to head the First Cavalry Division along the Burmese border. A cavalry officer judged Manat's promotion "unthinkable" without political influence. At the same time, Major General Picharnmet Muangmani became head of the Third Army in the North. Critics claimed this promotion was also "unthinkable" given his lack of combat experience, and attributed it to association with Thaksin and his brother (*BP*, 19 March 2003). In August 2003, two other classmates, Major General Jirasit Kesakomol and Major General Anupong Paochinda, became respectively deputy chief of the First Army and commander of the First Infantry Division (historically critical because of its location in the capital) (*BP*, 19 March 2003, 29 August 2003).

The rise of Thaksin's cousin, Chaisit Shinawatra, was more spectacular. Chaisit's military career was solid without being special. He gained a scholarship to the US military college in Virginia, fought with US forces against communists in Laos in 1969–70, served in intelligence operations against the communists, and then worked mainly in the southern border zone. In 1999, Surayuth transferred Chaisit to an inactive post for having presided over the opening of the TRT Party branch in Songkhla. After Thaksin became prime minister, Chaisit was rehabilitated and boosted up the hierarchy. In 2001 he became a lieutenant general and commander of the First Army Corps; in 2002 a full general and the assistant army commander; and in August 2003 the army commander. A military analyst noted: "Never before in the military records has a 3-star general risen to a full general in one year." Chaisit claimed: "It's neither strange nor impossible that the prime minister and the army chief would share the same family name" (*BP*, 24 October 2002). Thaksin said: "The best decision has been made, based on national interests." When this failed to stifle comment, he added: "The promotion can be justified rationally. There must be no more criticism. Everyone must accept the decision" (*TN*, 24 and 30 August 2003; *BP*, 29 August 2003). Chaisit later appointed his own brother-in-law as army intelligence chief (*BP*, 31 March 2004).[4]

Thaksin's classmates also prospered in the police. Chidchai Wannasathit, became assistant police chief and secretary-general of the Narcotics Control Board (*BP*, 20 March 2001). Police Major General Surasit Sangkapong was put in charge of the Government Lottery Office which had been a source of secret funds for earlier military dictators and which had increasing revenues from government's displacement of the underground lottery (*TN*, 29 September 2003). But again the most spectacular rise was reserved for someone with special connections.

Phrieophan Damaphong had met Thaksin at the cadet school. He went in parallel with Thaksin to study for an M.A. in criminology at Eastern Kentucky University. On return, he was launched onto a fast-track career in the police. Apart from his personal talents, he had the backing of his father's weight and reputation, and also the support of two other powerful patrons, Police General Prayun Komarakun na Nakhon and Police Lt General Tanu Homhuan. Phrieophan held posts in special branch, crime suppression, immigration, tourist police, central investigation, and drug suppression— a span of departments that suggests he was being groomed for a high position. Even so, Thaksin accelerated this rise. Phrieophan was appointed to assistant national police chief in 2003, and deputy in 2004, vaulting over four more senior candidates. He would only have to vault over three more[5] to become national police chief on the incumbent's retirement in September 2004 or at the following opportunity (Bangna 2004; *BP*, 1 October 2002).

Thaksin's network also extended into the senior ranks of the civilian bureaucracy. His brother-in-law, Somchai Wongsawat, was permanent secretary in the Justice Ministry. Purachai Piumsombun as justice minister got into a conflict with Somchai. Even though Purachai was an associate of Thaksin since cadet school, a founding member of TRT, a putative successor to the TRT leadership, and highly popular (he regularly topped polls measuring popular approval), he was removed from the justice ministership within days.

A central piece of Thaksin relationship with the military was General Chavalit Yongchaiyudh. Thaksin appointed him first as defense minister, and later as a deputy prime minister overseeing projects involving cooperation with the military. Shortly after, Thaksin gave adviser posts to fifty-three of the large number of surplus generals who had no substantive job. This group is widely believed to have been instrumental in planning policies to control dissent.

Thaksin's relationship with the uniformed services was far from simple. His nepotistic promotions angered more senior candidates. He had to handle the traditional rivalry between army and police, and initially annoyed the army by removing them from special security operations in the southern border area, and showing uncertainty in policy towards the Burmese border. But the armed services needed his patronage just as much as he needed them. He gave the army a major role and a major new reason-for-being in the anti-drug campaign of 2003. He shunted Chuan's handpicked army chief, Surayuth, to the largely symbolic role of Supreme Commander and showed little interest in Surayuth's reform agenda. He had no interest in media liberalization and encouraged the military to retighten their control over broadcasting. He restored the military's influence over foreign policy, especially concerning neighbors (*BP*, 2 March 2001). He released the brake on arms spending imposed since the crisis. In 2003, he restored a 3 billion baht cut from the military procurement budget by the Budget Bureau; approved all procurement proposals for 2005–13 including two frigates and thirty-three Blackhawk helicopters; and told the armed forces: "Whatever they want to buy, even if it costs billions, I am willing to support if they have good reasons and supporting facts." Analysts estimated he had increased the average procurement from 17 billion baht to 24 billion baht a year (*BP*, 3 and 13 September 2003).

In sum, he promised to be a patron of the military who would protect them against threats to their interests, and return some of their prominence in society. In return, Thaksin gained a powerful source of support—especially through his kin, marriage, and class networks—which gave him extra leverage against other political actors including rival politicians and civil society.

OVERTHROWING THE BUREAUCRATIC POLITY

In particular, this is a new era in which policy is decided by politicians. . . . Henceforth, politicians have to tell people what they are going to do, what policies they have to improve things. . . . Once people have chosen a party, politicians then lay out the strategy with the ministries and departments to make an implementation plan. (Radio, 27 July 2002)

Once the Thaksin government, following the resolution of the asset case, began to understand its unusually powerful position, it embarked on an ambitious project to remake the political system that had developed over the previous twenty years.

Under the military rule that lasted with few interruptions from the 1930s to 1980s, the senior bureaucracy had accumulated power without competition from elected politicians or civil society. In the 1980s, parliamentary politicians challenged the bureaucrats' power. At first, there were some bad-mannered clashes. The Chatichai Cabinet of 1988–91 in particular replaced many senior officials, emphasizing the new dominance of elected ministers. But the final result was not a revolution but a compromise. Senior bureaucrats had to share power and profit with elected ministers, and often align themselves to political factions. But in return, the structure and culture of the bureaucracy was left largely untouched. This historic compromise paved the way for the era of "money politics." Politicians invested large sums to gain election to parliament and to maneuver their way into a ministership. Similarly, some officials were prepared to pay large sums to climb the last few rungs up the ladder. Bureaucrat reform was constantly discussed but never implemented.

The Thaksin Cabinet first repeated the Chatichai tactic of making many changes to senior bureaucratic appointments. But it also went further. In October 2002, it implemented a comprehensive remapping of the bureaucratic structure, changing it from fourteen to twenty ministries, reassigning several departments, and making a large number of senior appointments, promotions, and transfers.[6] This remapping removed some of the duplication of functions that had raised the cost and increased the time of securing any bureaucratic decision. But this streamlining was far from complete. More importantly, the scale of the change signaled the intention of the executive to impose its will on the bureaucracy more aggressively than in the past. Next, the government removed the Budget Bureau's overall command of the budget, thus increasing the ministers' authority over government funds. Then the NESDB planning agency was sidelined. Other reforms to increase political control and enforce performance standards on bureaucrats were drafted but then delayed until the initial changes were absorbed (*BP*, 20 February 2002; *TN*, 24 February 2002).

Thaksin appointed more businessmen to positions on statutory boards (normally occupied by officials), and proposed to modify regulations to allow appointment of non-officials to senior posts like permanent secretaries. The government announced a "war on corruption," which conspicuously targeted officials rather than politicians. Again, the impact was more symbolic than systematic. The first high-profile case concerned the Bangkok tollway system, where investigations found an elaborate scheme to embezzle tollway fees. The issue had obvious political appeal to the middle-class Bangkok motorist. The amounts involved were impressive. However, ultimately only mid-level personnel were charged, and there was no attempt to expand this "war" to other bureaucratic fronts.[7] The government also launched proposals to downsize the bureaucracy through enforced early retirement of officials judged to have poor performance.

The main result of all these moves was to make the bureaucracy more responsive to political command. Several senior officials retired, particularly from the foreign service. Others attached themselves to the TRT in order to secure favor. The party drew up plans to extend this politicization down the bureaucratic pyramid. In late 2002, the press uncovered that TRT cadres in every province were drawing up lists of local officials and assessing their political leanings as pro-TRT, pro-opposition, or neutral. In the subsequent outcry, the party disowned the exercise, but not before a senior party manager had confirmed its existence in an interview. Phumtham Vejjayachai, deputy secretary-general of TRT, explained: "We can never be complacent because the next election will be a do-or-die battle. . . . We have to be prepared. We have to resort to every strategy. And we have to know every area of the battlefield" (*TN*, 13 November 2002).

Senior bureaucrats had retained authority in part because they had the machinery for policy making, while politicians usually did not. Thaksin and TRT set out to change this too. Again Chatichai had pioneered change in the late 1980s by assembling a policy-making team under party control, but subsequent governments had not developed this practice further. As his chief policy adviser, Thaksin recruited Pansak who had headed Chatichai's Ban Phitsanulok policy team, and used other team members in various roles.[8] The TRT cabinet assembled a much larger and more active set of advisory teams than any previous government.[9] Thaksin trawled the universities for willing talent, recruited from his colleagues in the business world, and transferred people from within his own family companies. This greater party control of policy making was especially prominent in economic affairs. Thaksin assembled an inner economic cabinet of five or six members including his first finance minister, Somkid, his chief adviser Pansak, and business colleagues including Thanong Bidaya.

Thaksin also set out to change the culture and status of the bureaucracy. In several speeches, he argued that bureaucrats were inferior to businessmen because they did not contribute directly to the national economy. He launched schemes to make officials more involved in promoting economic growth. The first was directed at diplomats. During his short spell as foreign minister in 1995, Thaksin had laid down a new "vision" for the ministry as "economics before politics" (Thaksin 1999, 174). Now he extended the same idea under a scheme of "CEO ambassadors." Envoys were recalled to Bangkok to attend seminars on business management principles, and instructed to take a more active role in promoting Thailand's economic interests abroad. He told a meeting of ambassadors in Tokyo: "This [CEO] system will be a test of the ambassadors' performance. And those who don't perform will be ousted, definitely. . . . We have a lot of good and bright people in the bureaucracy. But none of them are brave enough to create good jobs for the nation" (TN, 19 November 2001).

The same thinking was applied to "CEO governors." After a pilot scheme in five provinces, all governors were called to Bangkok to attend seminars where they were instructed by international management consultants on business school thinking and practice. Thaksin lectured them on the findings of the latest management theorists and futurists, and stressed that bureaucratic practice would have to change to this "modern" culture:

> With this CEO Governor model, I'm challenging the governors whether they are really managers. . . . In the language of business, it's called profit comes from risk. Those who take no risks have no chance of making profits. So if you take risks, use your abilities to solve the nation's problems, and get well accepted, you will feel proud that this is something you brought to a successful conclusion. It will make you happy. (Pran 2004, 375–6)

The "CEO governors" were given new authority over the line-ministry bureaucrats in their provinces, told they were responsible for provincial economic growth, and subject to more stringent assessments of their performance. Each had to draw up a provincial plan on the model of a corporate business plan. Most of these plans targeted growth through tourism (*TN*, 1 November 2003; *BP*, 18 November 2003).

CRUSHING INFLUENCE

The influential figures create "social costs" and strip others of their opportunities. (Press, 20 July 2003)

The political parties of the 1990s were built bottom up. Politicians won elections principally on the basis of their local standing. Individuals in the localities joined a *phuak* or clique; cliques grouped into electoral factions, factions into parties, and parties into government coalitions. Switching parties was common. Binding factions together into a party depended a great deal on money. These groupings constantly shifted, creating an "instability" which business found inconvenient. The fact the system was built bottom-up meant the government was often responsive to local pressures but unresponsive to big business interests.

Thaksin and TRT set out to overturn this structure. The 1997 constitution made a start by introducing the party list, creating some separation between executive and legislature, and reducing the size of the Cabinet. Many fewer constituency MPs now made it to the Cabinet. But Thaksin and TRT pushed the change much further by shifting the fount of political patronage. In the past, the local bosses elected to parliament justified themselves to their constituents by securing the budget for roads, schools, colleges, hospitals, airports, industrial estates, dams, irrigation projects, famine relief schemes, and other political goods in their home constituencies. Under the new TRT system, the central government became the source of village funds, agrarian debt relief, cheap health care, OTOP schemes, cheap computers, and other offerings. Electors had chosen TRT in 2001 in part because of its innovative promises, though undoubtedly many had simply found the promises incredible, and local influence had still played a large part. Thaksin believed that the party's track record in power, and a host of new promises (land distribution, assets to capital, sustained economic growth) would ensure more would vote along party (rather than local) lines at the next election. In December 2003, he told a party rally in Pattaya:

> I utterly believe that whoever the [TRT] party chooses [as candidates], the people will elect them. . . . The party works for the people and so they trust the party. Individuals are not a big matter. . . . I tell politicians used to the old system, today the people have changed, so will you change? The old votebank system no longer exists. Influence no longer exists. In today's society, people have access to information, and so people select what is of most benefit for themselves. Petty sums like a couple of hundred baht no longer have any meaning for people. (Thaksin 2003g)

While shifting the fount of political patronage, Thaksin also launched an attack on the local power of the old-style provincial politicians. This was tricky, since Thaksin had welcomed at least a hundred into the TRT Party to achieve his election success, and welcomed others as coalition partners. Indeed, when TRT absorbed NAP in 2002, it acquired Suchat Tancharoen, the man who Thaksin had identified three years earlier as the most dubious of all provincial politicians (Thaksin 1999, 196–8).[10]

In May 2003, Thaksin launched a campaign against the "dark influences" behind all kinds of illegal activity.[11] This was an ambitious initiative. Some of the most successful provincial businessmen were those who strayed across the line dividing legal from criminal activity. With the establishment of parliament and elective local government, such figures had been able to convert their wealth into political positions, or influence over those who held them (McVey 2000).

For more established and respectable businessmen and politicians, such figures offered unfair competition (because of the size of their illegal profits), and brought both business and politics into public disrepute. Bangkok magnates who wished to set up a business in the provinces, or run for a provincial constituency, were irritated that they had to gain the support of such powerful local figures. Closing down the godfathers would remove a source of competition in both business and politics. It would also shift the criteria for success in elections away from local "influence," towards membership of a national party with a policy agenda. The interior minister explained: "I want the elections to be clean and fair competition under rules. I do not want to see influential people using their power to force people to go to the polls" (*TN*, 19 February 2002). Thaksin said: "Influence which buys votes is a barrier to proper democracy. It's a vicious circle. Corrupt politicians use their power to recoup their investment. I want politicians who treat politics as service to the people, not as an investment."[12]

The first move in the campaign targeted two Kanchanaburi local bosses who were clearly identified with the opposition Democrat Party. Perhaps by coincidence, at the same time another major godfather associated with the Chat Thai Party (Somchai Khunpleum, Kamnan Po), was arraigned on murder and corruption charges. Also around the same time, government agencies laid charges concerning the construction of the Khlong Dan waste treatment plant in which several politicians were involved.[13]

Government ordered provincial governors and police chiefs to draw up lists of their "influential people" but the results were often counterintuitive. Some notorious provinces apparently had none (Suphanburi, Chonburi, Nakhon Sawan). The effort to identify influential people was obviously itself subject to influence. "We all know there are debts and gratitude," mused a Cabinet source (*BP*, 18 July 2003). Thaksin admitted "real influential figures" including "national level politicians" escaped inclusion (*BP*, 25 May 2003, 2 July 2003). A government committee eventually compiled a list of 700 hardcore "mafia" and another 2,000 influential people. Thaksin repeatedly announced that past deeds would be forgotten but any future "influential" activity would invite the full force of the law. But he also repeatedly extended the deadline for a government crackdown. Government invited owners of unlicensed firearms to surrender the hardware or face prosecution in the future. Some were turned in or abandoned, but this was only a small percentage of the estimated 10 million illegal arms in the country (*BP*, 9 September 2003).

PROMOTING PARTY DOMINANCE

The world understands me. The minority is the minority. It is the majority we have to listen to. (Press, 1 September 2001)

TRT also began to build something like a mass party. Prior to the 2001 election TRT recruited members using a system modeled on pyramid selling. In 2003, it claimed almost 11 million members, far more than any rival, though the Election Commission noted that several members held duplicate membership in another party (table 6.1).

Table 6.1 Membership of political parties, 2003

Party	Members	Duplicates
Thai Rak Thai	10.9	2.3
Democrat	3.8	1.4
Chat Thai	2.3	-
Chat Phatthana	3.7	1.5
Ratsadon	0.6	0.3

Source: *TN*, 24 November 2003, from the Election Commission of Thailand

But the party had only a sketchy national structure. By April 2004, it had three branches in Greater Bangkok and another nine upcountry (compared to 193 Democrat branches).[14] Its major activity was large rallies in Bangkok and provincial centers as a setting for the party leader's speeches. To some extent, the party was glued together by money. In December 2003, party sources leaked that allowances paid to TRT MPs were being raised from 50,000 to 200,000 baht per month, with a bonus of 800,000 baht for festivities during New Year and Songkran (*TN*, 2 and 3 December 2003).[15] A TRT source described how MPs went to collect part of this "social tax" each month from a TRT office in the Shin Corp building, and another part from their faction leader (*Thai Post*, 20 September 2003). If this were true (Thaksin refused to acknowledge questions on the matter), the annual bill at the new rate would be between 600 million and 900 million baht. This money did not appear to be coming from party donations, which under the constitution had to be reported to the Election Commission. In 2003, the TRT reported 30.6 million of donations of which 16.4 million came from Pojaman Shinawatra (*TN*, 19 January 2004).

Over 2003–4, the TRT ventured into local government elections. This was new. Hitherto these elections had been fought without party labels. Much of the impetus to involve TRT and other parties in local elections came from the bottom up. During 2003, some groups contesting municipal polls adopted the TRT Party name. In fact, the party had a rule banning the use of its label in local elections but made no attempt to police this rule. In December 2003, Thaksin had the ban removed (*TN*, 3 December 2003). At elections for Provincial Administrative Organizations (PAOs) in early 2004, almost all the victorious teams ran under a party banner.

In 2003, government had amended the local government laws in ways which made the position of PAO president much more attractive than before. The PAOs' budgets were increased. They took over many tasks formerly administered centrally including building local roads and other infrastructure. The president became directly elected and had considerable executive powers. As a result of this increasing power and the declining status of an MP, several former MPs and a few ex-ministers sought election to this post. Some used a party label in hope it might supplement their local standing. Sitting MPs gave support to such candidates in hope of strengthening their local base and their chances at the next parliamentary election. Faction bosses within the TRT Party also got involved in order to strengthen their weight against one another within the party. As a result of these conflicting pressures, several teams competed to run on the TRT ticket in some provinces. Rather than attempting to adjudicate between these rivalries, in twenty-nine provinces, the party allowed competing teams to run in the same constituency under the TRT banner. In the most high-profile example in Chiang Mai, three teams claimed the TRT banner, while in Chiang Rai one team backed by Thaksin's sister, Yaowapha, ran against another backed by the TRT secretary-general (*BP*, 10 February 2004). In some provinces, the rival TRT teams distinguished themselves by a different campaign color, or a suffix to the party label. But elsewhere the confusion was absolute. In three provinces, there were similar intraparty contests between Democrats.

The result was that for the first time local elections across the country were run on party lines. Only in seven provinces were there direct party-party contests. Elsewhere the contests were fought between a party and independents, or between rival factions of the same party. In the end, TRT won forty-seven provinces, the Democrats thirteen, Chat Thai five, Chat Phatthana two, and independents seven (*MS*, 1231, 19–25 March 2004, 6–7).

The interplay between local influence and central party control was also highlighted in a by-election in Songkhla in February 2004. TRT allowed three potential candidates to compete for the candidacy by building local support. The party then conducted a local poll so that Thaksin and his inner party associates could select the most promising contender. Thaksin gave speeches about the party platform. But at the same time, TRT was estimated to have spent 70 to 100 million baht, mostly in 300-baht handouts to voters, and to have pressured officials to act as canvassers (Askew 2004).

In practice, local influence was far from being suppressed or bypassed. Snoh Thienthong, the old political godfather who had led his faction of provincial politicians into TRT in 2000, constantly reminded Thaksin that he commanded the party's biggest faction

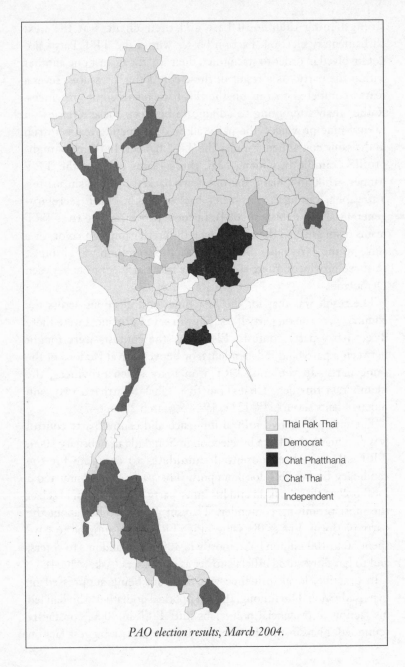

PAO election results, March 2004.

Thai Rak Thai
Democrat
Chat Phatthana
Chat Thai
Independent

and deserved respect. He claimed: "Whether the prime minister can remain in power or not depends on me" (*BP*, 11 July 2001). He opposed the government's attempts to strengthen the center's institutional control over the provinces. He objected to the scheme of "CEO governors" because it increased central power over the provinces. He objected also to a proposal to make village headmen and *kamnan* appointed by the center rather than elected by the locality. Thaksin argued that as new elective local government bodies had been formed, the village headmen and *kamnan* should be appended formally to the bottom of the administrative pyramid so they could serve as the center's "eyes and ears" at the grassroots.[16] Snoh successfully campaigned for this proposal to be withdrawn (*TN* 1, 3, and 4 February 2004). Snoh and his followers were active in the 2004 PAO chairman elections in order to strengthen the foundations of local influence.

CONCLUSION: BIG MONEY POLITICS

On 6 January 2001 we won by a *landslide*. In July 2005, we will win by an *avalanche*. (Speech, 28 December 2003, italicized words spoken in English)

Thaksin and TRT set out to remake the Thai political system. The "money politics" which Thailand evolved over the 1980s and 1990s amounted to a power deal between the senior bureaucracy and local politicians. It spread the national budget more widely, but a lot finished up as inflated construction profits or bureaucratic graft.

The 1997 constitution aimed to end this system by strengthening the executive, increasing transparency, adding checks and balances, decentralizing power, and empowering the citizenry.

But the new big business politicians see a different way ahead. They want a powerful central state to mobilize national resources and manage the society. They welcomed the constitution's provisions for strengthening the executive, but they sabotaged the checks and balances, empowerment, decentralization, and scrutiny.

Thaksin has begun to build a new political structure in which power is centralized in a political party financed by big business.

He intimidated and politicized the senior bureaucracy while denigrating bureaucratic practice as inferior to the CEO culture of business. He rehabilitated the military after its post-1992 decline, and tied it to himself by kinship, connection, and patronage as an instrument to control dissent. He made the "CEO governors" into extensions of executive authority into the provinces.

He wants to pull up the local roots of Thai politics by attacking "influence" and by switching the source of political goods. While people once looked to their local godfather to get them paved roads, electricity hookups, and water supply, he wants them now to turn to the TRT government for village funds, debt relief, cheap health care, land deeds, and a route out of poverty. This is potentially a massive change in the political culture. It aims to replace the old personal bonds, the *phuak*, with a direct, universalized relationship between citizen and state (Pitch 2004). All qualify for a loan from the village fund, for a 30-baht hospital visit, for a cheap TV, for a chance to turn their assets into capital. All are Thais loving Thais.

Of course, things are not quite so clear-cut, not least because the old political bosses are still a major part of TRT and are resisting this attack on their bases of power. Thaksin believes more electors will choose TRT at future elections because of its policies, but in practice, the party will still have to negotiate with local influence.

Thaksin aims to replace "money politics" with "big money politics." Big money is now power. And so gaining power, and holding onto it, are inseparable from the generation of big business profits.

7

POWER AND PROFIT

In Thailand, the coincidence of political leadership and commercial leadership is absolutely traditional. All through the early modern era, the kings and courtiers were the merchant princes. In the expansion of a modern economy at the turn of the twentieth century, kings and favored nobles were the biggest landlords, bankers, urban property developers, and investors in modern industries. After the rise of military dictatorship, generals were a fixture on the boards of any companies of significance.

All the major businesses in the Shinawatra empire originated from a government concession. The enormous wealth generated in a handful of years—as Surathian noted in admiration, more than earlier Thai business dynasties could expect to accumulate in three generations—resulted in very large part because these businesses were monopolies or oligopolies protected by government power. This does not mean that Thaksin is "not a (real) businessman" as some have claimed. Hunting and exploiting political concessions is just as much a business as, say, running Wal-Mart, but the context is different and also the skills required. The state created the context. Thaksin found the skills to exploit it.

Maintaining the profit flow from such businesses depends on continual management of this political context. Concessions are not simple one-time grants. The overall telecom industry is not governed by any set of regulations or real master plan. Rather, the industry is based on a series of deals hatched between a handful of state agencies looking for new revenue opportunities on the one side, and a handful of businessmen looking for profits on the other. As one TOT executive said about the era when the concessions were created: "All we were thinking about at that time was how to sidestep the law" (*TN*, 15 May 2002). Deals can always be adjusted, extended, or reinterpreted. Any change or any new deal may affect the profit-making opportunities of other deals. Management of a telecom business means continual management of the political context.

The 1997 constitution attempted to change the context by banning concession holders from direct involvement in politics:

> A member of the House of Representatives shall not . . . receive any concession from the State, a State agency or State enterprise, or become a party to a contract of the nature of economic monopoly with the State, a State agency or State enterprise, or become a partner or shareholder in a partnership or company receiving such concession or becoming a party to the contract of that nature. (Clause 110)

But this restriction extended to the MP alone, not his family. Thaksin resigned from all positions in the Shinawatra companies, and transferred his shareholdings to his wife and children. Legally he was now separate from his concession-based business empire. But the gap was no more than the width of the dining table.

This interlocking of business and politics is not confined within Thailand. The leading edge of the Shinawatra business empire overflows Thailand's political boundaries. The IPStar satellite is by far the group's most ambitious, visionary enterprise. It has high profit potential but also high risk. The project involves designing a new generation of satellite that can outstrip existing providers in terms of cost and speed. According to its backers, the technology is patently superior. Yet many technically superior projects fail in the marketplace. The ambitious Iridium project, which collapsed in 1997, was just one recent example. To succeed, the IPStar project has to attract customers from many countries. Some of the most important potential customers are governments. Although Shin executives protested again and again that Thaksin played no part in selling the project, it is very hard to believe that no words were passed during the Thai prime minister's many meetings with his regional counterparts. When the Shin group belonging to the family of the Thai prime minister works in Burma with a company belonging to a son of the ruling triumvirate, and competes in Cambodia against a company belonging to the prime minister, it is clear that the telecom business, national or regional, is political.

Thaksin regularly insisted he made no use of his position as prime minister to assist the Shinawatra businesses. It may be fair to say that most Thai would view such use of power as one of the privileges of leadership, and be amazed if he were not to make use of such privilege. At a telecom industry gathering in late 2003, Thaksin proudly took the credit for the sector's revival from the crisis:

> Right now I am trying to steer the whole ship to the shoreline. Whether it's people I like, people who like me, or people who hate me, we're all trying to survive. . . . Even those people I dislike, even if I wanted to kick them off the ship, I cannot. We must move together. (*BP*, 19 December 2003)

MOBILE PROFITS

> You can be proud of me because I am not bad, I just have too much. (Press, 19 April 2001)

At the turn of the millennium, the cost of owning a mobile phone in Thailand was significantly higher than in most other countries (Somkiat and Tharathon, 2002). The two main players avoided a price war. Handsets were locked to SIM cards, blocking out third-party providers, and reducing customers' ability to shop around. One sign of the industry's large profit margin was the existence of a vast grey subsector of service technicians, expert at tweaking phones to steal back some of that margin. In 2000, AIS made a profit of 6.6 billion baht, around 3,300 baht from each customer—ten times the same figure for rival Ucom. Even though the Shin group comprised over thirty companies, its Thai mobile phone business totally dominated, providing between two-thirds and four-fifths of total profits. But the business faced three threats in the late 1990s.

First, the arrival of several new players promised to change the nature of competition. With their privatization now mooted (though, as it turned out, distant), CAT and TOT were interested in launching new mobile phone ventures in which they were shareholders and managers rather than just licensors. Jealous of Shin's spectacular profits, other companies in the telecom sector (Samart, TelecomAsia, Loxley, etc.) were also keen to enter the mobile business.

In mid 1996, CAT entered into a venture with Loxley and IEC to start a new mobile phone network. The venture, which came to be called WCS, bought some unused bandwidth owned by Ucom, contracted Canada's Northern Telecom to construct the network, and was on the point of launching in mid 1997 when the Asian crisis struck. CAT made another deal with the Samart group and Telekom Malaysia, which also bought unused bandwidth from Ucom and launched its network under the name DPC in May 1998. CAT made a third deal with a subsidiary of the Hong Kong company, Hutchison, which launched another network under the name Tawan Mobile in April 1998. In addition, TOT licensed its fixed-line supplier TT&T to launch a PCT network planned for 2000. And in May 2000, Shin's main competitor, Ucom/TAC, entered into a joint venture with Norwegian Telenor which strengthened both its finances and its technical potential. Finally, the communications minister in the Chuan government, Suthep Theuksuban, directed TOT to launch another network known as ACT Mobile with the specific purpose of undercutting the inflated price levels of the duopoly. The contracts were signed in the dying days of the Chuan government in January 2001.

As it turned out, it was not marketing or political clout that protected Shin from this avalanche of competition, but the 1997 crisis. The WCS venture fell apart. The TT&T project was abandoned. Tawan Mobile launched but had no money for marketing; a year later it had only four thousand of its projected fifty thousand subscribers. DPC survived but was unable to offer any serious competition. However, this respite was temporary. Once the crisis eased, the duopoly faced the possibility of up to five new players.

The second threat was regulation. The 1997 constitution proposed to move beyond the era of cozy deals by setting up a regulatory body:

> Transmission frequencies for radio or television broadcasting and radio telecommunication are national communication resources for public interest. There shall be an independent regulatory body having the duty to distribute the frequencies under paragraph one and supervise radio or television broadcasting and telecommunication businesses as provided by law. (Clause 40)

The charter required the law to establish this commission be passed within two years. The Chuan government decided to split the broadcasting and telecommunication sectors into two separate commissions. The legislation was completed in 1999, and the procedure for selecting the members set in motion once the new Senate, which made the final selection, was elected in early 2000.

The third threat was liberalization of the telecom sector from 2006 under commitments to the WTO.

In sum, a government-protected, high-margin, effectively unregulated, and hence highly profitable duopoly in which Shin's AIS had a dominant share faced the prospect of transformation into a highly competitive market with heavyweight international players and proper regulation in the public interest.

The fact that that prospect did not materialize over the subsequent four years—or even show much sign of materializing—was not a matter of chance.

MANAGING COMPETITION

> In this era, it is said that an organization must be versatile and capable of adapting frequently. . . . It is now time that is scarce, not capital. We compete with speed. (Speech, 21 August 2003)

The number of potential mobile phone competitors with AIS was thinned down by several means. After the 2001 election but before formally taking office, Thaksin announced he would review Suthep's price-busting ACT Mobile network. On his first day at work, the incoming minister of communications ordered the review, and six weeks later the project was suspended (*BP*, 15 and 22 February 2001, 30 March 2001). In May 2001, the Council of State ruled that the project was improper as it had not been licensed by the National Telecommunications Commission (which had not yet come into existence; see below). CAT and TOT protested vigorously that they needed such a project for their revenues beyond privatization, and threatened to continue defiantly. For the next year and a half, the project floated in limbo while the government repeatedly revised the privatization plans for the two agencies. Eventually it was launched in November 2002 but without a technical advantage or marketing budget to give any hope of success. By June 2004, it had lost 900 million baht (*BP*, 14 June 2004).

The already launched DPC network was simpler. Shin Corp bought out Samart's share in February 2000, then forced out the Malaysian partner in July 2001 (*BP*, 7 February 2000, 19 July 2001). Subsequently the network was merged with AIS, and DPC continued life as a Shin subsidiary.

The other two potential competitors were more difficult. Hutchison had begun building its network with CAT. Shortly after taking office, Thaksin twice rubbished its CDMA technology in public. He said CDMA was failing worldwide, and the project should be scrapped (*TN*, 20 November 2001). Like ACT Mobile, the project then floundered while CAT's future was repeatedly recast. It was eventually revived in January 2002 as a 65:35 joint venture between Hutchison and CAT, and launched in February 2003. The real reasons for rubbishing the technology then became apparent. The network provided faster downloads which made it attractive for fashionable novelties like transmitting photos. By the end of 2003, Hutch had gained half-a-million users and was rated the second most preferred network (*TN*, 28 February 2003, 15 January 2004).

The WCS project, which had been on the cusp of its launch program when the 1997 crisis struck, initially collapsed and joined the flotsam of distressed assets left behind by the crisis. It was sold first to Ucom and then to CP TelecomAsia in early 2000. Six months later, TelecomAsia announced that the European company Orange would take a 49 percent share and provide the technology. The service was launched in late 2001 with high expectations that Orange's success in other markets would make a difference.

Realizing that the Hutch and TA Orange launches meant the old duopoly had disappeared, Ucom (now trading under the brand name DTAC) launched a price war in April 2002. It broke the lock between the handset and SIM, forcing others to follow suit, and allowing for much more flexible competition. It offered aggressive price deals, again forcing others to follow. DTAC and TA Orange also refused to pay the TOT interconnection charge (200 baht per subscriber per month), which disadvantaged them in competition with Shin.[1] They claimed the charge was unfair and hence illegal under the new telecom law. TOT responded by threatening to block the subscribers of these two networks from calling into TOT's landline network. The house committee on communications opposed TOT's move, and Thaksin personally delivered them a reprimand (*TN*, 10 April 2002). The fledgling TA Orange soon crumbled. DTAC held out longer but finally recognized that it simply lacked the political torque.

AIS responded to the price war by following the market down but maintaining a slight price premium over its competitors. It made no big investment in technology to provide the novelty services offered by rivals, but relied on the quality of its network built up over many years, its retail systems, and customer base. With its higher margin and larger number of subscribers, it had the revenues to blast away its competitors with saturation marketing. From 2001 onwards, AIS was one of the nation's largest spenders on advertising. Its full marketing budget was 1 billion baht in 2001, and 2 billion in 2002 (*TN*, 4 January 2001, 11 February 2002).

With plummeting prices, heavy marketing, and a recovering economy, the mobile phone market spurted. The total number of

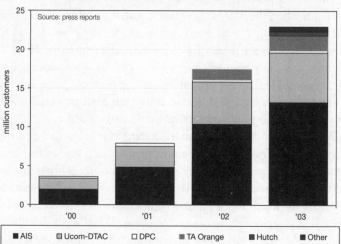

Fig 7.1 Mobile phone customers, 2000–2003

subscribers grew sixfold from 3.5 million at the end of 2000 to 22 million by the end of 2003 (fig 7.1). The dominant share of AIS was not threatened; its subscriber base grew from 2 million at the end of 2000 to 13.2 million three years later. In 2003, AIS had a two-third's share of total revenues, compared to 25 percent for DTAC, 9 percent for TA Orange, and less than 1 percent for the remainder (including Hutch) (*TN*, 23 September 2003; figures not full year). Although the price war slashed margins, the expansion of the market more than compensated. Rather than losing its profitability in the face of competition, AIS prospered spectacularly, delivering 3.8 billion baht profit in 2001, 11.4 billion in 2002, and 18.5 billion in 2003 (table 7.1 and fig. 7.2). Helpfully, in December 2003, Cabinet raised the mobile phone allowance for senior officials (C9 upwards) from 1,000 to 4,000 baht a month to "increase efficiency and mobility in the CEO-style management" (*TN*, 30 March 2004).

TelecomAsia's partners lost their stomach for such an uneven battle. Despite massive marketing investment, TA Orange had captured only 1.9 million subscribers and saw no prospect of profits. Verizon sold its 10 percent stake in July 2003 (*BP*, 18 July 2003).

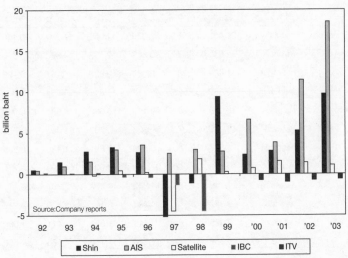

Fig 7.2 Shin group company profits, 1992–2003

Orange sold 39 percent of its 49 percent stake in March 2004, probably incurring a huge loss (*TN*, 10 March 2004).

AIS survived the avalanche of new competition. Indeed, it turned the threat of competition into an opportunity to confront another of the three threats—the 2006 liberalization. After the price-cutting market boom, it was predicted that by 2006 the market would be saturated, lessening the prospect of any new international entry.

MANAGING REGULATION

> People who do good will get good results. We cannot tolerate moral hazards because the nation will suffer. Thailand must become the most transparent nation in the region. (Speech, 21 August 2003)

The process for selecting members of the new regulatory National Telecommunications Commission, established under the 1997 constitution, began in 2000. Under the enabling act, a selection committee was formed of senior figures from various

Table 7.1. Shinawatra company results, 1998–2002 (million baht)

		1998	1999	2000	2001	2002	2003
Shin Corp	assets	22,432	25,566	37,879	41,356	51,249	60,159
	revenue	12,935	17,711	10,682	12,392	14,876	20,570
	net profit	-1,408	9,387	2,384	2,820	5,281	9,723
	market cap	16,632	87,595	46,111	45,817	29,664	113,888
AIS	assets	38,079	39,864	59,170	113,538	126,085	124, 949
	revenue	17,449	25,873	39,730	60,738	81,366	90,463
	net profit	1,447	2,750	6,599	3,851	11,430	18,529
	market cap	49,608	121,500	97,200	119,601	104,193	249,775
Shin Sat	assets	11,149	11,144	11,832	14,377	20,307	25,116
	revenue	3,150	3,047	4,234	5,161	5,429	6,217
	net profit	2,925	280	711	1,563	1,411	1,080
	market cap	6,388	17,172	12,578	11,156	7,306	14,656
ITV*	assets			3,198	2,953	3,309	3,189
	revenue			1,203	932	1,467	1,701
	net profit			-776	-979	-770	-660
	market cap					4,945	35,700
SC Asset	assets						6,194
	revenue						1,020
	net profit						284
	market cap						11,235

Source: Company reports. * ITV was acquired in 2000 (see chapter 6).

categories of public life. This committee prepared a short list sent
to the Senate for final selection. On paper this procedure sounded
smooth. But the airwaves over which this commission would hold
sway were very valuable. Those currently enjoying that value were
unlikely to let the procedure take its own course. They formed a
National Telecommunications Association and plotted to pack the
selection committee and the nominee list with military efficiency.
But this strategy failed on one key point: the enabling act forbade
any conflict of interest between the selection committee and its

nominees. Besides, the plotters seemed so used to this sort of rigging that selection committee meetings were attended and even chaired by military men who were not committee members. A rejected candidate challenged the process; the Senate voted by an overwhelming majority that it had been "illegal, non-transparent, and unfair;" and the Administrative Court invalidated the whole process (*BP*, 5 May 2001, 7 and 8 February 2002). A round of appeals added further delay. The government showed no interest in speeding things up. The selection began again in late 2003. Again a solid phalanx of the short list had strong industry connections, suggesting the process would either deliver a commission amenable to the industry, or again be aborted (*TN*, 21 and 22 December 2003).

In 2001, a Telecommunications Business Act was passed to provide a framework for the commission when it finally appeared. During the bill's passage through parliament, the Senate inserted a clause limiting foreign shareholding in any new telecom venture to 25 percent. While Shin's AIS conformed to this rule, Ucom and other competitors did not. While the limit applied only to new licenses, it would create problems when the existing concessions were transformed into licenses. Despite a howl of protest, the legislation was passed in this form. The government subsequently agreed informally to alter the limit to 49 percent, but made no move to pass the legislative amendment (*BP*, 15 May 2002).

Since they had become part of the concession market and slated for privatization, CAT and TOT had lost any semblance of providing regulation. Besides, in time-honored fashion, the ruling party had recomposed the boards of these agencies with chosen nominees (*TN*, 24 July 2002). Moreover, while their privatization had been mooted since 1995, the timing was constantly delayed and the methods repeatedly revised. The Thaksin government instructed the two agencies first to privatize separately, then to merge, then to separate again, then to shelter under a common holding company, and then again to go their own ways. As these agencies constantly drafted and redrafted their business plans, they fell further and further behind their future rivals.

The effective source of regulation, thus, was the minister in charge. The disgruntled executive of a rival company remarked: "We've been playing in a football game where some of the players have referees' whistles in their pockets" (*TN*, 19 December 2003).

The immediate problem for regulation was unwinding the concession structure. Plans for the sector's future envisaged CAT and TOT evolving into companies that competed with the other players who currently were their concessionaires. That would mean breaking the licensor-licensee relationships, and finding ways to share revenues for services that crisscrossed between networks. Given the chaotic way the original concessions were evolved, this was not a simple matter.

The first task was to decide how to deal with the revenue-sharing payments that the concessionaires made to CAT or TOT. The concessions mostly had ten to fifteen years still to run, and the concessionaires had to share 15–25 percent of revenues. The Chuan government had commissioned the TDRI think tank to consider the problem. TDRI took the principle that any new arrangement should not change future expectations of revenue flows. It thus summed the estimated revenue each concessionaire would have to pay from 2006 to the end of the concession period, converted it into a capital sum, and proposed the concessionaires pay this amount by 2006 and then be free of all obligations. The telecom companies howled this proposal down. The heavy upfront payment, they claimed, would make them financially vulnerable in face of incoming foreign competition. After the advent of the Thaksin government, another study was commissioned from a university institute which passed the task onto a subsidiary run by a cousin of Thaksin's justice minister (*TN*, 16 January 2002). This IPI study proposed the concessionaires pay until 2006 and then simply stop, free of any future obligation. The difference between the TDRI and IPI proposals was between 70 and 290 billion baht by different estimates (*TN*, 16 and 20 January 2002). Critics said the concessionaires would profit under the IPI plan at public expense. Thaksin retorted: "I'm convinced no private companies are so thick-faced as to seek billions of baht extra profit. . . .

Nobody would think of doing something so shameless" (*Nayok Thaksin lem 2*, 98).

There the matter deadlocked. In the bureaucratic reform of October 2002, the telecom sector was moved under the new ICT ministry headed by Surapong Seubwonglee. He first wondered whether each concessionaire should negotiate its own settlement with its licensor. Then he proposed replacing the revenue sharing with an excise tax. Reputedly, this idea had originated inside Shin Corporation (*BP*, 24 May 2003). Certainly Shin's head, Boonklee Plangsiri, welcomed it enthusiastically as the "best way out for everybody" (*TN*, 26 December 2002). Certainly also the shareholders of the concession firms liked it. The sector's shares jumped at the initial announcement, and jumped again when the proposal was finally implemented (*TN*, 26 December 2002, 22 and 29 January 2003). Thaksin justified the proposal on nationalist grounds. After privatization, CAT and TOT could be acquired in some part by foreign investors, and then the revenue-sharing payments "will have to be shared with [foreign] investors. In such a scenario, the government will not get the full amount, so it's better to have private telecom operators directly pay the Excise Department" (*TN*, 26 January 2003). The proposal was enacted through an executive decree, a procedure normally in the case of financial matters used only in an emergency. The Constitutional Court rejected a challenge to this procedure with one judge explaining that the excise director had told the court that government needed the extra cash "to reduce public debt and create investor confidence" (*BP*, 2 May 2003).

In fact this arrangement was only a very partial solution to the problem. Concessionaires now paid 10 percent of their revenues as excise to the Finance Ministry, and continued to pay the balance of the original revenue sharing to CAT/TOT. What would happen at privatization was still moot. The excise tax level could easily be adjusted downwards, though Thaksin accused critics who raised this point of "overreacting" (*TN*, 26 January 2003). Effectively, this arrangement killed off the TDRI proposal, while leaving the government with lots of flexibility. It also helped to block future competition. Any new entrant would have to pay the same excise tax while competing against existing players whose networks were already established and substantially amortized (Somkiat 2003). Stock investors certainly appreciated this moment: from this moment, the trajectory of AIS's share price separated from that of the market as a whole and climbed upwards (see below and fig. 7.3).

Later in 2003, Surapong's ministry also broached the question of sharing the charges for calls that crossed networks. Under the old system, all charges were collected and kept by the system where the call originated. As the mobile phone networks now had more subscribers than fixed lines, they were also the largest recipients of incoming calls. The mobile companies began to press for "interconnection" charges. Analysts reckoned these could increase the income of AIS by around 2.2 billion baht a year, while TOT and fixed-line concessionaires like TelecomAsia would lose equivalently.

The remaining regulatory issue was the supposed liberalization of the telecom sector under agreements with the WTO in 2006. However, this was less of a threat than at first assumed. In 1997, the Thai government concluded a liberalization agreement for telecoms with WTO, but its scope covered only fixed lines, telex, telegraph, and fax—in effect, past history. Wireless services, including mobile phones, were not covered. The pressure for liberalization in this subsector came not from WTO but from the several free trade agreements under negotiation, especially those with the US and Australia.

SATELLITES WITHOUT BOUNDARIES

> Apart from being the telecommunications center of east Asia, Thaicom is the collective pride of the whole Thai nation. I consider it the greatest success of my business life. (Autobiography, 1998–9)

The satellite business broadened the Shinawatra group's interests beyond the national boundaries. In the early 1990s, the group, like many other rising Thai companies, followed Chatichai's call to "turn battlefields into marketplaces." It started phone and TV businesses in neighboring countries and farther afield in Asia. But these businesses proved difficult to manage. Shin had to service local consumers with different cultural expectations, and compete against local entrepreneurs with better political connections. While serving as foreign minister in 1994, Thaksin was accused of being involved in a failed coup in Cambodia because of his business interests (*TN*, 16 November 1994). Whatever the truth behind the affair, the accusation itself showed the complexity of conducting such businesses across the political borders of the region with their recent histories of conflict.

Satellites soar way above these borders. They are hidden from public view. And selling their services is largely a form of business in which Thaksin had specialized—deals with government agencies.

Yet up to 1996, Shinawatra's satellite business was still around 90 percent inside Thailand. Over the next three years, that situation changed rapidly. Shinawatra's Thaicom 3 satellite was launched just as the 1997 crisis sank the Thai domestic market. Shinawatra became much more aggressive at seeking regional custom. It made its first sale in China in 1996. It entered India in 1997, selling to the Department of Space, Department of Telecoms, and over thirty television stations representing 40 percent of India's television market. It entered Burma in 1998, selling transponder space to the posts and telecommunications office and the state radio and television networks. It entered Cambodia in 1998 with a mobile phone business under the name CamShin. By the end of the decade, Shinawatra Satellite had customers in twenty-seven countries, and made around half of its income outside Thailand (Ukrist 2004, 61–2; Crispin 2002).

Also around 1996, the company began to seek a leap ahead in the satellite business. According to Shinawatra Satellite executives, they trawled the world looking for the next generation of satellite technology, and concluded they would have to back a totally new design. The result was IPStar, a satellite with much higher capacity, much faster speeds, and potentially much lower cost than the current generation.

The scale of the project's ambitions was matched by the scale of its difficulties. The project needed to attract customers across its footprint ranging from India to China to New Zealand. The 1997 crisis dulled the market on a regional scale. The escalating private and commercial use of the Internet initially seemed to provide a marketing opportunity. But these hopes collapsed in the pricking of the e-business bubble in 2001. Corporate customers were nervous of such an innovative venture, especially after disasters like the collapse of the Iridium network project. Both China and India were planning satellites with orbits that would conflict with IPStar. In early 2003, Loral Space, the US company building IPStar, applied for bankruptcy. Anti-Thai riots in Cambodia in January 2003 were a reminder that Shin's mix of business and politics had risks. Among the handful of Thai commercial offices targeted by the rioters was CamShin. Its mobile service had begun to encroach on the market leader known to belong largely to Cambodia's prime minister, Hun Sen. The US$350 million cost of IPStar required some heavyweight financing. In May 2002, Shin Satellite secured a loan guarantee for part of this (US$160 million) from the US Ex-Im Bank.[2] US lobbyists complained: "How is it that billionaires like Thaksin . . . can get the US taxpayers to subsidize their deals?" and tried to block the loan guarantee in Congress (*BP*, 2 September 2002, from *New York Times*). The planned launch of IPStar was delayed from 2002 to 2003 and then 2004.

While IPStar continued to court private and corporate customers,[3] its marketing strategy increasingly focused on government agencies. It especially touted the cost advantages for backward countries which had less installed capacity of more conventional communication services. Its first major customer was China Railway Communication Asia Pacific, which booked around 20 percent of the project's total capacity.[4] In January 2004, the Chinese agreed to adjust their satellite's orbit to accommodate IPStar. Shortly after, China's national satellite operator agreed to distribute IPStar terminals. Similarly in India, conflicts over orbits were resolved and Broadband Pacenet became an agent for IPStar terminals (*TN*, 24 February 2004).

Another target country was Burma. Shinawatra Satellite had reportedly first become interested in the Burma market after Thaksin visited there as foreign minister in 1994 and learned that a lease from a Hong Kong satellite would shortly expire. Eventually Shinawatra secured that deal in 1998. After becoming prime minister, Thaksin traveled to neighboring countries more often than any predecessor. Burma was the first country visited, just one month after taking office. In September 2001, Khin Nyunt, one of Burma's ruling military triumvirate, made the first return visit by a Burmese leader to Thailand in eleven years (*TN*, 3 September 2001). In May 2002, Shin Satellite signed a contract with Bagan Cybertech to extend and upgrade the usage of Shin satellites for broadcasting inside Burma, and to install IPStar terminals for use in upcountry phone and education networks. The managing director of Bagan Cybertech was Dr. Ye Naing We, the younger son of Khin Nyunt, who also attended the contract signing as the overseer of communications policy. Under another agreement, the staff of Bagan Cybertech and the Burmese post and telecommunication agency were sent for training in Shin's facilities in Thailand (*FT*, 24 April 2002; Ukrist 2004). IPStar's ground stations were tested in Burma (Crispin 2003). Khin Nyunt visited Thailand again in May 2004

The Thai press constantly speculated about the mixing of business and diplomacy in Thaksin's overseas travels. Shin executives, along with other businessmen, joined some of the trips. Most curious was a one-day lightning visit to India a few days after India had successfully launched a new satellite, and Shin Satellite's stock price had dropped 7 percent. Subsequently the Indian Department of Space extended its contracts with Shin for another six months (*MR*, 19 March 2002; Ukrist 2004). Dumrong Kasemset, head of Shin Satellite, explained this was "just a coincidence" (*TN*, 3 June 2002), and consistently denied Thaksin played any part in the company's marketing.

IPStar also got help on its home patch. In November 2003, the Board of Investment granted investment privileges for IPStar, including an eight-year tax holiday on imported equipment and on profits from overseas revenues. Normally such privileges were granted to attract new investment, not reward an existing company. Moreover, this level of privileges was designated for companies that are located in remote areas. The estimated value of these privileges was 16.4 billion baht over eight years (*BP*, 20 November 2003). Thailand's CAT granted a contract to IPStar for the first stage of a potentially massive distance education project. No bidding was called for this contract, as the CAT executive explained, because "there's only one satellite operator in Thailand" (*TN*, 20 January 2004).

If IPStar succeeded, Shin executives hoped it could be replicated in other parts of the world, taking the company global. But the technical novelty, high cost, repeated delay, and political complexity of the region meant IPStar remained both risk and opportunity.

PROPERTY

> If someone enters politics for himself, for power, for his clique, then he should go and read Buddhadasa's book on *thamma* and politics. He said that when politicians stop being selfish and reduce their greed, then the country will be fine. (Speech, 23 August 1998)

Surathian Chakthranont first met Thaksin in 1994. He was impressed that "even while the telecom business was booming, Thaksin was looking ahead to a time this business would decline. He had decided to diversify his investments into property that was secure and tangible" (Surathian 2003, 23).

The Shinawatra family accumulated a great deal of property. Surathian was hired—first as consultant, then as managing director—to run the company, SC Asset, which looked after most of these investments. Three office towers were built to house the Shinawatra group's various units in Bangkok. These buildings were not owned by the corporate entities, but privately by the family, which collected rents for use of the offices. This practice was quite common among Thailand's family-based corporations.[5] The family also owned land leased to AIS for base stations.

Besides such property linked directly to the business, the family also bought up plots of urban land and buildings, especially after the 1997 crisis when many property owners were bankrupt and prices dropped. When Thaksin made his statutory declaration of assets on becoming prime minister in early 2001, the family's total property was worth around 5.5 billion baht, including land and buildings worth half a billion baht, and investments of another 5 billion baht in property companies (see appendix 1).

The most troublesome of these investments was the Alpine Golf Club to the north of Bangkok. The 924 rai of land had been donated to a local Buddhist temple in the will of a female devotee in 1971. As temple property, the land was not legally saleable. But in 1990, Snoh Thienthong, as deputy interior minister, had the land transferred to a foundation, which then sold it on the same day for 142 million baht to a company in which Snoh's wife and brother were major partners. The land was then developed into a luxury housing development and golf course. After the 1997 crisis, when luxury investments suddenly seemed worthless, the Thienthong brothers wanted to liquidate this investment. Thaksin bought the golf course for 500 million baht in 1999. Thaksin's ownership gave the project a touch of glamour. He used the golf course for business entertainment, and managed to snare prestigious events like the Johnnie Walker Classic. The Alpine project became the "most lucrative" of all the property holdings managed by Surathian through SC Asset (*TN*, 14 January 2002).

In a parliamentary censure debate in May 2002, the opposition charged that the Thienthongs' acquisition of the land had been underhanded and illegal. Snoh had blocked the transfer to the temple, and contrived an illegal sale; hence, all subsequent transactions were also invalid. Snoh responded that the temple had never taken full possession of the land because it could not afford the title transfer fees (*TN*, 23 May 2002). However, in early 2001, the Council of State had found against Snoh and ruled that all transactions of the land since the 1990 legacy were invalid. A ministerial panel was hastily assembled which pointed out this would create an impossible legal tangle for subsequent purchasers.

The Land Department unilaterally overrode the Council of State's judgment and validated all existing land titles associated with the project (*BP*, 13 June 2001, 10 May 2002; *TN*, 2 February 2001, 16 May 2002). Although the legal position was still murky, the case then faded from public notice. A year later Surathian noted matters had been "completely resolved" (*TN*, 21 April 2003).

Around 2001–2, more of the distressed assets, which had fallen into the hands of banks and other creditors in the 1997 crisis, began to come onto the market. SC Asset was active in acquiring such properties including office buildings, a real estate firm, a ceramics exporter, and the operating lease on a convention center. Surathian said the group was looking for assets with "high yield, huge margin and short-term sales opportunities"—a subtle business strategy (*BP*, 30 October 2003). With the resulting land bank and a strong recovery in the property market in 2003, SC Asset announced it was turning towards residential developments. It launched three major projects worth 2.7 billion baht, with four more slated and several others on the horizon (*TN*, 21 April 2003; *BP*, 30 October 2003, 4 March 2004). In late 2003, the family made some consolidation of its property holdings by selling many of them to SC Asset and then listing that company on the stock market.[6] On the day the company was floated, the share price more than doubled its value, raising the net worth of the family by an estimated 2.3 billion baht (*TN*, 14 November 2003). In December 2003, Pojaman Shinawatra acquired a 33-rai city-center plot for 772 million baht in an auction held by the organization disposing of properties formally belonging to bankrupted finance companies (*TN*, 19 December 2003).

DIVERSIFICATION

> I'm happy with my [financial] status now. . . . There's no need for me to seek more profits. (Press, 4 February 2004)

Despite the success in defending the spectacular profitability of the AIS mobile phone business, it was inevitable that the business would eventually deliver diminishing returns. Shin was cash rich and needed to diversify. As the economy picked up over 2001–3, Shin spread into several new areas. All were in the service sector. Most depended to some extent on government regulations and licenses. Boonklee Plangsiri, the managing director of Shin Corporation, said:

> My goal is to build up Shin as a conglomerate. . . . We want our portfolio to be bigger, with a greater range of businesses. . . . We're not just looking at the trends in Thailand, but around the world. Entertainment, for one, is an interesting sector.
>
> We target raising the group's non-telecom business portfolio to 200 billion baht over the next five years from 40 billion baht currently. In the same time Shin's total portfolio is expected to reach 400 billion baht. (*BP*, 27 October and 18 December 2003)

In the new debt-based economy, one booming sector was finance. As part of its credit-based stimulus, the Thaksin government eased age and income limits on credit card ownership. Along with low interest rates, these changes created a boom in low-end financial services. In 2003, the number of credit cards jumped 20 percent to 6.7 million (*TN*, 11 March 2004). The sector leader, Easy Buy, had a turnover of 10 billion baht a year. Reportedly, Shin first tried to buy into this venture, and only then decided to launch its own. In December 2003, the group announced a joint venture with the Development Bank of Singapore (DBS) to provide financial services. The new venture, named Capital OK, would combine DBS's financial expertise and Shin's customer base to offer personal loans, hire purchase, and credit card services (*BP*, 11 December 2003; *TN*, 11 December 2003).

In early 2004, following reports of rising consumer debt, the Bank of Thailand announced it would retighten rules on credit card ownership, including banning direct solicitation of new cardholders. But when the new regulations were announced a few weeks later, they had been significantly watered down. Credit limits had been eased, and the ban on solicitation effectively removed (*TN*, 11 and 30 March 2004).

Another opportunity for diversification lay in tourism, one of the sectors targeted in the government's quest for competitiveness. At regional meetings, Thaksin urged neighboring countries to deregulate the airline business to promote tourism. At the ASEAN summit in Bali in October 2003, he signed "open skies" agreements with Cambodia, Singapore, and Brunei, and announced his support for low-cost airlines to establish themselves in Thailand. The Transport Ministry quickly removed the regulation setting a floor on air ticket pricing. A couple of weeks later, AirAsia, a low-cost carrier from Malaysia, announced it planned to extend to Thailand. The communications minister granted a license. Only then did it emerge that Shin had a 50 percent share.

A few days later, the Airports Authority announced it was granting Thailand AirAsia (TAA) a 50 percent discount on docking fees on grounds this would "promote tourism." Just three weeks earlier, prior to the announcement of the Shin stake in the firm, the authority had rejected such a discount as "impossible" because it would be unfair to competitors (*TN*, 4, 7, and 28 November 2003).

In late January, the Board of Investment gave TAA a package of investment privileges. This was unusual. Such promotional grants were usually offered to induce new investment, but TAA was already committed. The board explained that the project deserved help because it would promote tourism and create jobs. The main part of the privileges was an eight-year exemption from taxes, including customs dues on equipment imported for establishing ground services. In the same week, the deputy transport minister announced government would provide help with pilot training, and the air force would help with maintenance (*TN*, 29 January 2004). In February, TAA announced "we are heading towards profit in our first month" despite earlier predictions that "it would take us a year to make money."[7] In fact it took three months to turn a profit, but by that time its only competitor in the low-cost segment, One-Two-Go, was incurring losses and talking about giving up the "dogfight" within a couple of months (*BP*, 27 March 2004, 8 April 2004).[8]

Another service sector enjoying strong growth was entertainment. The Shinawatra group had bought into the only independent television station, ITV, in 2000. By 2001 Shin Corporation had a stake of around 55 percent. The station had originally been created in reaction to the government manipulation of news during the May 1992 political crisis, and was designed to be primarily a news station. Its charter limited entertainment to 30 percent of prime-time programing. The license fees were set during the heady days of the pre-1997 boom, and were significantly higher than the two stations operating under long-standing licenses from the army and the government. Barely into its stride when the crisis intervened, ITV had never turned a profit. Thaksin always insisted that he bought the station for its commercial potential not its political utility, and the prospectus painted a bright future when the company listed on the stock market in March 2002.[9]

But after Shin Corporation owned the station, the news content was lightened, and the investigative and analytical programs totally lost the sharpness that had made the station in its early years a real departure in Thailand's controlled broadcasting. The sacking of twenty-three journalists for protesting manipulation of their 2001 election coverage, the resignation of the ITV chairman, sacking of a news editor, and regular reports of journalists punished for overstepping a critical line, raised concerns that ITV was little more than a propaganda arm of the Thaksin government. Its ratings languished at no more than an 8 percent share of total viewing, and the company continued to make losses (770 million baht in 2002). Ironically, Thaksin had purchased a news station and then abolished news.

The solution was to convert ITV into an entertainment station in the teeth of established competition and in contravention of its original charter. In December 2003, ITV announced a deal with two of the most prominent forces in entertainment programing, the game show host Traiphop Limpraphat, and the soap-opera producer, Kantana. Each bought a 1.5 billion baht stake in ITV and undertook to move their shows from other channels to ITV (BP, 18 December 2003; TN, 19 December 2003). A month later, an arbitration board recommended that ITV's license fee be cut to a fraction of its existing level, and the limitation on entertainment programing during prime time be eased from 30 to 50 percent. The stock-market price of ITV leapt so far after these two announcements that the Traiphop and Kantana's investments were virtually self-financing (*BP*, 18 December 2003). The cut in the licence fee effectively transferred at least 17 billion baht from the government to ITV over the thirty-year concession.

The arbitration ruling was curious. ITV had petitioned the courts that government had breached its contract by allowing new advertising on rival channels (two cable networks, and the government's "educational" Channel 11). However, these reasons scarcely justified such a large revision of ITV's operating conditions and license fee. The scale of advertising on these rival channels was tiny, and ITV's revenues had been increasing despite this competition. It was curious too that ITV had made its deals with Traiphop and Kantana *before* the arbitration ruling that made it possible to relaunch ITV as an entertainment channel. The retired judge who cast the deciding vote on the arbitration panel admitted: "We wanted to keep iTV competitive" (*TN*, 2 February 2004). The Prime Minister's Office, which was ITV's licensor and hence the injured party under the arbitration ruling, pantomimed that it would challenge the ruling in order to defend the interests of the people. But ITV was clearly not concerned by this threat and completed the revision to its programing by 1 April 2004. The minister of the Prime Minister's Office wrung his hands in public about how difficult it would be to confront ITV legally, and helped ITV to circumvent the programing restrictions by simply redefining prime time (*TN*, 4, 10, 12 February 2004). ITV's original charter had in effect been ripped up.

Health services were also booming. The government's 30-baht health scheme had helped to divide the health care market into a socialized segment and a premium private segment. In addition, several hospitals had been able to develop an export segment with a customer base in neighboring countries of the region and in the Middle East. Private hospitals had recovered rapidly from the crisis (when many had been badly hit because of foreign loans, and several had changed hands) and were enjoying a boom. Thaksin's family had made investments in private hospitals prior to 2001. Later it was found that Vichai Thongtang was actively buying stakes in other hospitals. Since Vichai had acted as Thaksin's lawyer in the assets case, the press speculated that Vichai was acting on behalf of his patron (*TN*, 29 January 2004). Thaksin denied this.

Another company in which the family had a significant interest was Thai Military Bank (TMB). The bank had backed Thaksin from early days, and Thaksin had maintained the relationship, especially through Thanong Bidaya. In the 1997 crisis, TMB was especially badly hit because of large exposure to the sugar industry. In 2000, Thaksin invested 2 billion baht to help the bank survive, and thus acquired a stake of 7–8 percent (*FEER*, 13 December 2001). The Finance Ministry came to own 49 percent. The bank staggered through the next few years while the ministry sought a solution. Several local financial groups considered a buy-out, but backed away when they saw the extent of bad loans. Australia's ANZ Bank also took a look but declined for the same reason. Eventually in early 2004, Siam Commercial Bank seemed on the point of absorbing several banks including TMB into a new financial conglomerate. At this point, Thaksin's finance minister (Suchart Jaovasidha) managed to contrive a merger between TMB, the semi-public IFCT (a relic of early development policy), and Singapore's DBS. Unlike the Siam Commercial Bank plan, TMB would be the dominant part of this merged entity, while its remaining problems were buried in the larger context. The Shinawatra family share was expected to be around 2–3 percent.

After his son, Panthongthae, completed university, Thaksin helped him establish a photography and advertising business. In April 2004, the firm with the concession to develop advertising on Bangkok's new subway system announced it had been forced to surrender half the concession to Panthongthae's company (*TN*, 21 April 2004; *BP*, 22 April 2004).

As the economy picked up over 2002–3, the Shin group seemed like an octopus, extending its tentacles into many new areas of opportunity. At the end of 2003, a Shin executive promised, "Next year will see other investments. Shin is definitely looking to expand" (*BP*, 11 December 2003). A few months later, he predicted: "Within

the next three years, 20 million Thais or one-third of the population
will be our group's customers" (*TN*, 4 February 2004). In June 2004,
Boonklee predicted that the combined revenues of the Shin companies would grow from 90 billion baht in 2003 to 200 billion in
2004 and 400 billion in 2005 (*BP*, 12 June 2004).

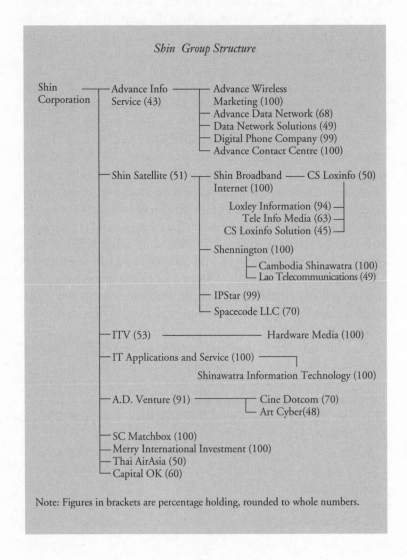

Shin Group Structure

Shin Corporation
— Advance Info Service (43)
  — Advance Wireless Marketing (100)
  — Advance Data Network (68)
  — Data Network Solutions (49)
  — Digital Phone Company (99)
  — Advance Contact Centre (100)
— Shin Satellite (51)
  — Shin Broadband Internet (100) — CS Loxinfo (50)
    — Loxley Information (94)
    — Tele Info Media (63)
    — CS Loxinfo Solution (45)
  — Shennington (100)
    — Cambodia Shinawatra (100)
    — Lao Telecommunications (49)
  — IPStar (99)
  — Spacecode LLC (70)
— ITV (53) — Hardware Media (100)
— IT Applications and Service (100)
  — Shinawatra Information Technology (100)
— A.D. Venture (91)
  — Cine Dotcom (70)
  — Art Cyber (48)
— SC Matchbox (100)
— Merry International Investment (100)
— Thai AirAsia (50)
— Capital OK (60)

Note: Figures in brackets are percentage holding, rounded to whole numbers.

CONCLUSION: THE FAMILY BUSINESS

As a prime minister, my motto is "you must be rich and don't stop becoming richer". . . . The rich should not be envied. (Speech, 21 August 2003)

In early 2004, *Forbes* magazine credited Thaksin with a worth of US$1.4 billion, around 55 billion baht. Slightly tongue-in-cheek, the magazine ranked him sixth on a sub-list of "Royals and Rulers," outpaced by four oil sheiks and the Prince of Liechtenstein.[10] In 2003, Shin Corporation's net profit was 9.7 billion baht, of which the Shinawatra-Damaphong family's share was 47 percent.[11] A newspaper estimated that the family's cash income from the Shin group was around 2.8 billion baht made up of 1.6 billion baht of dividends; 700 million baht from property rentals and other purchases (e.g., car rentals) which the Shin group made from companies directly owned by the family; 230 million baht from land sold to SC Asset; and 280 million baht in interest on loans to the companies (*KT*, 5 January 2004).[12] The income on several billion baht of other property and investments outside Shin is unknown.

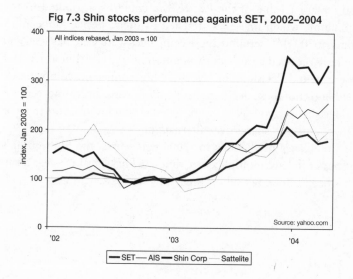

Fig 7.3 Shin stocks performance against SET, 2002–2004

Over the year 2003, the stock-market value of the five listed companies in the group almost tripled (from 146 to 425 billion), while the market as a whole grew by 117 percent. AIS was the third largest company in the market,[13] and Shin Corp the eighth. The five companies combined represented around 9.5 percent of market capitalization.

Since Thaksin became prime minister, the market capitalization of the three main Shin listed companies (Shin, AIS, Satellite) had multiplied almost 2.5 times. Among its main competitors, Ucom's capitalization had stayed roughly flat, while TelecomAsia had halved. The Shin companies had initially performed well after Thaksin's election triumph, but then wallowed through 2002, largely because of market concern over the growing competition, falling margins, and coming liberalization in the mobile phone market. The Shin group's success in overcoming this competition, maintaining market leadership, and managing the threats of liberalization had resulted in the group's two main listed companies (Shin Corporation and AIS) soaring ahead of the market in 2003 (fig 7.3). In the investment community, *hun thaksin* or "Thaksin shares" were a specific category, vaunted by most analysts and much favored by retail investors. By one estimate, no less than one-third of the market value of the *hun thaksin* could be attributed to the "premium" which investors attached to their special connections (Somkiat 2004).[14] Certainly these companies were well managed and regularly received awards in recognition of this fact. But a string of governmental decisions in favor of Shin-connected companies— whether or not these decisions resulted from any direct intervention by Thaksin or anyone else—were added reason for investors to favor these companies' shares over alternatives.

If Boonklee's predictions for 2004 come true, the Shin group's revenues will have multiplied five times in Thaksin's four-year term. It has been a good period for the family business.

8

CONCLUSION

At the end of 2003, Thaksin was flying. The economy had delivered the respectable rate of growth that he had been predicting all along in the teeth of doubt and criticism. The stock market had more than doubled within a year. His name had been adapted into the term for his economic policies, Thaksinomics. He had launched a war on poverty. Even some in the IMF had wondered if these policies might be a model for other countries. Over the previous three years, he had made enormous changes to Thai politics. He had put policy at the center of electioneering and political debate; pioneered a new relationship between leader and people; shaken up Thailand's famously torpid bureaucracy; begun to project himself as a regional leader in a way that no previous Thai premier had ventured; and largely achieved the "quiet politics" he desired. He boasted to a party gathering:

> You could talk about our government's achievements from ordering morning coffee to eating the evening meal. But for others in the past, even before the morning coffee arrived there would be nothing left to talk about. (Thaksin 2003b)

INTERPRETING THAKSIN

> I was determined that I must play some part in reversing the country's state of the economy. I was determined to utilize the pool of resources I have: my experiences, my knowledge, my network in government and business, and everything else to turn this crisis into opportunities for my Thai fellow citizens. (Speech, 8 September 2003)

In one sense Thaksin and Thai Rak Thai are creations of the 1997 crisis. Thaksin's decision to bid for the premiership was taken in the eye of the crisis. His initial goal was economic recovery. Handling the crisis wrecked the rival Democrats. The social dislocation created an audience for Thaksin's message of change. The constitution passed in the panic of the crisis created the opportunity for a new politics. The differential corporate impact gave him a financial advantage over competitors.

But in a longer perspective, Thaksin and TRT are products of the increasing power and sophistication of Thailand's urban society in general and Thai domestic capital in particular. Over the four prior decades, Thailand became much richer, more urbanized, more socially complex, and more exposed to the outside world. Protected by government and boosted by globalization, an elite of business families came to dominate the economy, mold new social values, and increasingly influence politics. The 1997 crisis was simply a final trigger for some of the biggest survivors to take a more directly active political role than before.

This business group—and much of a broader urban middle class—feels squeezed between globalization and democratization.

Globalization, which had formerly seemed such a useful ally of domestic capital and the middle class, was suddenly transformed into a threat in the form of IMF-mandated reforms, neoliberal ideologies, and ambitious foreign capital. At the same time, the internal growth of civil society and protest politics threatened to obstruct access to "national" resources, and introduce new interests and agendas into the work of the Thai state. The fundamental ambition of Thaksin and TRT is to control the state in order to restore its major purpose, evolved over the previous four decades, of promoting economic growth by creating a benign and positive environment for domestic capital. That means managing globalization. It also means cushioning discontent, suppressing dissent, and blocking the infiltration of new ideas (like participation, people-centered development, community rights) onto the state's agenda.

In power, Thaksin and TRT have pursued this ambition in three main directions: stimulating growth, managing society, and remaking politics.

Growth has been restored to its prime place in economic policy—growth out of the crisis, and then growth to first-world status on an accelerated path. This growth is to be achieved by a more active "developmentalist" intervention by the state than had marked the pre-crisis period, in particular through state-directed credit, policies to build competitiveness, and efforts to deepen capitalism and incorporate more of the nation's people and resources into the legitimate market economy. Recognizing that the Thai economy has become significantly and irreversibly globalized over recent decades, these policies follow a dual path. On the one hand, attempts are made to upgrade Thailand's position within global production chains by becoming an attractive site for foreign investment. On the other hand, special attention is paid to developing the potential of domestic capital in segments of the economy still at least partially shielded from global forces—mainly in service sectors, and the grassroots economy.

In statistical terms, the first three years of these policies were a spectacular success. GDP revived. Incomes and consumption rose. Thousands of companies bounced back. Thailand escaped having a "lost decade." But in reality, this recovery depends a great deal on the old export economy. The government is now embarking on a massive program of state projects in an attempt to lead an investment revival. This new economic direction has a strong internal logic, and a good starting track record. But it also entails a large number of risks. Household debts are at a record high. Cronyism is entrenched. Quasi-fiscal financing is not subject to any system of scrutiny and approval. Political leaders are too interested in the speculative markets of stocks and property to allow prudent controls. The social reaction to Thaksin's ambitious economic transformation is only just beginning to emerge.

The TRT government's second agenda is to have peace and quiet in society and in public space. Developmentalist states pursuing catch-up economic strategies (Korea, Taiwan) have tended to be repressive, particularly in order to control the price of blue-collar labor. But controlling labor is less critical in Thailand. The main export industries are not as dependent on blue-collar labor as the steel mills and shipyards of earlier examples. Labor organization has been weakened by law and force. Even if Thailand's reserve of labor is drying up, neighboring countries still contain a large pool. The business groups around TRT are concentrated in service industries. Thaksin and TRT are interested not so much in repressing labor as disciplining the society as a whole.

The tools for this task include carrots and sticks. Far more than any previous Thai government, Thaksin and TRT recognize the need to share more of the benefits of growth, and to get rid of the country's remaining poverty. But at the same time they try to delegitimize all non-formal politics and close down political space. "The people" stand at the center of Thaksin's rhetoric, but their role is passive. Thaksin sees democracy as a tool of growth, a historical partner of capitalism, not as an ideal. He mentions rights only as an irritating foreign imposition. He views the rule of law as subordinate to "management." The government tries to suppress protest politics through above-board law and legislation, and also through the old covert methods of the security state. It controls the media through rules, money, and intimidation. It wants to block dissent and contrive a feel-good atmosphere by micromanag-ing news content. Behind these efforts lies a conviction that nationalism stirred up by the 1997 crisis can be channeled into support for economic growth, while other agendas which might distract from this single-minded focus should be allowed no play.

Thaksin's economic vision may be fixed on the future and the first world, but his social vision is medieval.

The TRT's third agenda is to restructure the political system for the long term, building on some of the foundations laid by the 1997 constitution. Thaksin's government set about undercutting the residual power of the bureaucracy, and the foundations of local "influence." It began to construct a centralized party that took control of policy making away from the bureaucracy. It switched the source of political goods from the local boss to the central party. Thaksin also partially rehabilitated the military from its political and economic decline in the 1990s, and brought it under political control through personal networks and nepotistic ties to serve as a tool of the political executive against opposition and dissent. Thaksin's political project is to replace both the residual power of the bureaucracy, and the bottom-up, provincially focused system of political parties, with a powerful executive and a centralized party supported by business firms. In practice, this remaking of the political system depends heavily on money, with the corporations grouped around the government possibly providing funding of around a billion baht a year.

Thaksin is head of the family that has a controlling stake in one of the largest business empires in the country. The super-profits that built this empire were created from government-granted oligopolies. In all the important component companies of this empire, profits are highly sensitive to government rules and decisions. Shin executives strenuously deny any political favoritism, and have begun to hurl lawsuits at people who suggest otherwise. Yet Shin companies have fared well since Thaksin came to power, even in comparison to their peers and rivals. A stream of government decisions has seemed to contribute to this success. Stock-market investors show by their preferences that they believe Shin companies' special status commands a market premium.

Thailand's experience under Thaksin is far from unique. There are strong parallels elsewhere, especially in Latin America (Jaya-suriya and Hewison 2004). In several countries, a national elite or oligarchy has felt squeezed between the twin poles of globalization and democratization. They have reacted by forming cross-class alliances to capture state power, and then using redistributive "populist" policies to retain it. They practice dual economic strategies that try to profit from globalization while simultaneously protecting internal interests. They espouse universalist ideologies which imagine away class conflict. This pattern has been labeled "neoliberal populism" or "globalized populism."

Thaksin fits this model with two variations. First, the elites elsewhere tend to be old political elites (generals, landlords, technocrats) who can work as the front for domestic capital. But in Thailand, Thaksin and TRT have closed the gap between big business and politics. These two are now Siamese twins, joined at the hip. This results in greater emphasis on economic growth, and stronger motivation to remodel the political system. Second, Thailand has had no history of mass politics, no nationalist uprising, no revolution. Political parties have no strong roots at all. The civil society that rose over recent years proved very fragile under attack. Meanwhile, Thailand's authoritarian state has been gradually bypassed, but never overthrown. Whereas Latin American populists often have to orchestrate a mass party to manage popular aspirations, Thaksin and TRT find it simpler to revive old forms of authoritarianism. Suchinda Kraprayun, the last military prime minister installed by a coup junta, hailed Thaksin as "a most suitable man for the job" (*TN*, 7 August 2001). There is a hard edge to Thaksin's brand of "globalized populism."

DOWNSLOPE?

You know an apple is a very sweet fruit. If you make it into apple juice, it is even sweeter to drink. But in the process of making the juice, the apple must be chopped up and crushed into small pieces that will look ugly. . . . Thailand is the same as an apple. It is going through that same process of juice-making. It will be ugly until it gets better. (Press, 29 October 2001)

Not everyone agrees with Thaksin and TRT's rush for growth by mobilization of all available resources, management of a passive society, and return of the authoritarian state. Liberals believe government's proper role is to clear away the oligopolies and other distortions that prevent a truly competitive capitalism working efficiently. They want a society in which rights, freedoms, and opportunities are guaranteed by the rule of law, and a political system with checks and balances on the use of power. This lobby criticizes Thaksin and TRT for destroying the institutions and beliefs built up with difficulty over the past decades' successful resistance against military rule. The communitarian or localist lobby values the society's diversity and peaceability above the fixation with growth. It prioritizes learning, self-reliance, and participation, as summarized in the king's concept of sufficiency. This lobby criticizes Thaksin for undermining local communities' self-reliance by handouts, attacking civil society, and reinforcing the old pattern of a patrimonial government ruling over a passive people.

At the end of 2003, Thaksin and TRT seemed in a more powerful position than any previous elected Thai government. Thaksin predicted the party would sweep at least 400 of the 500 seats at the next election, and rule for a total of twenty or twenty-four years. But this supreme confidence was challenged over the next few months. The phrase *kha long*, "on the downslope," popped up in the media and was constantly repeated. "I don't know why so many problem issues seem to be coming up at the same time," he muttered to his radio audience.[1] His entourage talked darkly of a conspiracy to unseat him.

In his annual birthday speech on 4 December 2003, the king said:

> The sufficiency economy . . . has to progress. It is not only about growing enough to eat. There must be enough to set up schools, and support the arts. Then it can be said that Thailand is moving ahead. . . . Sufficiency also matters in governance and other disciplines, in economics, in political science . . . without sufficiency, things do not work, they are messy. . . . Sufficiency is not only about the economy; sufficiency in thinking and doing anything makes it possible to survive. . . .
>
> I know the prime minister does not like to be criticized because

criticism makes us angry. But let me tell you about criticism; even when I was forty to fifty, when the Princess Mother praised me, said I was clever, and she liked what I did, she would add, don't get carried away. She said every time, don't forget yourself, don't float. She used the word, float, float, float, keep your feet on the ground. . . .

The way I understand it, a CEO does not have to take responsibility . . . the seven deputy prime ministers must take the responsibility . . . they then push it to the permanent secretaries . . . then the permanent secretary does not have to take responsibility. . . . his deputy must; then the deputy says there is the department head; in this way, nobody is taking responsibility. So in the end, who takes the responsibility? The CEO citizen, all the CEO citizens take the responsibility. . . . Government today is strange, it goes back to the old way . . . the citizens take responsibility for everything. . . .

However, the prime minister is responsible for everything. So he must accept criticism. . . . If one person is responsible, people will point at one person. . . . Read the newspapers. If they say the government did wrong and acted too violently, go and check. . . . If their criticism is correct, thank them. If it is not right, tell them it was not right, go easy.[2]

A close aide quoted the king saying: "If you are dishonest, even just a little, may you be cursed and have bad luck. . . . the wealthier, the more corrupt" (*TR*, 21 March 2004; *Thai Post*, 21 March 2004). In January 2004, the bird flu epidemic reached Thailand. Although birds had been dying for two months, the government denied the epidemic, threatened newspapers with legal action, and flatly lied to a European Union health commissioner. It owned up only after a renowned medic went public with the facts (*BP*, 29 January 2004). Some wondered whether this behavior had anything to do with the big CP chicken conglomerate's close relationship with the government. The epidemic had been covered up for two months (partly by buying the silence of affected farmers), while big chicken exporters profited from inflated international prices. CP was allowed to manage the epidemic internally within its factories, rather than being submitted to the enforced cull imposed on smaller producers in infected areas. CP also took the opportunity to vaunt the superiority of its "closed" systems, and would probably benefit in the long term from the difficulties of smaller producers (Chanida and Delforge 2004). Throughout the incident, Thaksin seemed more concerned by the impact on the economy, stock market, and big business than the implications for the health of nation or world.

Also in January, the labor union at the Electricity Generating Authority of Thailand (EGAT) came out strongly in opposition to plans to corporatize the authority and float 30 percent of its shares on the stock market. The government hoped to rush through the plan with an executive decree, while EGAT hatched a plan to pretty up its asset value by a share swap with two power-plant companies. The EGAT union had a record of opposing past privatization plans, and some sympathy from parts of management. When the government refused to make a deal with workers on pay and share offerings, the union began mass rallies on 23 February 2004. It appealed for public support by accusing the government of sacrificing consumer interests for the sake of cronyist gains from the share sale. It pointed to the experience of the PTT corporatization, when large shareholdings went to associates of the government and the share price was subsequently ramped (see chapter 4). Unions in other utilities and activist groups provided sympathetic support, raising the rallies to fifty thousand people. Bangkok opinion polls showed public concerns over cronyist profiteering and future power prices. Thaksin's response revealed perhaps too much of his personal fears: "If I back down, I can tell you the economy and the stock market will crash. . . . The SET index would nosedive. . . . The baht will depreciate. I just can't back down" (*BP*, 29 February 2004). The head of NESDB predicted: "If we can't stop this mob, this could be the end of this government" (*TN*, 31 March 2004).

Rallies continued through March and April. The union then threatened to cut off power supplies to government agencies and companies that were in arrears on their bills, and to contrive a slowdown by mass leave-taking. Thaksin threatened to fire the EGAT management and railed against his ministers for mishandling the affair. He also had to backpedal. The plan for a fast executive decree was abandoned; the timetable scrapped; the proposed share swaps unwound; and new rules announced to prevent cronyist allocation of shares. The climbdown had implications for the government's ambitious program of future corporatizations designed to raise 80 billion baht.[3]

In parallel with these growing problems, the transition from 2003 to 2004 was marked by a stream of stories about the Shin empire's successes—IPStar's investment privileges (estimated value 16.4 billion baht), Thailand AirAsia's cheap landing rights, SC Asset's capital gain (2.3 billion baht), Capital OK's plans, and ITV's fee reduction (17 billion baht). Shin Corp's annual profit jumped 84 percent to 9.7 billion baht, equivalent to the annual income of the inhabitants of a moderate Thai provincial city (e.g., Ubon, Rayong).

Also in early 2004, the long-running problems in the three Muslim-majority provinces in the far south took a violent turn. Of all the rising problems, this was the most complex and tragic.

THE SOUTH

There's no separatism, no ideological terrorists, just common bandits. . . . In some places, it's conflict between local politicians. In others it's conflict over the profits from drugs and vice. Elsewhere it's a result of personal conflict. Sometimes there is politics in the background too. In sum, it's very varied, but no ideological terrorism. (Radio, 27 July 2002)

Areas in southern Thailand populated mainly by Muslim Malay-speakers were brought under Bangkok by military expansion in the late eighteenth century. From then onwards, these areas intermittently raised revolts and sought help from the Malay states to the south. Pattani, which had been a major port and political center for centuries, became the ideological focus of this resistance. Before and after the Second World War, when Bangkok tried to integrate outlying regions and impose some cultural uniformity, new separatist organizations appeared and were violently suppressed. Bangkok continued to control the area by semi-colonial rule with large roles for the army and police, and with studied neglect, which made the area one of the poorest regions.

From the mid 1970s, overt separatism declined in parallel with the gradual extension of democratic politics. But the rump of the organizations continued to exist and to command some popular sympathy. The Muslim communities' first line of cultural defense was *pondok* schools run on Islamic principles. Local students often found it difficult or culturally unpleasant to ascend the Thai education system, and many progressed from the *pondok* schools to Islamic institutions overseas. With the growth of the wealth and political ambitions of the oil states in the Middle East, more students from this area went to study in the Middle East, especially in Wahabist institutions. Some returned to be local teachers and religious leaders.

The tensions of the south were complicated by the rising antagonism between the US and the Islamic world. After the al-Qaeda attacks on the US in September 2001, Thaksin attempted to keep a little independence from the US in public to avoid provoking local Muslim sensibilities, while in private committing full support to the US according to long-standing treaty obligations. This was difficult in view of President Bush's demand that countries align themselves clearly. It became more difficult after the Bali bombings of October 2002, when the US took more interest in suppressing militant Islamic networks in Southeast Asia. Militants had been able to pass through Thailand unscathed, with authorities hoping they would be reluctant to disturb these convenient arrangements by committing a terrorist act locally. But the US agencies began to put heavy pressure on the Thai military.

In June 2003, Thaksin visited the White House and Bush conferred on Thailand "non-NATO ally status." On 11 August 2003, a CIA-backed operation captured the senior al-Qaeda figure, Hambali, in Thailand and spirited him away. Thailand's alignment was now clear. In October, Thailand sent 447 non-combat troops (mostly medics) to Iraq. Thai Muslims objected, and public feeling over this commitment became worse after two of the troops were killed and the disaster of the American invasion became more apparent.

Meanwhile, the far south's unique position as a cultural enclave under semi-colonial rule meant it was uniquely sensitive to the Thaksin government's centralization of power, renewed stress on Thai culture, and rehabilitation of the military. From 2002 onwards, the region felt under increasing pressure. During the war on drugs in 2003, the death toll was high with some possibly victimized by the security forces. In June during Thaksin's visit to Washington, three prominent community leaders were arrested and charged with membership of Jemaah Islamiyah, apparently to impress President Bush. As security forces became more concerned over possible links to militant Islam, the frequency of searches and seizures increased, especially in *pondok* schools. According to the National Human Rights Commission (2004), many people were beaten or abducted. An activist lawyer, Somchai Neelaphaijit accused the police of barbarically torturing arrested suspects. A few days later on 12 March 2004, he disappeared. Four police officers were subsequently arrested and accused of abducting him. Chavalit let slip in parliament that he knew Somchai was already dead (*BP*, 26 March 2003).

In response to this pressure, some people turned for defense to Islam and the ideal of an independent Pattani kingdom.

This downward spiral was complicated by the turf war among the uniformed services. As elsewhere, the border generated lucrative businesses in smuggling of rice, people, drugs, arms, and consumer goods. The army and police who controlled the region had become deeply involved with these rackets jointly with local businessmen and gangsters. In 1995–6, government had set up a joint police-army command in an attempt to neutralize rivalries. But the turf wars continued, and escalated after Thaksin came to power and disrupted both the police and military hierarchies. In early 2002, police and army engaged in open propaganda warfare, accusing each other of running drugs, smuggling, prostitution, and other rackets (*BP*, 21 and 22 March 2002).

In May 2002, Thaksin tried to end this warfare by dissolving the joint police-army command, and giving the police the upper hand.

Probably this only provoked the soldiers and their gangster clients who lost out. Violence continued sporadically and then escalated dramatically in early 2004. On 4 January, a large haul of weapons was looted from a military camp. The police accused the army of manufacturing the "raid" to cover up arms sales by "insiders" to rebels in Aceh. The army reacted with angry public denials.

Through 2003, sporadic violence increased in the three southernmost provinces but on an old pattern of school arson, railway bombings, and attacks on police posts. After the 4 January 2004 attack, when government declared martial law and sent extra police to the region, the pattern changed. Now other officials and some civilians were attacked and killed on almost a daily basis. By April, over sixty had died. Some of the victims were Buddhist monks suggesting an attempt to stir religious animosity. Significantly, this brought no mass reaction. Local people strenuously denied there was any communal hatred in the area, and blamed the problem on the persistence of semi-colonial control, the arrogance of officials (especially those sent from Bangkok), and the joint racketeering of men in uniforms and their gangster clients.

From 2002 onwards, Thaksin blamed the disorder on "common bandits, just like in other provinces," while strenuously denying any role for separatism or international militant Islam (*Nayok Thaksin lem 3*, 5–6). His solution was to pour in development funds while cracking down on violence.

The security agencies diagnosed the problem as more serious. Defense minister Thammarak believed "we are not dealing with ordinary bandits, but with insurgents with a separatist ideology" (*BP*, 4 March 2004). He suggested 10 percent of Islamic students who had studied abroad had been recruited by militant organizations (*TN*, 30 July 2003). General Panlop Pinmanee of ISOC claimed there were 500 "active separatists" and 70,000 sympathizers in the three southernmost provinces (*BP*, 31 March 2004). In late March, two TRT MPs and one senator were accused of planning the 4 January weapons raid. The senator, Den Tohmena, was son of the separatist leader from the 1940s. The evidence for their involvement came from a local *kamnan*, used car dealer, and political canvasser who figured on the police list of "influential people" (*TN*, 23 March 2003).

In March 2004, Thaksin seemed to realize the military-driven heavy-handed policy would not work. He decided to "make a U-turn" (*TN*, 5 May 2004). On 9 March he shuffled the Cabinet, removing Thammarak and Wan Muhamad Nor Matha from overseeing the southern operation. He sent down Chaturon Chaisaeng who returned with a dramatically different diagnosis. Chaturon said: "Police must stop torturing, abducting and murdering people" (*BP*, 8 April 2004). He proposed withdrawing the Bangkok police, lifting martial law, giving amnesty, leaving the *pondok* schools alone, and replacing teachers and officials by local people. Thaksin also visited the region and returned with a more complex interpretation than before. He believed poverty, lingering separatism, local political conflict, corrupt officials, and gangster businesses all played a role. In addition, he hinted that these problems were being stirred up to undermine his government. His solution was yet more development funds along with campaigns against the "poor youths paid to commit the atrocities" and the "inhuman people" behind them.[4] Some in the security forces strongly opposed this interpretation. They argued that separatism was not only a major factor but was also now linked to international Islamic militancy with fearful potential (*BP*, 24 April 2004). They blocked Cabinet discussion of Chaturon's plan—perhaps the last straw.

On 28 April 2004, seven groups attacked police posts in the three provinces. One group retreated to the historically important Krue Se mosque in Pattani. They shouted radical slogans and invited martyrdom. The security forces obliged, attacking the mosque with anti-tank weapons and killing thirty-two people inside. In all, 108 people died along with five from the security forces in one of the worst days of violence in modern Thai history.

Subsequent reports showed that radical organizations had gathered strength over the previous year as the region felt increasingly under pressure. A week before the 28 April outbreak, the National Human Rights Commission had issued a statement:

The present problems result from the reactions of Muslim brothers and sisters who decided to stand up and fight after having accumulated grievances and frustrations over a long period. . . . For example, police captured and tortured people to secure confessions. . . . Many cases of missing persons have not been investigated. (NHRC 2004)

There were also suggestions that the security forces had helped provoke the violence to build a case for more severe repression. Thaksin stuck to the argument that poverty and drugs were the real problem, and that the youths were manipulated by "masterminds" that used separatist ideology as cover.

Some interpreted the violence as a perennial minority problem. But over the prior two decades, the far south had found a way to exist in uneasy but largely peaceful balance with the Thai state. Thaksin's policies and outside pressures had disturbed this balance in a tragic way.

LOOKING AHEAD

I will stay another five years, two terms [in total], as there will not be any challenge left for me. I will go and teach. There will be no poverty, no "mafia", no societal ills. (Speech, 21 August 2003)

Shorn of the rhetoric, Thaksinomics is a pragmatic approach to achieving growth by relying on the outside world, while protecting enclaves for domestic capital, and redistributing enough to achieve social peace. The current strategy of priming investment in the public sector, extending quasi-fiscal financing, promoting SMEs, and multiplying microcredit can work as long as the external environment remains favorable, and the obvious internal risks are contained.

But will the cronyism, nepotism, and conflict of interest endemic to Thaksin's system ultimately prejudice the aim of growth? Thaksinomics has no mechanism to force those who win favors from the regime to deliver efficiency in return. In the Philippines, a small group of "oligarchs" with a base in land and banking have been able to dominate politics and economy resulting in high private profits but overall economic stagnation (Hutchcroft 1998). Thailand's prospects are hopefully different. To date, Thailand has not developed an oligarchy in the sense of a rather stable politico-economic elite. Rather, there tends to be more competition and higher turnover. More importantly, the economic sectors dominated by the TRT inner circle are not as central to the economy as land and banking in the Philippines. The telecom sector in Thailand contributes only 3 percent of GDP (Ravadee and Apirudi 2000). The service sectors favored by the TRT inner circle have low linkages to the rest of the economy. Even if cronyism leads to inefficiency, the extent of the damage should not be great. The real risks of cronyism and conflict of interest under Thaksin lie in the potential for mismanaging another asset bubble, and the possibility that investments in education, technology, and environmental care will be paid only lip service because they are not critical for the inner circle's profits. The political costs of Thaksin are a larger problem than the economic risks. When a country becomes a company, and government becomes management, then people are not so much citizens with rights, liberties, and aspirations, but rather consumers, shareholders, and factors of production. Thaksin has rolled back a quarter-century of democratic development. He hopes to transform Thailand from a beacon of democracy in Southeast Asia into another illiberal one-party state. Optimists still believe that Thailand's democratic movement will revive. But some fear another round of the violence that has punctuated the country's modern history.

What then are the political prospects? Thaksin would like a stable, unchallengeable one-party dominance similar to Malaysia or Singapore (Thitinan 2003, 288). He hopes to achieve this through the ballot box. The slow recovery of the Democrat Party from its eclipse in 2000–1 makes this imaginable. But over a longer term, it may be more difficult.

Lee Kuan Yew was able to build a Chinese ethnic nationalism in Singapore based on fears of the outside threats to a small island.

Mahathir built a Malay nationalism on fears of the economic power of the resident Chinese. For Thaksin and TRT, there is no such long-standing threat. As the crisis recedes, globalization metamorphoses back from threat to friend. While the foreign press and UN agencies are easy targets for Thaksin's nationalistic posturing, they are not demons that walk through the nightmares of the average Thai.

Besides, a key difference between Thaksin and Mahathir or Lee is that the latter two did not count among the richest businessmen of their country. Capitalism is about competition. When capitalists enter government, market competition and political rivalry become confused. Even within the inner circle of Thaksin's business supporters, the relationships are very delicate. Bangkok Bank drifted away after Thaksin lost sympathy with the "old banking system." CP is torn: its agricultural businesses probably benefit under the Thaksin government but in the telecom field, designated as the corporation's future, CP is dying in the face of Shin's growing dominance. The Maleenont family's TV Channel 3 lost valuable program content to ITV, and will face increasing competition for advertising revenues. Outside the charmed circle of TRT, other business interests must be concerned by growing evidence of the monopolization of opportunities.

Significantly, the Thaksin camp interpreted the stirring of opposition in early 2004 as a clash of capitals. Sondhi Limthongkun analyzed the opposition as "old capital" fighting a rearguard action against the domination of "new capital."[5] Thaksin spoke of "interests which benefited under a weak government" now gathering against him.[6]

Thailand might move, not towards one-party dominance, but perhaps a two-party system of competing coalitions of capital, rather similar to the US pattern. Yet this would still leave the political system in the grip of a narrow plutocrat elite. Some intellectuals proposed that the only escape from this fate lay in another round of constitutional reform. Rangsan Thanapornphan had analyzed in detail how the 1997 constitution empowered big business. The drafters had concentrated on preventing the political corruption of provincial construction contractors, and had totally failed to imagine Thaksin and the financial resources of Shin Corporation. Amorn Chantharasombun, the lawyer whose 1993 book had outlined the political reengineering of the 1997 constitution, has called for a new political movement with the single objective of making another constitutional revision. But Thaksin and TRT are in a much stronger position to resist such a movement than Banharn Silpa-archa was in 1995. Besides, the ease with which big business bent the 1997 constitution to its own benefit suggests there are strong limits on what can be achieved by constitutional tinkering.

The emergence of any new political force is another matter. The novelty and ambition of TRT's agenda has inevitably created disgruntlement and dissent, especially within the elite—military factions displaced by nepotistic promotions; bureaucrats forced into new roles; businessmen outside the circle; proponents of the liberal and communitarian agendas sidelined by TRT's domination of political space; and civil society groups of all kinds. In addition, rural protesters, organized labor, victims of the drug war, Muslims, and chicken farmers all have reasons for dissatisfaction.

But perhaps, the biggest unknown of Thai politics now is the impact of Thaksin's new role for "the people" in Thai politics. In the electoral campaign of 2000–1, and the popularity campaign of 2001, Thaksin and TRT deliberately set out to raise people's expectations of the benefits available through the political process. Indeed, Thaksin's rhetoric ("every breath we think of the people"), the party's universal policies, the intimacy of Thaksin's weekly radio chats, the ambition of the party's promises ("everybody will have land to make a living and every home will have electricity and tap water"), and its new slogan ("TRT's heart is the people") have constructed "the people" as a factor in Thai politics in a new way. In Thaksin's version of the social contract, this "people" exists only to surrender its rights and wait for government to deliver the political goods. In its logic and inspiration, this formula is the old paternalist state in new clothing. It assumes the forces that broad-ened political space in the 1990s can be controlled permanently. But what now will "the people" really tolerate, really want, and really do?

EPILOGUE:

POLITICAL FOOTBALL

On 11 May 2004, Thaksin told the press he was close to finalizing purchase of a 30 percent stake in the English soccer club, Liverpool, for around 4.6 billion baht. Seconds later, the government spokesman said that "Thailand as a country" was buying the team. In this moment, the confusion between public and private, Thailand and Thaksin, Shin Corp and Thailand Company, seemed to be complete.

In fact, the story was more complex. As in the assets case three years earlier, large sums of money, confusion between public and private interests, and conflict between constitutional law and political popularity, were all at work.

Shin Corp had announced since 2003 that it was looking for international investment opportunities in the entertainment field. Thaksin had been openly in the market for a football club, and had already been rebuffed by Fulham. His people had told the press that the Liverpool purchase would involve a consortium of TRT billionaires: Thaksin, Suriya Jungrungruangkit, Charoen Siriwattanapakdi, and Prayuth Mahakitsiri.

Possibly "Thailand as a country" suddenly appeared as the purchaser because someone pointed out that Thaksin was about to do something unconstitutional. Section 209 of the charter clearly disallows any minister from such a purchase. Thaksin had not even spoken of Shin Corp (or Pojaman) as the buyer, but had been proudly using the first person pronoun. Yet at the same time, he had used two ministers, another TRT MP, the government spokesman, and several officials to conduct the negotiations. He had held the meeting with a Liverpool executive in Government House. For a "private" purchase, all this seemed a little inappropriate.

Possibly also, the shift to "Thailand as a country" was politically inspired. The prospective purchase had attracted enormous media attention. Watching English football—and, even more, gambling on it illegally—had become hugely popular over the past decade. Arranging for "Thailand as a country" to buy a team seemed a brilliant way to get off the "downslope" of recent months. Thaksin claimed that the Liverpool purchase would help upgrade Thailand's football league; Thai youth would be inspired to kick drugs and kick a ball; and Liverpool branding would help sell Thailand's "One Tambon, One Product" goods all over the world. Over-enthused sports journalists dreamed of Thai players in the Liverpool team. Hopeful entrepreneurs imagined Thai brandnames emblazoned across Liverpool jerseys during global telecasts. Six years earlier, Thailand was being crushed by globalization. Now "Thailand as a country" could buy a highly symbolic global property.

But neither the economics nor the politics were quite so easy. Thaksin had been invited into the deal as a white knight to fend off an aggressive bid by Liverpudlian property developer Steve Morgan, who wanted to dilute existing shareholdings and take control. Thaksin's offer was less threatening to existing owners. But some fan organizations objected on grounds of Thaksin's human rights record. Banners shouting "Say no to Thai blood money" were waved at Liverpool matches. A poll by the *Liverpool Echo* found 87 percent in favor of Morgan. Nationalistic objections were raised, even by Britain's minister of sport. A Liverpool fan remarked acidly that he would prefer a shareholder who could name three Liverpool players, after Thaksin could manage only two.

Moreover, how would "Thailand as country" buy a football team? For several days, this question was kicked all over the park. At first, Thaksin said he would use public money so the shareholding would be "owned" by "all" Thais. This brought immediate charges of inappropriate use of public funds. Thaksin switched to a purchase by "the people" with no use of "tax money." That soon changed into a lottery. Punters would buy 1000 baht tickets and in return get a 200 baht share and a chance to win a billion baht prize. The shareholding would be managed by a holding company in which the Sports Authority (i.e., tax money) had a 60 percent share.

But this proposal brought a storm of criticism. Law academics suggested the purchase would be unconstitutional. Financiers advised it was hugely risky and probably unwise given Liverpool had failed to pay a dividend in 2003. Social activists fumed against the government's flagrant encouragement of gambling. Economists noted that the lottery deal was really an upfront tax of 400 percent which would probably fall mostly on the poor. Lawyers pointed out that special lotteries were permitted only for charitable purposes. The Sports Authority doubted it could legally act as a holding company.

At the outset, Thaksin had said: "whether to buy it personally, invite a consortium, or use government money has yet to be decided. . . . I'm thinking of using it as the country's brand, to help the poor" (*KT*, 11 May 2004). In one thought, he could slip from a personal investment to poverty relief. In his mind at least, the two were somehow the same. When Shin Corp head, Boonklee Plangsiri, emerged as part of the negotiating team, the confusion between private and public interests was further confirmed.

But others wondered what were the benefits to "Thailand as a country" rather than "Thaksin as a politician"? Would buying into Liverpool really inspire Thai kids to be as soccer-mad as Brazilians? Why not build stadiums all over Thailand, rather than one in England? What value would the Liverpool logo add to a pack of Yasothon rice crackers? Would Liverpool (club or city) really allow its name to be used in such a way? What kind of mentality imagined that "Thailand's brand" could be "Liverpool"? Even the mass circulation daily *Thai Rath*, which had been generally pro-Thaksin, came out strongly against the deal as a "grand illusion" (*TR*, 31 May 2004).

In short, the proposal stood accused of being unconstitutional, unethical, illegal, fanciful, bad business, and riven with conflict of interest. Now pinned back deep in his own half, Thaksin protested that he was not "crazy."

Indeed, this project was a logical extension of Thaksinomics. If Thailand is a company as much as a country, why should it not act just like a multinational holding company or hedge fund, buying up properties in the international marketplace. Why limit the investor-citizens to ownership in Liverpool alone. Why not several football teams. Why not buy a piece of Britney Spears. As the Liverpool deal imploded, Thaksin threw up the idea of "Thailand" buying into an international automobile firm.

Like nothing before, the Liverpool deal exposed the essential confusion between business and politics, Thailand and Thaksin, Shin Corp and Thailand Company, the CEO and the premier, political power and commercial benefit, populism and capitalism, country and company.

Thaksin backed away from the project, sighing that the Thai people were not yet advanced enough to understand and embrace his vision. He cancelled the billion baht lottery saying he had not thought earlier that it might tempt the poor to plunge even further into debt. He insisted this climbdown was no loss of face because he was not bothered by such things: "If I'm on a ten-wheel truck and have to jump off, I'll jump" (Radio broadcast, 5 June 2004).

STATEMENT OF ASSETS AND DEBTS

Pol Lt Col Thaksin Shinawatra, prime minister,
on entering office 15 March 2001

		Number (shares)	Baht
Assets			
1	Cash		1,000,000.00
2	Deposits		
2.1	Commercial banks, 2 accounts		
2.1.1	Bangkok Bank		3,235,018.11
	Bangkok Bank		3,484.08
	Total		3,238,502.19
3	Investments		
3.3	Other investments, 13 places		
3.3.1	OAI leasing	1,106	1,060.00
3.3.2	OAI Asset	1,000	10,000.00
3.3.3	SC Office Plaza	10,000	100,000.00
3.3.4	PC Property	25,999	259,990.00
3.3.5	Upcountry Land	1,000	10,000.00
3.3.6	Phramaisuri Property	4,900	490,000.00
3.3.7	OAI Consultant and Management	10	100.00
3.3.8	V Land Property	999	99,900.00
3.3.9	Caspian Holdings (Cayman)	1	0.43
3.3.10	AEA Investors Inc.	10	42.87
3.3.11	LFD Investors II LP	2,350	8,891,824.25
3.3.12	RMC Investors LLC	21,148	79,632,254.94
3.3.13	MBI Investors LP	6,194	23,322,895.77
	Total		112,818,068.26

4 Money loaned
　Mr Panthongthae Shinawatra　　　　409,200,000.00
　Ms Yinglak Shinawatra　　　　　　　20,000,000.00
　Total　　　　　　　　　　　　　　　429,200,000.00

5 Land, 2 pieces　　　　　　　　　　　　535,850.00
　Huai Yap, Amphoe Muang, Lamphun
　Huai Yap, Amphoe Muang, Lamphun

8 Rights and concessions
　Policy, Muang Thai Life Assurance　　7,307,973.00
　Policy, Thai Life Insurance　　　　　　254,475.00
　　　　　　　　　　　　Total　　　　7,562,448.00

9 Other property　　　　　　　　　　14,800,000.00

GRAND TOTAL　　　　　　　　　　569,154,868.45

Debts
3 Debts with documents
　Loan guarantee, Thanachat Finance　　60,329,589.04

GRAND TOTAL LESS DEBTS　　　　508,825,279.41

Khunying Pojaman Shinawatra,
wife of Pol Lt Col Thaksin Shinawatra

Assets

1	Cash		1,000,000.00

2 Deposits
2.1 Commercial banks, 20 accounts

2.1.1			895,559.13
2.1.2	Siam Commercial Bank		158,461,586.67
2.1.3	Siam Commercial Bank		-
2.1.4	Siam Commercial Bank		5,070,583.58
2.1.5	Siam Commercial Bank		2,082,143.30
2.1.6	Siam Commercial Bank		528,064.81
2.1.7	Siam Commercial Bank		894,651.88
2.1.8	Siam Commercial Bank		42,566.68
2.1.9	Siam Commercial Bank		2,000.00
2.1.10	Siam Commercial Bank		-
2.1.11	Siam Commercial Bank		7,491.68
2.1.12	Siam Commercial Bank		200,100,690.62
2.1.13	Siam Commercial Bank		5,000,000.00
2.1.14	Siam Commercial Bank		5,000,000.00
2.1.15	Bangkok Bank		1,295,328.50
2.1.16	Bangkok Bank		12,969,676.08
2.1.17	Bangkok Bank		450.23
2.1.18	Bangkok Bank		10,000,000.00
2.1.19	Si Ayutthaya Bank		20,569,090.89
2.1.20	Siam City Bank		1,032,889.51
		Total	423,952,773.56

2.2 Other financial institutions, 2 places

Thai Farmers Mutual Fund		50,570,112.55
Krung Thai Thanakit Investment Fund		10,231,421.23
	Total	60,801,533.78

3 Investments
3.2 Registered investments, 4 places

3.2.1	TCM Plus Fund	483,286	698,009.94
3.2.2	Thai Military Bank Mutual Fund	20,000,000	201,400,000.00
3.2.3	Thai Farmers Bank Loan Fund	18,000	18,000,000.00
3.2.4	Siam City Credit Investment Fund	800	8,000.00
		Total	220,106,009.94

3.3 Other investments, 22 places

OAI Property	10,980,000	109,800,000.00
OAI Leasing	100	1,000.00
OAI Asset	1,000	10,000.00
SCK Estate	1,550,000	15,500,000.00
SC Office Plaza	10,000	100,000.00
BP Property	16,817,500	168,175,000.00
PT Corporation	9,990,000	99,900,000.00

Upcountry Land	1,000	10,000.00
Phramaisuri Property	4,900	490,000.00
World Supplies	3,559,900	35,599,000.00
OAI Consultant and Management	47,999,950	479,999,500.00
V Land Property	4,999	499,900.00
OAI Education	22,499,997	75,924,970.00
Nawatakam Fund	1,877,993	5,624,979.00
Patthanakan Vetchakit	1,550,000	15,500,000.00
The Peninsula Travel Service	20,000	200,000.00
Rama IX Hospital	935,000	93,500,000.00
Hariphunchai Memorial Hospital	100,000	1,000,000.00
Alpine Golf and Sports Club	24,899,987	166,666,580.00
Bangkok Telecom Engineering	999,994	9,999,940.00
Udomwan	994	994,000.00
AIG Asia Direct Investment Fund	1,000,000	42,870,000.00
	Total	1,322,364,869.00

4 Money on loan, 10 loans

OAI Property	800,000,000.00
Upcountry Land	110,000,000.00
OAI Consultant and Management	32,000,000.00
SC Asset	18,000,000.00
Jao Khun Industry and Agriculture	160,250,000.00
Millennium House	38,654,158.90
Ms Busaba Damaphong	118,999,970.00
Mr Banphot Damaphong	450,385,225.00
Mr Panthongthae Shinawatra	5,056,348,840.00
Mr Phratak Likhitluasuang, Ms Kalayarat Panichsakun	3,000,000.00
Total	6,787,638,193.90

5 Land, 108 plots	387,760,646.00

6 Buildings
6.1 Residences, 4 places

6.1.1 Mae Rim, Chiang Mai	50,000,000.00
6.1.2 Charoensanitwong Rd, Bangkok	153,000,000.00
6.1.3 Hua Hin	93,000,000.00
6.1.4 Chareonsanitwong Rd, Bangkok	28,000,000.00
Total	324,000,000.00

6.2 Other buildings, 35 places

6.2.1 Two-story building, Dusit, Bangkok	1,000,000.00
6.2.2 Two-story building, Dusit, Bangkok	1,000,000.00
6.2.3 Two-story building, Dusit, Bangkok	1,000,000.00
6.2.4 Two-story building, Dusit, Bangkok	1,000,000.00
6.2.5 Two-story building, Dusit, Bangkok	1,000,000.00
6.2.6 Two-story building, Dusit, Bangkok	1,000,000.00
6.2.7 Two-story building, Dusit, Bangkok	1,000,000.00
6.2.8 Two-story building, Dusit, Bangkok	1,000,000.00
6.2.9 Two-story building, Dusit, Bangkok	50,000,000.00
6.2.10 Two-story building, Dusit, Bangkok	1,000,000.00
6.2.11 Two-story building, Dusit, Bangkok	1,000,000.00
6.2.12 Two-story building, Dusit, Bangkok	1,000,000.00

6.2.13	Two-story building, Dusit, Bangkok	1,000,000.00
6.2.14	Two-story building, Dusit, Bangkok	1,000,000.00
6.2.15	Two-story building, Bangkok Noi, Bangkok	1,000,000.00
6.2.16	Two-story building, Dusit, Bangkok	1,000,000.00
6.2.17	Three-story building, Bangkok Noi, Bangkok	1,000,000.00
6.2.18	Three-story building, Bangkok Noi, Bangkok	1,000,000.00
6.2.19	Three-story building, Bangkok Noi, Bangkok	1,000,000.00
6.2.20	Three-story townhouse, Lat Phrao, Bangkok	1,000,000.00
6.2.21	Three-story townhouse, Lat Phrao, Bangkok	1,000,000.00
6.2.22	Three-story townhouse, Lat Phrao, Bangkok	1,000,000.00
6.2.23	Three-story townhouse, Lat Phrao, Bangkok	1,000,000.00
6.2.24	Three-story townhouse, Lat Phrao, Bangkok	1,000,000.00
6.2.25	One-story shophouse, Chanthaburi	1,000,000.00
6.2.26	Two-story townhouse, Nothaburi	1,000,000.00
6.2.27	Two-story house, Phasi Charoen, Bangkok	1,000,000.00
6.2.28	One-story house, Bang Lamung, Chonburi	1,000,000.00
6.2.29	Two-story house, Pathumthani	1,000,000.00
6.2.30	Royal Park unit, Bangkok	1,500,000.00
6.2.31	Sanchon Pattaya unit	5,564,152.00
6.2.32	Sanchon Pattaya unit	3,615,616.00
6.2.33	Sanchon Pattaya unit	9,000,000.00
6.2.34	Century Heights 1 unit, Bangkok	8,650,000.00
6.2.35	Sukumwit House unit, Bangkok	4,000,000.00
	Total	110,329,768.00

7	Vehicles, 10	
7.1	BMW	1,500,000.00
7.2	Toyota	30,000.00
7.3	Toyota	90,000.00
7.4	Toyota	1,700,000.00
7.5	Mitsubishi	700,000.00
7.6	Porsche	4,000,000.00
7.7	Ferrari	9,000,000.00
7.8	Benz	9,000,000.00
7.9	Benz	9,000,000.00
7.1	Benz	9,000,000.00
	Total	44,020,000.00

8	Rights and concessions	
8.1	Policy Thai Life Insurance	244,075.00

9	Other property	276,380,000.00

GRAND TOTAL	9,958,597,869.18

Debts
3	Debts covered by documents, 3 cases	
3.1	Deposit pledged, Siam Commercial Bank	100,000,000.00
3.2	Deposit pledged, Siam Commercial Bank	100,000.00
3.3	Deposit pledged with personal guarantee, Siam Commercial Bank	10,000,000.00
	Total	110,100,000.00

GRAND TOTAL LESS DEBTS	9,848,497,869.18

Children of Pol Lt Col Thaksin Shinawatra below age of legal status

2.2 Deposits at commercial banks, 5 cases

Siam Commercial Bank		7,669.76
Siam Commercial Bank		703,936.43
Siam Commercial Bank		550,000.00
Siam Commercial Bank		703,936.43
Siam Commercial Bank		550,000.00
Total		2,515,542.62

3.3 Other investments, 16 cases

OAI Property	98,939,999	989,399,990.00
OAI Leasing	5,498,699	44,996,990.00
OAI Asset	39,995,999	399,959,990.00
SCK Asset	12,999,999	128,999,990.00
SC Office Plaza	89,999,998	199,699,980.00
SC Office Park	49,999,999	809,999,980.00
BP Property	9,749,999	97,499,990.00
PT Corporation	59,999,999	599,999,990.00
Upcountry Land	25,995,999	299,959,990.00
Phramaisuri Property	3,389,999	323,999,900.00
World Supplies	28,199,999	281,999,990.00
V Land Property	9,399,900	9,399,900.00
OAI Education	67,499,998	227,774,980.00
Nawatakam Fund	5,625,000	16,875,000.00
Alpine Golf and Sports Club	59,799,973	333,333,153.00
Bangkok Telecom Engineering	1	10.00
Udomwan	2	2,000.00
Ek Realty	10,000	100,000.00
Total		4,764,001,823.00

8 Rights and concession

Insurance policy OAI		283,310.01
Insurance policy OAI		244,853.34
Total		528,163.35

GRAND TOTAL   4,767,045,528.97

GRAND GRAND TOTAL   15,124,368,677.56

Note: Information from the National Counter Corruption Commission

SPEECH OF PRIME MINISTER
THAKSIN SHINAWATRA
ON THE POLICY FOR PREVENTION AND
SUPPRESSION OF DRUGS, AT THE MEETING HALL,
SUAN DUSIT RATCHAPAT INSTITUTE, 3 P.M.,
TUESDAY 14 JANUARY 2003

Deputy prime ministers, ministers, senior officials, provincial governors, provincial police chiefs.

Today is an important day in solving the country's drug problem. I invited all of you to this meeting so you will properly understand our policy on this matter—how we view this problem, and how we would like to solve it—so you will have a clear idea of the direction. Today I'd like to talk very clearly and that may not be so elegant. If you are not happy with what you hear, tell me, so we can work together comfortably, as once we start the work and assign the responsibilities, it must be done to the full. Today I may have to speak in a very straightforward manner, as sometimes if we try to talk in a roundabout way and believe we understand one another well, in fact that is not the case.

The government and I believe that drugs are destroying the security of the country. When there is conflict in our neighbors, every group involved in the fighting has to use a lot of money. The various groups forced to fight one another need a lot of money. Those living in the forest, who need cash to buy weapons, must get it from drugs because that is the quickest and easiest way. Thus, if our neighbors are peaceful, there will be no fighting and the drug affair will become a lot less severe. If you look carefully, you will see that drugs come from countries where there is fighting. Policy towards our neighbors is thus crucial in solving the drug problem and the increase in drugs. So now that our policy is taking shape, we have to make things clear both with our neighbors and with those implementing the policy domestically.

I believe that drugs have damaged Thailand a great deal. Today it is time for us to unite our forces to solve this problem seriously. I can no longer tolerate people who view drugs as something ordinary. I will not tolerate policies that fail. I will not tolerate dishonest people involved directly or indirectly in the distribution of drugs, whoever they are, because I think we have tolerated too much already, and now the country's youth has been very badly damaged. We are entering the age of the knowledge society, but the brains of the nation's youth are being destroyed. Drugs may be a consequence of many other problems including the education system, dens of vice, and other causes, but we don't have time now to talk about such matters in detail.

Today we will focus on suppression, on solving the drug problem by using the area approach. I am not telling you to do things which are not backed up with good logic. Several provinces have already done these things and achieved good results—led by Kalasin, which has dared to declare itself a drug-free province, because it worked comprehensively and systematically. The governor and provincial police chief worked together very well. The governor had good relations with the communities, with local politics. After Kalasin declared itself a drug-free province, I checked up in several ways, and it's true. Chiang Rai is another example of a province which was serious about suppression and rehabilitation, including using some police stations for rehab, and seizing assets. Sometimes people were shot dead and had their assets seized as well. I think we have to be equally ruthless. The drug sellers have been ruthless with the Thai people, with our children, so if we are ruthless with them it is not a big deal. I believe we are forced to be so. It's not something we have to be cautious about. Nonthaburi is another province which has had good results through cooperation between communities and the police.

Using the area approach, the provincial governors and police chiefs have to cooperate closely, not prepare to stab one another in the back but work in unison. Both governors and police chiefs were invited today so a clear message can be sent that you have to work together. If you can't work together and go on fighting, then the work will not succeed. At the provincial level, the governor has to be the leader. He has to preside over the province's drug activity with the provincial police chief as his deputy. Then the work has to be subdivided by districts. At the district level the district officer is the head, and the district police chief is his assistant. I want to see every square inch x-rayed. In the next three months, it has to be done seriously. At the end of three months, there will be an evaluation. If today the governor, provincial police chief, district officer, district police chief do not themselves know who is selling drugs in their locality, it shows lack of efficiency, because if you are really working then you know everything. If you don't, it is because you are not committed, because you don't give importance to drugs.

Do you know that today almost three million Thai children take drugs, and around 700,000 are seriously addicted? Many are in jail. The jails we built to hold around 80,000 criminals now have over 300,000 inmates of which 80 percent are drug related. We have issued a new law that views drug users as patients who need rehabilitation. This principle will increase flexibility. Many offices have to give their support to the effort of solving drug addiction problems including the ministries of health, interior, education, culture, labor, justice, and tourism and sport. We have to work together. We have to understand that drugs is a vital issue, a threat to national security, something we must fight and defeat, something where people will get hurt but we must prevail. Using the area approach to solve the drug problem means the three methods already mentioned—suppression, rehabilitation, and prevention.

Suppression has to be serious. I think the police already know all the various dens of vice that distribute drugs. There is no police station chief that does not know such things, because even the taxi drivers do. Don't make the interior minister or his deputy have to do the duties of the police suppression unit. You all know everything; it's just a question whether you will do anything or not. Today if you do nothing, I will do you. We have allowed the society to suffer because of this matter for a long time. Why is it necessary to wait for a policy, for someone to give orders? The laws are already in our hands. Things that are wrong cannot be ignored. The dens of vice which distribute drugs have to be dealt with decisively. Today we are sending out a loud warning message that from now to the end of January all the service establishments that spread vice and tolerate drugs must stop doing so. The first of February is D-day. Three months ahead on 30 April there will be an evaluation. You must x-ray every square inch of your area. If drugs are still distributed in your area, it means you are not efficient. I don't believe there is any police station chief who doesn't know which of the officers in his stations is selling drugs. If you know and do nothing, then it shows you know what's going on. Don't be afraid. Nobody has more connections. Those with the biggest connections are the people. Officials who fear the influence of the mafia should not be officials. You have no reason to fear that you will be threatened or punished for doing your duty. Just come to see me. I will protect you all. Just eradicate what is destroying the nation. If you are good officials, you must not fear any influence.

Today we are giving everyone two weeks to get ready. If drug traders are listening they must make up their minds whether to stop selling or carry on. If they don't stop, there is a chance they will be dealt with in every way, both life and limb. Those who trade, those who have entertainment places and allow the "mad drug" sellers to operate inside them—these service establishments must be dealt with. If they want to remain open and do business in peace, they must not allow these things to happen, or else there will be proceedings. From 1 February 2003, everybody will be dealt with. I want you to x-ray every sort of place, as I've said.

Be very clear, you must x-ray every square inch in your area and show there is nothing left. From 1 February onwards, anyone who fails to stop selling drugs will be dealt with, whatever kind of seller they are. Assets will be seized too. On asset seizure, if today any citizen has a clue that their neighbors are unusually rich, without any obvious occupation, and without reason why they became rich, give the information, as it will give us a lead and we will make sure they do not escape. Take the example of one successful asset seizure in the central region. Fifty million baht of assets were seized. But the evidence was not enough to nail the leader who is a former national-level politician. We have been following his activities until today, but it is difficult to do anything. As we know but cannot do anything, we have to keep watch and keep the pressure on. Assets have to be seized in full, so when they are dead there is no inheritance left for their descendants, because these people are destroying the nation. The ONCB (Office of the Narcotics Control Board) has to study how officials should be rewarded for asset seizures. There must be a clear system of rewards and punishments. Those who do good will have good done to them, and those who do evil will be punished. So if you are successful at suppression, there must be rewards for asset seizure. You will have the honor and reward of money that is untainted, and you will be happy. But let me warn you. We must not arrest scapegoats, and we must not have mercy towards drug traders. Those who are sick or addicted, you must treat with mercy, consider them people that have made mistakes or been led astray, who need to be rescued and cured. With the traders, you must use hammer and fist, that is, act decisively and without mercy. Police General Phao Sriyanon once said "There is nothing under the sun that the Thai police cannot do." So I'm confident that drugs are something that the Thai police can deal with. Do it to the full. Provincial governors must give support and work too. If there is failure, both the provincial governor and provincial police chief will go together. So let the rewards and punishments be very clear. When there is any suspicion that someone is involved, bring it out in the open, and then don't let up. Investigate. Find the evidence for a court case. Punish. But quickly. If procedures impede or delay exposing a drug suspect, then the procedures have to be changed. Don't protect bad people. I think that involvement with drugs is so evil that we should give absolutely no pardon at all.

Let me repeat, all the dens of vice and distribution points for drugs, deal with them decisively. Don't be polite. Don't have even the slightest feeling for them. Don't care for little things. Do not allow the situation to arise where the senior-most police raid an area but it fails. Today, I consider whatever bad happened in the past is forgotten. But from 1 February we will begin a new life for our nation, for our youth, our children and children's children. If any officer can't work because there are people over him, maybe a favorite of a more senior officer, in whatever branch of officialdom, just send the details directly to me. I will give protection and fairness to every official of every unit who does his duty of suppressing drugs straightforwardly but is not treated fairly. So let both commanders and subordinates be properly looked after. If anyone has a problem, or cannot get things done on their own, send details to me, to the prime minister's secretary. We will keep it secret and look after you.

If there is any problem over budget in the next three months, let the officer in charge of the unit arrange support from their own budget first, and if it is not enough, ask for extra from the budget bureau. In three months' time, drugs must be dealt with in every square inch of Thailand because we have district offices and police stations overseeing every square inch. So we will x-ray every square inch, seize the assets of anyone suspected of being unusually rich without reason. In this work, separate the good officers from the bad, from the dregs of officialdom. It must be obvious who is efficient and who is not efficient. So you must all give your utmost efforts to this task. That means the next three months will be especially tough, and after that the system will come together of its own accord. And after that we can think of many other things. Those who don't care will not know, but if you really care, you will know, and once you know, you will come together. Governors, police chiefs, district officers, station heads will meet together to identify the methods for prevention, rehabilitation, and suppression. I guarantee that after these three months, you will have a completely different understanding about drugs compared to today. You'll come back talking in another language, a language that understands that things are like this because of that. And then we will be able to deal with this matter. Today let me call on you to give your utmost efforts to this serious task for the next three months. If some drug traders die, it will be a common thing. We have to send a message that they have to quit. Traders will get no return except risk to their own lives, risk of being arrested, and of being finished off because all their assets are seized. Whenever the chance of profiting from a crime is greater than the chance of punishment, or when the punishment is not severe enough, some people will choose to make a living by crime, without thinking about right or wrong.

So use these three months to the full. Give your utmost for the country, for your children, for the future of the nation. I believe we can deal with it. I'm not at all worried. If all you officials do your utmost, I don't think there is anything beyond our ability. I have confidence in your abilities. But you must give your utmost. Senior officers must specially look after the budget so that the work of these three months is successful. Today, go back and make preparations. From 9 a.m. on 1 February everything must be done down to the details and with sincere cooperation.

When we talk about the task, we must also talk clearly of the rewards. The Office of the Narcotics Control Board (ONCB) as the unit for policy, study, support, and coordination must quickly amend regulations by the end of January 2003, for instance, the reward money, bonuses for arrests, and other related matters. At 9 a.m. on 1 February 2003, rewards and punishments will come into operation immediately until 9 p.m. on 30 April 2003, when matters will be reviewed. Police commanders will report to the national police chief, the prime minister, and the deputy prime minister (General Chavalit Yongchaiyudh). Provincial governors will report to the under-secretary of the Ministry of Interior. Both achievements and obstacles must be reported so we can conclude how to solve the problems and proceed further. Don't make it like a shower of rain that soon evaporates away. When we have things clear, then we can proceed without any let-up. I will talk with neighboring countries so they give their full cooperation in every form and dimension. I think we have tolerated this matter for too long already. Today we should not tolerate it further. If we think about parents sending their children to school just for them to get drugs and AIDS, we have to feel their devastation. If we don't think anything, then we don't feel anything. But if we think properly, we'll see that all our Thai children, innocent kids, who don't know what they're doing, are sometimes tricked by the drug traders in some way or other. I don't think these are things the police don't know about, but it's a question only of commitment, because the police have many levels. The police on the ground know everything, but whether the commanders take an interest or not, nothing in this world is secret. Today buying drugs is as easy as buying chewing gum. It's harder to buy chewing gum in Singapore than drugs in Thailand. Sometimes you can order them, like pizza.

Officials who have been effective against drugs, let their seniors create channels for these people to rise in government service faster than usual, according to the principle of rewards and arrest bonuses. But be careful that the heroes and villains are not the same people. Don't let this happen. The investigation must be clear. Don't let the same person play the hero in the open, but the villain in the background. Don't let yourselves be fooled. All officers must be watchful and precise. Good people must be rewarded and bad people punished. Prevention is the duty of many ministries because it concerns education, sport, culture, and science, to encourage the youth who today are still innocent to quit the drugs circle. And we need cooperation from the temples, schools and parents.

At today's Cabinet meeting, I told the ministers that the sports facilities of the army, the Thai Sports Association, and the education ministry, should be used to the full. Let people come to take exercise and play sport. Organize lots of competitions. If a province wants a Premier's Cup, tell me and I'll give one. Same with prizes. If kids love sport, they will love health, and if they love health they won't get involved in vice. The government has passed laws to help parents. On such matters, don't wait for the policy. If there's a law, then it has to be enforced. If there is to be some relaxation, you will be told. If you are not told, it means there is no relaxation, you must apply all the laws that you have. Help the parents. Act as their eyes and ears. Do whatever is right so society is orderly and everyone falls back in line.

For prevention, apart from the importance of sport and other creative activities, provincial governors and heads of government offices must help think up other projects. Many different activities don't need much budget—less than what gets wasted on useless construction projects in which the prices are inflated by collusion. Now we have bidding by computer, which saves at least 20 percent of the budget. If we spend 50 billion baht in a year, the savings are 10 billion and they can be used for creative activities and still have a lot left over. Arranging creative activities so kids and youth have something creative to do is to get them out of the system. So I don't begrudge any budget spent on creative activities or rewards for good people.

Provincial governors, you must always think of yourselves as the big bosses. You have to give the orders, follow up, evaluate, advise, hold meetings, and fine-tune the strategy. Please don't have boundaries among yourselves, borders, walls dividing the government agencies in your province. The governor has the duty to break down the walls between government agencies, between all the representatives of government agencies in your province. Use your power as a leader. A leader must indicate clearly that he will deal severely with drugs. All those still involved will be done for. But if the leader is passive, doesn't talk about the drug issue, doesn't drive it, others will be passive too. So the leader has to determine the culture of the organizations in that place. The provincial governor and police chief must determine clearly that drugs are an evil matter, a matter that must be dealt with severely, something that is unacceptable, intolerable. But if the provincial governor and police chief are passive about this issue, then the whole province will be passive, and the province will be heaven for drug traders. I feel sorry for parents, especially the poor who find the money to send their kids to school only to discover they have sent them to be ruined. If they knew their kids would be ruined, they would choose to keep them in the paddy fields instead. So we have to help them, arrange all kinds of activities. The budget bureau will help find something to support them. I will use the country's budget economically, for the maximum benefit, especially for building human resources, building people, building human respect. This is very important because we must have 63 million Thai people of good quality, strong in body, mind, and intellect, not weaklings who act like semi-ghosts, semi-humans. One million people have been ruined by drugs. I can't accept this. You must be wholehearted about prevention.

There are many methods of rehabilitation we can use to help. We had a seminar on this, and assigned the justice minister, interior minister, and deputy prime minister (Chaturong Chaisaeng) to study the matter and decide on the direction and details to be proposed this March. But at the provincial level, the governor must call a meeting of all government agencies to make a plan for rehabilitation and prevention.

The idea of rehab communities is interesting. I'm no expert. The ONCB must prepare documents to disseminate information on this, especially about the successes in many places, and distribute them for all the governors to be informed. ONCB is the research agency which must communicate what has succeeded in one place to other places so they can be copied and known and applied. Things may not be 100 percent useable but must be adapted because culture varies from place to place. We must understand the word "adapt." The rehab communities have succeeded in several places, such as rehab at the police station, at the police kiosk. But some who pass through rehab today get hooked again and have to go to rehab again. If we have rehab every day for everyone, soon it will be over. Today over 300,000 people who are in jail for drugs cannot be brought out for rehab because there is nowhere to do it. So we must bring down the curtain on drugs; then, if they come out even without rehab it will still be like rehab because they won't know where to buy drugs. Importantly, now the health ministry has issued a ministerial regulation about codeine ingredients. We must follow this all the way through, because it is constantly changing. Sleeping pills and anaesthetics all get used. Pharmacies sell them without a doctor's prescription. These are businessmen without social responsibility and must be punished.

So if there is anything that needs to be controlled but there is no current law, study what law is needed, so that government officials and police can do their duty without being sued. For example, before there was no ministry regulation controlling the sale of caffeine. Now the government has made one. Codeine is an ingredient in cough medicine popular in the south. The government has acted on this today, because these things can be applied very quickly. I have seen the state of kids in various communities who are taking drugs and it's pitiful. There are many drug sellers in communities like Khlong Toei. They get rich and then move on, go out to Minburi or Nong Chok, and leave their sale network in Khlong Toei. It's like MLM (Multi Level Marketing), setting up lower levels. We must turn MLM back against them, turn their method back against themselves, that is, chase them from the police, from top to bottom, from the bottom to the community, create a suppression network to find the information to work back up the chain, and seize their assets. You need not be afraid of any influence, even if there are politicians or whoever behind them. You can meet me any time. If politicians are involved, arrest them, deal with them severely, whatever party, whatever name. Anyone who sells drugs is destroying the nation. Let me say this very clearly. However many times I say it, it will be the same. If you come across influence, if you are intimidated, come to see me. I'll stand by you and I'm ready to give you justice. Nobody has such influence or merit with me that I have to fear or defer to the extent that I will tolerate their involvement with drugs. You can all rest assured. Act decisively. If someone threatens to move you or punish you because of drug suppression work, come to see me any time.

On rehabilitation, let all agencies gather their thoughts on what else can be done. I don't have knowledge of everything but I appeal to all agencies to help. At present we have brought some drug convicts out to the Citizens' Development School, and detained some instead of imposing fines. The detention centers are now overflowing. At some places there is not enough water for bathing. Now we must bring drug users punished under the old law out for rehab and give them an opportunity to return to society. Most of the petty traders are housewives who, during the economic crisis when prices went up and there was no work, were invited to become sellers under the MLM system. Recently I went to see Kaset Yothin School in Chiang Mai. I found that 90 percent of the female convicts were small drug vendors who had been arrested. They sell petty amounts of drugs, because they think the police won't arrest women. So we need cooperation on the issue of rehab communities and forced rehab. Any government agency that is ready to help can go ahead, so we can complete rehab quickly, and bring down the curtain quickly.

Each of the six deputy prime ministers has a region of responsibility. You must follow up matters closely, give encouragement and support, and evaluate the progress in the provinces under your responsibility. Government inspectors (*phu truat ratchakan*), chairman of the advisors, please help oversee every area, go and check what is beyond the capacity of the province and has to be reassigned at the government level. Please take decisions on my behalf to ensure these three months are highly successful. Let every area have a boss, that is the provincial governor and the police chief, and below them the district officer and station heads, and the Bangkok Police Chief, and the station head in every locality, but it does not mean the police chief is free of responsibility, even though there is no province, the police chief must oversee all units under his command just as if he were a provincial police chief. The deputy prime ministers have to doublecheck matters for the prime minister, but not to the extent of doing the duty of a police officer. Just oversight is enough. Give encouragement to the implementers, coordinate, and solve immediate problems so the work can proceed smoothly. Anything that requires an emergency budget can be arranged. You can order it on the prime minister's behalf. In these three months, don't waste any time. There are no weekends. For these three months there are no holidays. You can take a rest, but you cannot take a rest from the responsibility. You can take a rest, but the responsibility will still be there. So for these three months, get in the frame of mind, make a plan, a strategy, work systematically and absolutely continuously.

In addition, about news. We must help one another. I believe all you deputy prime ministers will help solve your problems so you can work to your utmost. Know the government is beside you. Work to your utmost. We are beside you, ready to help you work to the best of the skills you have acquired, and with the ideal and commitment to work to preserve a peaceful population, overcome problems, and increase well-being.

When the US makes war against terrorism, they do it with full commitment, pour in all their resources, and use every kind of influence they have, use every level of politics to deal with this matter. I think that task is more difficult than a domestic drug problem because they have to work all over the world. So today we have to make war on drugs, have to attack, and that is not beyond our ability. I have confidence in you, especially as I was a military cadet. I know that if the police work seriously they can do anything, deal with anything. I am really confident. I'm confident that my friends and colleagues can do it. The provincial governors must give support. You must plan together, and think together. For sure, in any organization not all the people are good people, and not all are bad people either. The bad people are fewer than the good, or else Thai society could not survive. But we must unite to deal with the bad people. None of you must flinch.

I hope that in these three months, these ninety days, everyone should make preparations, have a meeting plan, and think together well. In these three months, work to the best of your ability, in every area, without diversion. Wherever they show their heads, arrest them all. And in the end we will have information that will enable the police, especially the officers at the center, to make out the "jigsaw" and be able to crush the whole system. I myself shall travel to neighboring countries in February to create the understanding to solve all the problems. I will do this in parallel. I am giving orders here because I will be working as well. We will be working in parallel. Not one thing will be overlooked. Government agencies must have no boundaries between them. Help one another to the full. Use the full power of the land. And for sure, three months will not be enough, for sure. There must be rehab and many other things following on. Let me just say one thing. One day I went to play golf and had a caddy around thirty years old who was quite good looking. I asked whether she was married. She replied no. I was surprised and asked why, with such an appearance, she was not married. She replied that around her home everyone was on drugs and she did not know why she should get married, just to get bashed about. Don't you see how sad this story is? She said around her home everyone was on drugs. This is an ordinary person speaking. Wherever I go I like to ask the villagers one or two questions, so I can think about them.

This shows how bad the situation is today, because the impact goes right down to the village, the countryside, and the poor. Before it was only the slums in Bangkok, but now it is in every school at every level. Almost every famous school has drugs. So-called "white" [i.e., drug-free] schools are white because of the smoke. This is the truth. And today the attitude of many teachers towards kids is different from teachers in the past. Then they felt that students were like their own children and treated them with compassion. Nowadays the behavior of some teachers towards kids is not good. The compassion and fairness towards kids has deteriorated. Teachers think their duty is to finish teaching in the evening and then go to give special classes. Kids lack warmth. Parents have no time because they have to work hard for a living. At the schools, the attitude of teachers is deteriorating. These things have changed a lot. So today we have to help one another in every form. We have to turn back to the good things in the past. Everyone should help one another.

Today we do not have much time to discuss together. The main purpose is to hear the policy. I apologize that this has been like one-way communication, but let us be of one mind in pooling our efforts. Whoever has the manpower and the facilities must help. If there is no budget, it doesn't matter. If you need a budget, use your own first and if there really is no budget, make a proposal. I'll arrange things; you need not worry. I will take full responsibility to ensure these three months have real value, that they make history in dealing with drugs in Thailand. I hope that in these three months, we will be of one mind for the future of our children, to eradicate drugs, and to give rise to common wisdom about solving the drug problem in the long term, through both rehabilitation and suppression. After the three months for which we are pooling our efforts, a new wisdom will emerge, a more systematic thinking. After that, in March, after the deputy prime minister (Chaturon Chaisaeng), the justice minister, and interior minister, carry out the three tasks already assigned to you, we will get a picture of the things you find during these three months of eradication, and will be able to solve things completely in the long term. But in these three months, I believe there will be a lot of arrests, especially of traders. As for the dens of vice, they will gradually be brought under regulation so they cannot distribute and sell drugs at all. RCA, where you can buy ecstasy like from a chewing gum vendor, will be totally stopped, and hopefully fully cleaned up. In these three months, the six deputy prime ministers should not go overseas. Go to the provinces instead. Go to provide support, go to solve the problems on the spot in every province you oversee.

Good luck and thank you again for all your efforts for our nation.

	17 February 2001	14 June 2001	9 October 2001	5 March 2002 (Chat Phatthana
Prime minister	Thaksin Shinawatra	Thaksin Shinawatra	Thaksin Shinawatra	Thaksin Shinawa
Deputy prime minister	Chavalit Yongchaiyudh	Chavalit Yongchaiyudh	Chavalit Yongchaiyudh	Chavalit Yongch:
	Suwit Khunkitti	Suwit Khunkitti	Somkid Jatusripitak	Somkid Jatusripi
	Pitak Intarawityanunt	Pitak Intarawityanunt	Pitak Intarawityanunt	Pitak Intarawitya
	Pongpol Adireksarn	Pongpol Adireksarn	Pongpol Adireksarn	Pongpol Adireks:
	Dej Boonlong			Korn Dabbaransi
PM's Office	Krasae Chanawong	Krasae Chanawong	Krasae Chanawong	Krasae Chanawo
	Thammarak Issarangkura	Thammarak Issarangkura	Thammarak Issarangkura	Thammarak Issa
	Chaturon Chaisaeng	Chaturon Chaisaeng	Chaturon Chaisaeng	Pongthep Thepk
	Somsak Thepsuthin	Somsak Thepsuthin	Somsak Thepsuthin	Somsak Thepsut
				Suwat Liptapanl
Interior	Purachai Piumsombun	Purachai Piumsombun	Purachai Piumsombun	Purachai Piumso
	Sombat Uthaisang	Sombat Uthaisang	Sombat Uthaisang	Sombat Uthaisan
	Sora-at Klinpratum	Sora-at Klinpratum	Sora-at Klinpratum	Sora-at Klinprat
Defence	Chavalit Yongchaiyudh	Chavalit Yongchaiyudh	Chavalit Yongchaiyudh	Chavalit Yongch:
	Yuthasak Sasiprapha	Yuthasak Sasiprapha	Yuthasak Sasiprapha	Yuthasak Sasipra
Finance	Somkid Jatusripitak	Somkid Jatusripitak	Somkid Jatusripitak	Somkid Jatusripi
	Suchart Jaovisidha	Suchart Jaovisidha	Suchart Jaovisidha	Suchart Jaovisidl
	Varathep Rattanakorn	Varathep Rattanakorn	Varathep Rattanakorn	Varathep Rattan:
Foreign	Surakiart Sathirathai	Surakiart Sathirathai	Surakiart Sathirathai	Surakiart Sathira
Industry	Suriya Jungrungruangkit	Suriya Jungrungruangkit	Suriya Jungrungruangkit	Suriya Jungrung
	Pichet Sathirachaval			
Agriculture	Chucheep Harnsawat	Chucheep Harnsawat	Chucheep Harnsawat	Chucheep Harns
	Prapat Panyachartrak	Prapat Panyachartrak	Prapat Panyachartrak	Prapat Panyacha
	Nathee Klibthong	Nathee Klibthong	Nathee Klibthong	Nathee Klibthon
Communications	Wan Muhamad Nor Matha	Wan Muhamad Nor Matha	Wan Muhamad Nor Matha	Suriya Jungrungr
	Pracha Maleenont	Pracha Maleenont	Pracha Maleenont	Pracha Maleenor
	Pongsakorn Laohavichian	Pongsakorn Laohavichian	Pongsakorn Laohavichian	Pongsakorn Laol
	Nikorn Chamnong			
Labour	Dej Boonlong	Dej Boonlong	Dej Boonlong	Dej Boonlong
	Laddawan Wongsriwong	Laddawan Wongsriwong	Laddawan Wongsriwong	Laddawan Wong
Science	Sonthaya Khunpleum	Sonthaya Khunpleum	Sonthaya Khunpleum	Sonthaya Khunp
Education	Kasem Wattanachai	Thaksin Shinawatra	Suwit Khunkitti	Suwit Khunkitti
	Chamlong Krutkhunthod	Chamlong Krutkhunthod	Chamlong Krutkhunthod	Sirikorn Maneeri
		Sirikorn Maneerin	Sirikorn Maneerin	
University	Sutham Saengprathum	Sutham Saengprathum	Sutham Saengprathum	Suwat Liptapanl
Health	Sudarat Keyaruphan	Sudarat Keyaruphan	Sudarat Keyaruphan	Sudarat Keyarup
	Surapong Seubwonglee	Surapong Seubwonglee	Surapong Seubwonglee	Surapong Seubw
Commerce	Adisai Bodharamik	Adisai Bodharamik	Adisai Bodharamik	Adisai Bodharam
	Suwan Valaisathian	Suwan Valaisathian	Suwan Valaisathian	Suwan Valaisathi
				Newin Chidchot
Justice	Pongthep Thepkanchana	Pongthep Thepkanchana	Pongthep Thepkanchana	Chaturon Chaisa
Environment				
Culture				
Tourism and Sport				
Social Developmenr				
ICT				
Energy				

LISTINGS

3 October 2002 (bureaucratic reform)	8 February 2003	8 November 2003 (Chat Phatthana out)	9 March 2004
Thaksin Shinawatra	Thaksin Shinawatra	Thaksin Shinawatra	Thaksin Shinawatra
Chavalit Yongchaiyudh	Chavalit Yongchaiyudh	Chavalit Yongchaiyudh	Chavalit Yongchaiyudh
Korn Dabbaransi	Korn Dabbaransi	Somkid Jatusripitak	Wan Muhamad Nor Matha
Vishnu Krua-ngam	Vishnu Krua-ngam	Suwit Khunkitti	Chaturon Chaisaeng
Phrommin Lertsuridej	Purachai Piumsombun	Chaturon Chaisaeng	Suchart Jaovisidha
Chaturon Chaisaeng	Somkid Jatusripitak	Purachai Piumsombun	Thammarak Issarangkura
Suwit Khunkitti	Chaturon Chaisaeng	Vishnu Krua-ngam	Purachai Piumsombun
	Suwit Khunkitti	Bokhin Polakun	Vishnu Krua-ngam
Wan Muhamad Nor Matha	Wan Muhamad Nor Matha	Wan Muhamad Nor Matha	Bokhin Polakul
Pracha Maleenont	Pracha Maleenont	Pracha Maleenont	Pracha Maleenont
Pramuan Ruchanaseri	Pramuan Ruchanaseri	Pramuan Ruchanaseri	Pramuan Ruchanaseri
Thammarak Issarangkura	Thammarak Issarangkura	Thammarak Issarangkura	Chettha Thanajaro
Somkid Jatusripitak	Suchart Jaovisidha	Suchart Jaovisidha	Somkid Jatusripitak
Suchart Jaovisidha	Varathep Rattanakorn	Varathep Rattanakorn	Varathep Rattanakorn
Varathep Rattanakorn			
Surakiart Sathirathai	Surakiart Sathirathai	Surakiart Sathirathai	Surakiart Sathirathai
Somsak Thepsuthin	Somsak Thepsuthin	Phinit Jarusombat	Phinit Jarusombat
Sora-at Klinpratum	Sora-at Klinpratum	Somsak Thepsuthin	Somsak Thepsuthin
Newin Chidchob	Newin Chidchob	Newin Chidchob	Newin Chidchob
Wan Muhamad Nor Matha	Suriya Jungrungruangkit	Suriya Jungrungruangkit	Suriya Jungrungruangkit
Pichet Sathirachaval	Pichet Sathirachaval	Nikorn Chamnong	Nikorn Chamnong
Nikorn Chamnong	Nikorn Chamnong	Wiset Kasemthongsi	Wiset Kasemthongsi
Suwat Liptapanlop	Suwat Liptapanlop	Uraiwan Thienthong	Uraiwan Thienthong
Phinit Jarusombat	Phinit Jarusombat	Chettha Thanajaro	Korn Dabbaransi
Pongpol Adireksarn	Pongpol Adireksarn	Adisai Bodharamik	Adisai Bodharamik
Sirikorn Maneerin	Sirikorn Maneerin	Sirikorn Maneerin	Sutham Saengprathum
Sudarat Keyaruphan	Sudarat Keyaruphan	Sudarat Keyaruphan	Sudarat Keyaruphan
Pracha Promnok	Pracha Promnok	Chamlong Iamchaengphan	Sirikorn Maneerin
Adisai Bodharamik	Adisai Bodharamik	Wattana Muangsuk	Wattana Muangsuk
Wattana Muangsuk	Wattana Muangsuk	Pongsak Raktaphongpaisan	Pongsak Raktaphongpaisan
Purachai Piumsombun	Pongthep Thepkanchana	Pongthep Thepkanchana	Pongthep Thepkanchana
Prapat Panyachartrak	Prapat Panyachartrak	Prapat Panyachartrak	Suwit Khunkitti
Uraiwan Thienthong	Uraiwan Thienthong	Anurak Jureemas	Anurak Jureemas
Sonthaya Khunpleum	Sonthaya Khunpleum	Sonthaya Khunpleum	Sonthaya Khunpleum
Anurak Jureemas	Anurak Jureemas	Sora-at Klinprathum	Sora-at Klinprathum
Surapong Seubwonglee	Surapong Seubwonglee	Surapong Seubwonglee	Surapong Seubwonglee
Pongthep Thepkanchana	Phrommin Lertsuridej	Phrommin Lertsuridej	Phrommin Lertsuridej

ABBREVIATIONS

ABAC	Assumption Business Administration College
ASEAN	Association of Southeast Asian Nations
AIS	Advance Info Services
AMLO	Anti Money Laundering Office
BAAC	Bank of Agriculture and Agricultural Cooperatives
BOT	Bank of Thailand
CAT	Communications Authority of Thailand
CDMA	code division multiple access
CEO	chief executive officer
CP	Charoen Pokphand
DBS	Development Bank of Singapore
ECT	Election Commission of Thailand
EGAT	Electricity Generating Authority of Thailand
EXIM	Export-Import Bank of Thailand
FCCT	Foreign Correspondents Club of Thailand
FTA	free trade agreement
GDP	Gross Domestic Product
GHB	Government Housing Bank
GSB	Government Savings Bank
IFCT	Industrial Finance Corporation of Thailand
IMF	International Monetary Fund
IPRI	Intellectual Property Institute
ISOC	Internal Security Operations Command
KTB	Krung Thai Bank

MCOT	Mass Communications Organization of Thailand
MOTC	Ministry of Transport and Communications
MP	member of parliament
NAP	New Aspiration Party
NCCC	National Counter Corruption Commission
NGO	nongovernment organization
NHRC	National Human Rights Commission
NIDA	National Institute of Development Administration
NPKC	National Peacekeeping Council
NPL	nonperforming loan
OECD	Organization of Economic Cooperation and Development
ONCB	Office of the Narcotics Control Board
OTOP	"One Tambon, One Product"
PAO	Provincial Administrative Organization
PTT	Petroleum Authority of Thailand
SET	Stock Exchange of Thailand
SICGC	Small Industry Credit Guarantee Corporation
SIFC	Small Industries Finance Corporation
SIM	subscriber identity module
SME	small and medium enterprises
SMED	Small and Medium Enterprise Development Bank
TAA	Thailand AirAsia
TAMC	Thailand Asset Management Corporation
TDRI	Thailand Development Research Institute
TMB	Thai Military Bank
TOT	Telephone Organization of Thailand
TPI	Thai Petrochemical Industry
TRT	Thai Rak Thai Party
UN	United Nations
UNHCR	United Nations High Commission for Refugees
WTO	World Trade Organization

Note: Abbreviations of sources appear on page 285.

SOURCES OF THAKSIN QUOTATIONS
INTRODUCING EACH SECTION

2: Family and Business. Tax farms and caravans (Thaksin 1999, 29); Silk (Thaksin 1999, 31); Education (Pran 2004a, 53–4); The concessions (Sorakon 1993, 93); Business and political competition (Pran 2004a, 101); Crisis (Thaksin 1999, 149); Conclusion (Thaksin 1999, 157).

3: Political rise. From moral force to loving Thais (Thaksin 1999, 232); Thaksin and big business (Pran 2004, 401–2); Thaksin and small businessmen (*BP*, 27 December 2000); Thaksin and rural discontents (*TN*, 23 December 2000); The 2001 elections: Campaign and result (Thaksin 1999, 97); Thaksin in power (*BP*, 18 February 2001); Parliamentary power (*BP*, 28 January 2002); Conclusion (*DN*, 11 September 2003).

4: Thaksinomics. Growing to the first world (*BP*, 30 September 2003); Country=company (*BP*, 28 April 2001); Stimulating demand (Thaksin 2001d); Directing credit (*BP*, 26 July 2001); Nurturing competitiveness (*BP*, 2 October 2003); Deepening capitalism (Thaksin 2003d); Financing Thaksinomics (Pran 2004, 121); Going dual track (Thaksin 2001e); Promoting regionalism (Thaksin 2001b); Facing realities (Thaksin 2001a); Conclusion: Reward and risk (Thaksin 2001c).

5: **Managing society.** Social contract and moral leadership (Thaksin 2002); Nationalism and capitalism (*Nayok Thaksin lem 2*, 96); Controlling protest and NGOs (*TN*, 23 June 2003); Managing media (*Nayok Thaksin lem 1*, 176–7); Silencing public intellectuals (*TN*, 29 November 2002); Waging war on drugs (Thaksin 2003a); Social order and Thai culture (Phijitra 2003, 233); Conclusion (Thaksin 2003g).

6: **Remaking politics.** Managing the constitution (*Nayok Thaksin lem 3*, 145–6); Bringing back the military (Thaksin 1999, 56); Overthrowing the bureaucratic polity (*Nayok Thaksin lem 3*, 122); Crushing influence (*BP*, 20 July 2003); Promoting party dominance (*BP*, 1 September 2001); Conclusion: Big money politics (Thaksin 2003g).

7: **Power and profit.** Mobile profits (*TN*, 19 April 2001); Managing competition (Thaksin 2003d); Managing regulation (Thaksin 2003d); Satellites without boundaries (Thaksin 1999, 143); Property (Pran 2004, 399); Diversification (*TN*, 4 February 2004); Conclusion: The family business (Thaksin 2003d).

8 **Conclusion.** Interpreting Thaksin (Thaksin 2003f); Downslope? (*TN*, 29 October 2001); The south (*Nayok Thaksin lem 3*, 120); Looking ahead (Thaksin 2003d).

NOTES

PROLOGUE: 4:30 P.M., 3 AUGUST 2001

1. Before the 1997 crisis, the Thai baht exchanged at roughly 25 to the US dollar. When Thaksin came to power in early 2001, the rate was around 43, rising to 39 in mid 2004.

2. Pojaman Shinawatra was fined 6.3 million baht by the Securities Exchange Commission for failing to report transactions involving the nominees. Thaksin commented: "It is not an immoral wrongdoing." (*TN*, 20 and 21 October 2001).

3. Issara Nithithanprapas was the judge who publicly claimed he had been "unsuccessfully lobbied." He subsequently became the court's president. His wife was demoted from her job as permanent secretary of the Prime Minister's Office.

2: FAMILY AND BUSINESS

1. Thaksin's autobiography, edited by Walaya, is mostly narrated in the first person, presumably from edited interviews.

2. Thaksin, however, relates that Thongdi was "shot" (Thaksin 1999, 30). So does Plai-or (1987, 53).

3. One rai is equivalent to 0.16 hectares or 0.4 acres.

4. *Lukchin* literally means "child of Chinese." It was first used to distinguish those born in Thailand of Chinese parentage from first-generation immigrants, and later became a more general term for Thai nationals of Chinese descent.

5. The four were: Sujin Jaovisidha, Bangkok municipal councilor and MP, elder brother of Suchart, TRT minister; Somphon Keyuraphan, Khorat MP, father of Sudarat, TRT minister; Anan Chaisaeng, Chachoengsao MP, father of Chaturon, TRT minister; and Chai Chidchob, Buriram *kamnan* and MP, father of Newin, Chat Thai minister. See *"Yon roi 'phak phi' ngao adit 'Thai Rak Thai' 2512"* [Looking back

to the "ghost party", past shadow of Thai Rak Thai in 1969], *Nation Sutsapda*, 604, 29 December 2003.

6. The college was part of the Assumption group. Earlier it had offered free schooling, but later became so popular that parents had to pay a large *betchia* (tea money, bribe) to get children admitted.

7. Thanom Kittikhachon and Praphat Charusathian were right-hand men of Sarit Thanarat, the military strongman who took power by coup in 1957–8. After Sarit's death, they became prime minister and interior minister respectively, until they were felled by the student uprising of 14 October 1973.

8. This passage was part of the original magazine version of Thaksin's autobiography, but was cut out of the book version (see Thaksin 1999, 87).

9. Perhaps the most intriguing finding of the research is that among students enrolling at Sam Houston State, those electing to study criminal justice have the least respect for the rule of law when they arrive. Most of the thesis consists of tables generated by SPSS. The text (excluding appendices) is fifteen thousand words. There is no reference to Thailand and the text talks of "our legal system," meaning the US.

10. For example, in General Prem's first Cabinet in 1980, the ministry had one full and three deputy ministers. Of these four, one was a civilian and the others represented each of the three branches of the armed services.

11. The Chatichai Cabinet resigned and was reconstituted on 8 December 1990. Montri signed the IBC contract on 7 December (Sorakon 1993, 76).

12. When Sunthon died in 2001, his wife and minor wife contested the estate. Writs filed in the court estimated the estate's total value at 4 billion baht, and some relatives and associates pitched it at 6 billion. As the press began to speculate that some of this magnificent amount may have come through his role in Shinawatra's satellite, the government moved to control the story by appointing an investigative committee. The case between the wives was quietly settled out-of-court. The investigative committee suppressed all information. Purachai Piumsombun only said vaguely that Sunthon "did not have even 1 billion" and claimed it would be "against Thai tradition" to investigate further (TN, 24 March 2001, 1 and 5 January 2002).

13. The issue went to constitutional arbitration, which was not finalized before the government fell. Thaksin argued that his family interests were only 48.7 percent and thus he "was not the major vote, the definite owner" (Thaksin 1999, 167).

14. The PCT service amounted to a mobile phone linked to a landline service. On these grounds, TOT allowed the concession as an extension of TelecomAsia's landline business. For technical reasons (some hardware was unreliable in tropical conditions), the project was long delayed and then unsuccessful.

15. The Veterans Organization was probably fronting for a big business group. Neither the satellite nor mobile project had materialized when Chavalit's government was felled by the economic crisis in November 1997.

16. Poosana Premanoch and Somchai Benjarongkun became minister of the Prime Minister's Office and deputy health minister, respectively, only twelve days before the Chavalit Cabinet fell in November 1997.

17. Thanong became finance minister on 25 November 1996, and resigned on 24 October 1997, just twelve days before the Chavalit government fell on 6 November.

18. With thanks to Thanong Khanthong of the *Nation* for letting us see his fuller account of these events.

19. Singapore Telecom had been a minority stakeholder in the Shinawatra paging business since the beginning.

3: POLITICAL RISE

1. Introducing Kotler at a Bangkok seminar, Somkid said that Kotler's article on "Political marketing" had "introduced me to the application of marketing in the political arena. As you may surmise, this paper has had real impact on my political career as I was able to apply many concepts to the election campaign that brought the Thai Rak Thai Party a landslide victory" (*TN*, 10 October 2001). See also Nelson 2001, 409–10.

2. It was followed by *Rak nagara* [Roots of the city], which was based loosely on the British colonial takeover of the Shan states a century ago. Curiously, Siam figured in the plot as a colonially minded oppressor.

3. Chuan was a lawyer by training, but his public demeanor recalled traditional bureaucrats, and his strategy as premier was to refer everything to the bureaucracy.

4. As the Thai language has several consonants representing the same sound, each is distinguished by a common word that it initializes. This letter is known as ท, *tho thahan* or "T army."

5. Provinces served as multi-member constituencies, with up to eight seats (eighteen in Bangkok); candidates were not allowed to be members of political parties and were not allowed to campaign, only to announce their candidature.

6. The quality of the TRT campaign gave rise to speculation (e.g. Nelson 2001, 286–7) that the party had hired foreign consultants in political marketing who had been kept concealed so as not to conflict with Thaksin's nationalist aura. This may be true, but is not necessary. There was little that was expertly "political" about the marketing of Thaksin and TRT. They were sold much like any other product. Thaksin had been an aggressive user of marketing methods and especially brand advertising since the pager wars in the early 1990s (one of the authors of this book worked in an advertising company servicing Thaksin at that time). He set up his own advertising agency, SC Matchbox, in 1991 to serve the group, and the resources of this agency were mobilized for the TRT campaign. As the entertaining book *Branding thairakthai* shows, the party and its leader were sold from the start by strong branding, a distinctive image, simple and single-minded messages, an integrated approach to communication, and constant repetition. The head of the Shinawatra agency argues that TRT did not use more money than its rivals, but maximized its value through standard marketing principles (Nichapha 2003, 128–9).

7. The NAP campaigned under the slogan: "To help a tree grow we have to water

its roots. To revive the country we must help the poor" (*BP*, 23 November 2000). Chat Thai chose "Reform agriculture thoroughly to solve the country's problems." The Democrats held a conference to protest that they were misunderstood and really had a rural program (*BP*, 24 April 2000).

8. This ad appeared in Thai in most newspapers in the first week of December 2000.

9. The old political families that lost included: Asavahame in Samut Prakan, Angkinan in Phetchaburi, Moolasartsathorn in Surin, Manasikarn in Phitsanulok, Iasakul in Nong Khai, Harnsawat in Pathumthani, Lik in Kamphaeng Phet, Yubamrung in Thonburi, Lertnuwat in Chiang Rai, Khamprakob in Nakhon Sawan, Wongwan in Lamphun.

10. The most glaring loss by an old politico who had joined TRT was Yingphan Manasikarn in Phitsanulok. His wife won the neighboring seat as a TRT candidate by a large majority.

11. Previously, most constituencies returned two or three MPs, and each voter had as many votes as seats. In the new system, the country was divided into four hundred single-member constituencies. Under the so-called M+1 rule, the number of "effective" (i.e., sizeable) parties tends to be one more than the number of seats per constituency. So the previous multi-member system fostered many parties. In addition, Hicken (2001) argues that the somewhat unpredictable process for selecting a prime minister, and weaknesses in the prime minister's powers, multiplied the fragmentation in Thailand. The single-member system tends (by M+1) towards a two-party system.

12. Sombat was elected under the Seritham Party, which was absorbed into TRT a month after the election.

13. NAP made a pact with TRT just before the polls in January 2001 (*TN*, 25 January 2001); voted for a merger a year later (*BP*, 28 January 2002); and formally merged in April 2002 (*BP*, 24 April 2002).

4: THAKSINOMICS

1. The most controversial among these bills established a bankruptcy court and allowed limited foreign ownership of property.

2. The NESDB claimed most of the funds were used for agriculture or business, only 2 percent for repaying old debt, and 0.1 percent for household expenses. The Chamber of Commerce estimated 40 percent was used to repay existing debt, 20 percent for luxuries, 5 percent for productive investment, and the remainder in various ways. The Northern Farmers' Alliance survey of 1,336 villages found more than 70 percent of funds being used either to pay old debts or for purchase of items like mobile phones and motorcycles (*BP*, 5 July 2003). These items could of course be productive investments.

3. A TRT source explained the stand-off between the government and bankers in this way: "For example, they [bankers] ignored government requests for them to approve more loans. At the same time, they demanded so much from the government, such as their request for the government to amend the TAMC Act to enable them to mark their collateral value to market prices, and not to evaluations by the Land Department." (*BP*, 11 September 2001).

4. A word of Chinese origin meaning an owner or boss, used especially for shopkeepers and small businessmen.

5. Speech to police officers in Phuket, televised on Channel 11 on 3 September 2003 (see also *TN*, 2 October 2003).

6. A cousin of Suriya, the industry minister, secured 2.2 million shares, the single highest holding; Prayuth Mahakitsiri and his wife came second and third with 3.6 million between them; a relative of a Pruetthichai Damrongrat, TRT MP from Bangkok, got 1.7 million; and a relative of another TRT Bangkok MP, Wichan Minchainan, got 0.3 million (*TR*, 28 February 2004). The Securities Exchange Commission found no wrongdoing. Thaksin said: "Don't think they are devils. Please give them a chance" (*TN*, 7 February 2002). In six stock offerings in state enterprises in 2003–4, the Mahakitsiri was the top buyer overall, spending almost 500 million baht. Next came the Chalangkul family (related to Suriya), Charoen Siriwattanapakdi, and the Maleenont family (*TN*, 20 April 2004).

7.The term appeared in July 2001. Sometimes it was "dual track" and sometimes "dual track plus" with the "plus" supposed to signify the special emphasis on poverty.

8. The foreign chains had grabbed 45 percent of retail business (*BP*, 26 September 2003). Some 89 percent of traditional retailers claimed to have been affected (*TN*, 3 August 2002). However, consumers showed by their behavior that they liked the big new stores.

9. This was controversial. As the economy picked up, the baht tended to rise from the rate of around 43/US$ when TRT came to power. The Bank of Thailand bought US dollars, partly to stabilize short-term fluctuation in the exchange rate, but also to depress the upward movement to assist exports. Thaksin publicly advocated a higher baht. The Shinawatra businesses have a high degree of imports and little exports.

10. For example, the excise tax rate on the liquor produced by Charoen Siriwattanapakdi's group was reduced, while those on imported liquor were increased (*BP*, 23 January 2003). When Boonrawd launched a new beer against Charoen's Beer Chang, within days the Excise Department revised upwards the tax assessed on the Boonrawd product (*BP*, 20 November 2003).

5: MANAGING SOCIETY

1. Thaksin's weekly radio broadcast, 17 April 2004.

2. *Thamma* (dharma) means Buddhist teachings, or the right action from following them.

3. Addressing the National Institute for the Development of Knowledge on 19 March 2003, Thaksin said, "I'm someone who doesn't enjoy reading novels. I can sit and watch a [TV] drama with my children, but I have never read novels. I read a few stories about science, but not much. Yet I like reading textbooks or that sort of thing, research findings of various kinds. I enjoy that" (Pran 2004a, 72).

4. While speaking in Thai, Thaksin often used the English word "nationalism," rather than the Thai *chatniyom*. Probably he instinctively wanted to differentiate his externally focused, economic nationalism from the earlier internally focused, political nationalism of King Rama VI and Phibun Songkhram.

5. Thaksin replied that the decree route had been used because, "Of course we have more MPs, but they [the opposition] can outclass us because they are very good at playing games" (*TN*, 14 August 2003). The TRT government had never come close to losing a parliamentary vote.

6. In both these cases, pressure was exerted through management. *Siam Rath* was owned by Chatchawan Kong-udom, better known as Chat Taopoon, who claimed that he no longer owned Bangkok's most famous illegal casino. Government had plans to suppress such casinos. Chairman of the *Bangkok Post* was Suthikiati Chirathiwat of the Central Group, which, early in the Thaksin government, had been accused of irregularities in its lease of state land, and been obliged to negotiate a settlement for an unknown sum.

7. Based on an English-language daily, *The Nation*, the group also has a Thai business daily, Thai weekly newsmagazine, several magazines, book publishing, and broadcasting ventures.

8. This exchange with Prawase was especially resonant. Prawase had been prominent in the reform agenda of the 1990s, including the 1997 constitution and many projects to increase participation in policy making. He had swung his considerable popularity and moral presence in support of Thaksin in 2001 in expectation that Thaksin would be more visionary and reformist than the Democrats. Prawase is also a prominent lay Buddhist and follower of Buddhadasa. Thaksin's abuse of Prawase came after Prawase had advised, "Mr. Thaksin is a very able person but people still doubt whether he is a statesman or a business politician. A complete withdrawal from family businesses will give the prime minister more ethical power" (*TN*, 21 May 2003).

9. There were several different versions of this final figure, most in the range of 2,500 to 2,700. This figure came from the National Human Rights Commission (*BP*, 11 December 2003).

10. See the investigative articles by Surath Jinakul and Orasong Charasdamrong in *BP*, 2 and 23 July 2000.

11. In his birthday speech on 4 December 2003, the king talked about deaths in the drug campaign and responsibility for them: "It has been announced to foreigners as twenty-five hundred people. The police and military take responsibility for shooting or killing only a few, less than a hundred. I'm giving a warning in order to reduce tensions. The person who is feeling most stressed here is the deputy prime

minister. We don't say which deputy prime minister. Like on the news, they say the deputy prime minister said this or said that. We don't know which deputy prime minister. But in the end, that's it. Deputy Prime Minister Chavalit." Our translation from unofficial transcript at http://kanchanapisek.or.th/speeches/index.th.html.

12. Draft plan at www.culture.go.th/ops/panda/DraftMasterPlan.doc.

6: REMAKING POLITICS

1. During the no-confidence debate in May 2002, Democrat MP Sirichoke Sopha alleged that Shin Satellite had evaded 26 million baht of customs duty on shipments of equipment through misclassification. He played a videotape of a former Shin employee, Kornthep Viriya, known as Shipping Mu, who described how he handled the bribes. Kornthep was now on the run (*BP*, 26 May 2002). Kornthep's wife claimed he had been offered bribes and threatened. Shin Satellite sued Sirichoke for damages. In November he claimed to receive a letter from Kornthep saying: "They know where I am. I can't fight any longer. I have lost everything and have to beg for food now" (*TN*, 28 March 2003). Kornthep had fled to the hills in Chiang Rai and married a hilltribe woman. On 26 March 2003 he was shot dead. Thaksin denied any involvement. Police offered six alternative reasons why he might have been killed (*BP*, 28 March 2003). No arrests were reported.

2. Chatichai in 1988 also kept the defense portfolio but in practice left everything to the service heads (Ockey 2001, 198).

3. The wage bill consumed over 60 percent of the military budget. Plans were laid to reduce total numbers from 236,000 to 190,000 by 2007 (Ockey 2001, 202).

4. Chaisit justified the choice on grounds of his relative's role in military intelligence in the south, which was becoming more violent and more difficult to understand by the day.

5. Ahead of him in seniority are Pol Gen Kowit Watana, Pol Gen Amnuay Petchsiri, and Pol Gen Piya Jiamchaisri (*BP*, 3 February 2004).

6. The new ministries were: tourism and sports; culture; social development and human security; energy; natural resources and environment; information and communications technology. See appendix 3.

7. Overall, the frequency of corruption scandals under the Thaksin government was no less than under previous governments, but tended to be concentrated in certain ministries. The agriculture ministry, which initially had been entrusted to Chucheep Hansawat, produced a string of spectacular scandals. The education, labor, and health ministries were next in rank.

8. Surakiat Sathirathai became foreign minister, Narongchai Akraseranee became an economic advisor, and Bowornsak Uwanno became cabinet secretary. The others were Chatichai's son Kraisak (senator), Sukhumbhand Paribatra (Democrat, deputy foreign minister in the Chuan II government), and Chuanchai Atchanan (academic).

9. On taking office, Thaksin set up two overall policy-planning teams (Ban Phitsanulok and Ban Manangkhasila), a legal reform committee, economic team, personal advisory team, and political advisory team (*BP*, February 20, 2001).

10. Suchat Tancharoen had been involved in the loan scandals that led to the collapse of the Bangkok Bank of Commerce in 1995. He had also been accused of using influence to acquire large tracts of land in two provinces by manipulating land documentation. He became a deputy speaker of the house during the Thaksin government.

11. The campaign identified fifteen "influential targets": drug trade; manipulation of bidding contests; extortion at factories and service venues; illegal control of motorcycle taxis and other vehicles for hire; oil and goods smuggling; gambling dens and underground lottery rackets; trafficking in women and children; job scams; smuggling of laborers; tourism scams; hired gunmen; debt collection using force or intimidation; illegal arms trade; encroachment on public land; and extortion on public land and highways (*TN*, May 17, 2003; *BP*, May 22, 2003).

12. Speech to police officers in Phuket, televised on Channel 11 on 3 September 2003.

13. The plant, in Samut Prakan on the outskirts of Bangkok, had long been a focus of scandal. Allegedly, Wattana Asawaheme, the province's most prominent godfather, had made a billion baht from selling the land for the plant, while Banharn Silpa-archa and Suwat Liptapanlop had interests in the company contracted for the construction.

14. TRT branches at www.thairakthai.or.th/contact.asp, as of 29 April 2004; Democrats at www.democrat.or.th.

15. The new monthly allowance was variously reported as 200,000 or 250,000 baht, and due only to constituency MPs, though party-list MPs were protesting the discrimination.

16. Thaksin weekly radio broadcast, 31 January 2004.

7: POWER AND PROFIT

1. Under the original concession contracts, TOT levied this charge from concessions under CAT, but not from Shin. See chapter 2.

2. French COFACE also provided a guarantee for the remainder of the US$390 million loan that IPStar raised from a consortium headed by Citibank and BNP Paribas (Shin Satellite 2003, 7).

3. In 2003, IPStar signed agreements with Reach Global Services to distribute its services in Australia and New Zealand, and with Time Dotcom in Malaysia (Shin Satellite 2003, 7).

4. China Railway's interest in the project was curious. The organization had got into the telephone business in an attempt to make extra income from the cabling laid

for its internal communications system. But it was a minor player in China's highly competitive telecom market, and not obviously in a position to compete with the heavyweights.

5. See asset declaration in appendix 1. The following companies all owned property leased to Shin companies: OAI Asset (offices in Phahonyothin), OAI Property (Shin Tower 3), SC Office Park (Shin Tower 1), Upcountry Land (offices in south and northeast), World Supplies (office in Chiang Mai), PT Corporation (small offices in Bangkok and provinces), Phramaisuri Property (Shin Satellite's office), and Adrinarin (ITV) (*KT*, 5 January 2004).

6. The properties sold included those under OAI Asset, Upcountry Land, and V Land Property, and 30 percent of Shin Towers 1 and 2. The family kept direct control of PT Corporation, OAI Leasing, Phramaisuri, World Supplies, and a 70-percent share in the two office towers (*KT*, 5 January 2004).

7. Tony Fernandes, the Malaysian partner, talking to AFP on 16 February 2004.

8. One-Two-Go was launched in December 2003 by Orient Airlines, a small private carrier. Thai Airways began preparing to launch a low-cost subsidiary, Nok Air.

9. The press ad soliciting investors for this offering was headlined "Thailand's TV station needs the support of Thais," and claimed ITV had a "mission . . . to uncover the truth and expose wrongdoings for the better good of society."

10. www.forbes.com/maserati/billionaries2004/bill04land.html. Forbes evaluates the wealth of the individual, but includes the family when ownership is complex. Curiously, Forbes did not include Thaksin on their global billionaires list, where the estimated wealth of US$1.4 billion would have ranked him in the low 400s. Possibly this was because of uncertainty over the family holdings.

11. The major shareholders in Shin Corporation were Thaksin's daughter Pinthongtha (14.98 percent), brother-in-law Bannaphot Damaphong (13.77 percent), son Panthongthae (10.01 percent), and Ample Rich Investment (7.8 percent), a family holding company. The family had no direct holdings in the other companies (AIS, ITV, Satellite) but held 61 percent of SC Asset.

12. The dividend was estimated from the previous end-year and mid-year; the rentals and other purchases were estimated from the 2002 figures (declared in the Shin annual report available through www.set.or.th).

13. The two larger were PTT and Siam Cement.

14. If the return on a share over one year is calculated as (dividend + capital gain)/ (original price), then the average for the Thai stock market in 2003 was 58 percent, while ITV was 592 percent, Shin Corp 284 percent, AIS 139 percent, and Shin Satellite 101 percent. Somkiat (2004) shows that the Shin companies' outperformance of the market cannot be explained by other factors such as the companies' sector, scale, or financial gearing.

8: CONCLUSION

1. Weekly radio broadcast, 17 April 2004.

2. Two years earlier on the same occasion, the king had said: "I intend to talk about disaster. At present everyone knows that the country seems to face disaster, not development . . . because nowadays things seem in decline. As for the prime minister, he is sitting making a face. He is not feeling good when I say the country is facing disaster. But it is true, because whatever is done seems to have problems all the time. But the prime minister . . . he is *happy* but *happy* on the outside . . . inside, he is not feeling good. . . . There is this matter of conflict in thinking. . . . In English it is *double standard*. . . . This means we think what is good for ourselves . . . but when we talk to someone else, we say something else is good for them. This is *double standard* . . . it prevents progress. . . . In Thailand, there used to be little of it. Foreign countries had more. But now . . . we have some. So to solve the problems of hardship and disaster, we have to find out how to overcome this *double standard*. . . . Someone who has *double standard* may do well himself. . . . but having *double standard* within oneself is the most dangerous." Italicized words were spoken in English. These are our translations from the unofficial transcripts of the speeches at http://kanchanapisek.or.th/speeches/index.th.html. In November 2003, the king refused to sign an education bill. The government admitted there were technical inconsistencies due to careless drafting (*TN*, 26 November 2003).

3. This figure includes EGAT along with MCOT, TOT, CAT, electricity distribution agencies, and the Bangkok water supply (*TN*, 10 April 2004).

4. Weekly radio broadcasts, 17 and 24 April 2004.

5. *Mueang thai raiwan*, TV Channel 9, 9 April 2004.

6. Weekly radio broadcast, 10 April 2004.

BIBLIOGRAPHY

BP   *Bangkok Post*
DN   *Daily News* (Thai)
FEER   *Far Eastern Economic Review*
FT   *Financial Times*
KT   *Krungthep Thurakit*
MR   *Matichon Raiwan*
MS   *Matichon Sutsabda*
TN   *The Nation*
TR   *Thai Rath*

NB: The organization of the government website containing Thaksin's speeches keeps changing. Some of the references below may no longer work. At present, all can be found through www.thaigov.go.th/index-eng.htm and www.thaigov.go.th/index_t.htm, as can the transcripts of the weekly radio broadcasts.

Anuson ngan phrarachathan phlengsop phon. to. tho. samoe damaphong. [Cremation volume of Pol. Lt. Gen. Samoe Damaphong] Wat Thepsirin, Bangkok, 11 July 1999.

Arghiros, Daniel. 2001. *Democracy, Development and Decentralization in Provincial Thailand.* Richmond: Curzon.

Ariwat Sapphaithun. 2003. *Trakun Chinnawat* [The Shinawatra family]. Bangkok: Wannasat.

———. 2004. *Kit yang Somkit Chatusiphitak.* [Somkid's Jatusripitak's ideas] Bangkok: Wannasat.

Askew, Marc. 2004. "Taksin hits a wall of opposition in south Thailand." *Asian Analysis*, April, at www.aseanfocus.com/asiananalysis.

Baker, Chris. 2000. "Thailand's Assembly of the Poor: Background, drama, reaction." *South East Asia Research*, 8(1).

Bangna Bangpakong. 2004. "Phum chai dai tam roi pho, Phon. to. to. Phrieophan Damaphong." [Proud to follow in his father's footsteps, Pol. Lt. Gen. Phrieophan Damaphong] *Nation Sutsapda* 610, 9 February.

Brown, Andrew, and Kevin Hewison. 2004. "Labour politics in Thaksin's Thailand." SEARC Working Papers 62, City University of Hong Kong, March.

Buddhadasa Bhikkhu. 1986. *Dhammic Socialism*. Trans. and ed. by Donald K. Swearer. Bangkok: Thai Inter-Religious Commission for Development.

Callahan, William A., and Duncan McCargo. 1996. "Vote-buying in Thailand's Northeast." *Asian Survey*, 36.

Chanida Chanyapate and Isabelle Delforge. 2004. "The politics of bird flu in Thailand." *Focus on Trade*, 98, April, at www.focusweb.org.

Chumphon Phatraphon. 2002. *Thaksin ruai thaorai nae!* [How rich is Thaksin really!] Bangkok: Thawatchai Pitchphon.

Connors, Michael K. 1999. "Political reform and the state in Thailand." *Journal of Contemporary Asia*, 29.

———. 2003a. *Democracy and National Identity in Thailand*. New York and London: Routledge Curzon.

———. 2003b. "The reforming state: Security, development and culture in democratic times." In *Radicalising Thailand: New Political Perspectives*, edited by Ji Giles Ungpakorn. Bangkok: Chulalongkorn University Institute of Asian Studies.

Crispin, Shawn. 2002. "Shooting for the stars." *FEER*, 30 May.

———. 2003. "Big broadband dreams." *FEER*, 31 July.

De Soto, Hernando. 2000. *The Mystery of Capital: Why Capitalism Triumphs in the West and Fails Everywhere Else*. London: Bantam.

Faccio, Maria. 2003. "Politically connected firms." Owen Graduate School of Management, Vanderbilt University.

Gothom Arya. 2001. "Participation in Thai politics." Paper presented at the conference on "Thailand: The Next Stage," SAIS, Johns Hopkins University, Washington D.C., 30 November.

Government of Thailand (GoT). n.d. *The Eighth National Economic and Social Development Plan (1997–2001)*. Bangkok: NESDB.

Greenfeld, Liah. 2001. *The Spirit of Capitalism: Nationalism and Economic Growth*. Cambridge, Mass. and London: Harvard University Press.

Hewison, Kevin. 2000. "Thailand's capitalism before and after the economic crisis." In *Politics and Markets in the Wake of the Asian Crisis*, edited by Richard Robison et al. London: Routledge.

———. 2001. "Pathways to recovery: Bankers, businessmen and nationalism in Thailand." SEARC Working Papers 1, City University of Hong Kong, April.

———. 2002. "Responding to economic crisis: Thailand's localism." In *Reforming Thai Politics*, edited by Duncan McCargo. Copenhagen: NIAS.

———. 2003. "Crafting a new social contract: Domestic capitalist responses to the challenge of neoliberalism." In *Radicalising Thailand: New Political Perspectives*, edited by Ji Giles Ungpakorn. Bangkok: Chulalongkorn University Institute of Asian Studies.

Hicken, Allen D. 2001. "From Phitsanulok to parliament: Multiple parties in pre-1997 Thailand." In *Thailand's New Politics: KPI Yearbook 2001*, edited by Michael H. Nelson. Bangkok: King Prajadhipok's Institute and White Lotus.

Higgott, Richard. 2000. "The international relations of the Asian economic crisis: A study in the politics of resentment." In *Politics and Markets in the Wake of the Asian Crisis*, edited by R. Robison et al. London and New York: Routledge.

Hutchcroft, Paul. 1998. *Booty Capitalism: The Politics of Banking in the Philippines*. Ithaca: Cornell University Press.

IMF. 2004. *IMF Survey*, 2 February.

Jackson, Peter A. 2003. *Buddhadasa: Theravada Buddhism and Modernist Reform in Thailand*. Chiang Mai: Silkworm Books.

Jaran Cosananund. 2003. "Human rights and the war on drugs: Problems of conception, consciousness and social responsibility." *Thailand Human Rights Journal*, 1.

Jayasuriya, Kanishka and Kevin Hewison. 2004. "The anti-politics of good governance: From social policy to a global populism?" SEARC Working Papers 59, City University of Hong Kong, January.

Jitra Konuntakiat. 2004. "Nam sakhun nayok thai lukchin lae thammai chueng pen...Chinnawat." [Surnames of the Thai prime ministers of Chinese descent, and why Shinawatra] *Nation sutsapda*, 611, 16–22 February.

Kasian Tejapira. 2001. "Pisat poppiwlisam." [The populism devil] *Matichon*, 20 January.

———. 2002. "Post-crisis economic impasse and political recovery in Thailand: The resurgence of economic nationalism." *Critical Asian Studies*, 34, 3.

———. 2004. "Thi ma khong rabop Thaksin." [The context of Thaksin] *Matichon*, 20 February.

Kavi Chongkittavorn (2001) "Media reform in Thailand: New prospects and new problems." Paper presented at the conference on "Thailand: The Next Stage," SAIS, Johns Hopkins University, Washington D.C., 30 November.

Klein, James R. 1998. "The Constitution of the Kingdom of Thailand, 1997: A blueprint for parliamentary democracy." Asia Foundation working paper, March 8.

———. 2003. "The battle for the rule of law in Thailand: The role of the Constitutional Court." In *The Constitutional Court of Thailand: The Provisions and Working of the Court*, by Amara Raksasataya and James R. Klein. Bangkok: Constitution for the People Society.

Kotler, Philip, Somkid Jatusripitak, and Suvit Maesincee. 1997. *The Marketing of Nations: A Strategic Approach to Building National Wealth*. New York: The Free Press.

Lewis, Daniel Ray. 2003. *The Long Trip down the Mountain: Social and Economic Impact of Illicit Drugs in Thailand*. Bangkok: UN Office on Drugs and Crime, Regional Centre for East Asia and the Pacific.

LIF (Mulaniti sathaban thidin). 2000. *Khrongkan suksa kan thuekhrong lae chai prayot thidin lae matrakan thang setthasat lae kotmai phuea hai kan chai prayot thidin koet prayot sungsut*. [Study of land holding and usage, and economic and legal standards to maximize benefits] Bangkok.

Looney, Robert. 2003. "Thaksinomics: A new Asian paradigm." *Strategic Insight*, December.

McCargo, Duncan. 1997. *Chamlong Srimuang and the New Thai Politics*. London: Hurst.

———. 2001. "Populism and reformism in contemporary Thailand." *South East Asia Research*, 9 (1).

———. 2002. "Security, development and political participation in Thailand: Alternative currencies of legitimacy." *Contemporary Southeast Asia*, 24 (1), April.

———. 2002a. "Introduction: Understanding political reform in Thailand." In *Reforming Thai Politics*, edited by Duncan McCargo. Copenhagen: NIAS.

———. 2002b. "Thailand's January 2001 general elections: Vindicating reform?" In *Reforming Thai Politics*, edited by Duncan McCargo. Copenhagen: NIAS.

McVey, Ruth, ed. 2000. *Money and Power in Provincial Thailand*. Chiang Mai: Silkworm Books.

Missingham, Bruce D. 2003. *The Assembly of the Poor in Thailand: From Local Struggles to National Protest Movement*. Chiang Mai: Silkworm Books.

Narong Petchprasoet. 2000. *Kham prakat chatniyom mai*. [Declaration of new nationalism] *Setthasat kanmueang (phuea chumchon)*. [Political economy, for communities] 15. Bangkok: Chulalongkorn University Political Economy Centre.

Narongchai Bunyanonthachai. 2002. *Thaksin bon banlang nayok rathamontri: 2 pi rathaban thai rak thai*. [Thaksin in the premier's seat: Two years of the Thai Rak Thai government] Bangkok: Dok Ya.

Nayok Thaksin khui kap prachachon lem 1. [Prime Minister Thaksin speaks with the people, vol. 1] Bangkok: Public Relations Department, n.d.

———. *lem 2.* [Prime Minister Thaksin speaks with the people, vol. 2] Bangkok: Public Relations Department, n.d.

———. *lem 3.* [Prime minister Thaksin speaks with the people, vol. 3] Bangkok: Public Relations Department, n.d.

Nelson, Michael H. 2001. "Thailand's House elections of 6 January 2001: Thaksin's landslide victory and subsequent narrow escape." In *Thailand's New Politics: KPI Yearbook 2001*, edited by Michael H. Nelson. Bangkok: White Lotus.

NHRC. 2003. "Summary report on the Thai Malaysian Gas Pipeline Project." *Thailand Human Rights Journal*, 1.

———. 2004. "Kammakan sit sanoe matrakan dap fai tai 1 sapda kon koet 'mesa nong lueat.'" [Human Rights Commission proposed measures to extin-guish the fire in the south one week before "Bloody April"] *Krungthep Thurakit*, 30 April.

Nichapha Siriwat. 2003. *Branding Thai Rak Thai*. Bangkok: Higher Press.

Nidhi Aeusrivongse. 2002. "Thaksinomics." *Kyoto Review of Southeast Asia*, 1.

Nualnoi Treerat, Noppanun Wannathepsakul, and Daniel Ray Lewis. 2000. *Global Study on Illegal Drugs: The Case of Bangkok, Thailand.* UNDCP.

Ockey, James. 2001. "Thailand: the struggle to redefine civil-military relations." In *Coercion and Governance: The Declining Political Role of the Military in Asia*, edited by Muthiah Alagappa. Stanford: Stanford University Press.

Olarn Chaipravat. 2003. "Thailand's positioning in a new global economic paradigm." *Kyoto Review of Southeast Asia*, 4.

Panitan Wattanayagorn. 1998. "Thailand: the elite's shifting conceptions of security." In *Asian Security Practice*, edited by Muthiah Alagappa. Stanford: Stanford University Press.

Pansak Vinyaratn. 2003. "Asia finds its own way: The Thai roadmap." *Asia Times*, 30 May, www.atimes.com/atimes/southeast_asia/ee30ae02.html.

Pasuk Phongpaichit. 2002. *Withi chiwit withi su: khabuankan prachachon ruam samai.* [Ways of life, means of struggle: Contemporary popular movements] Chiang Mai: Silkworm Books.

———. 2003. "Financing Thaksinomics." *Chualongkorn Economic Journal*, 15, 3.

——— and Chris Baker. 2000. *Thailand's Crisis*. Chiang Mai: Silkworm Books.

———. 2002. *Thailand: Economy and Politics*. 2nd ed. Kuala Lumpur: Oxford University Press.

Phak thai rak thai. 1999. *Khana tham ngan phuea tit tam kan patibat ngan ratthaban.* [Working groups to monitor the government], pamphlet, 29 August.

Phijitra. 2003. *Kit yang Thaksin Chinnawat: Leader of Asia.* [Thought of Thaksin Shinawatra: Leader of Asia] Bangkok: Thai Media Network.

Pitch Phongsawat. 2004. "Senthang prachathippatai lae kan prap tua khong rat thai nai rabop Thaksin." [Democracy and state adjustment under Thaksin] *Fa dieo kan,* 2, 1 (Jan.–Mar.).

Plai-or Chananon. 1987. *Pho kha kap phatthanakan rabop thun niyom nai phak nuea pho. so. 2464–2523.* [Traders and development of capitalism in the north, 1921–80] Bangkok: CUSRI.

Porter, Michael. 2003. "Thailand's competitiveness: Creating the foundations for higher productivity." Presentation, Bangkok, 4 May.

Pran Phisitsetthakan, ed. 2004. *Thaksinomik lae CEO prathet thai.* [Thaksinomics and Thailand's CEO] Bangkok: Matichon.

———. 2004a. *Thaksinomik kap nayobai sangkhom.* [Thaksinomics and social policy] Bangkok: Matichon.

Prani Sirithorn Na Phatthalung. 1980. *Phu bukboek haeng chiangmai.* [Pioneers of Chiangmai] Bangkok: Ruengsin Publishers.

Praphat Pintobtaeng. 1998. *Kanmueang bon thong thanon: 99 wan samatcha khon chon.* [Politics on the street: Ninety-nine days of the Assembly of the Poor] Bangkok: Krirk University.

Purachai Piumsombun. 1983. "Itthiphon phon prayot lae phruethikam nai ongkan tamruat thai." [Influence, interests and behavior in the Thai police] *Warasan phattana borihansat* (Public Administration Journal), I, 23.

Ravadee Rattananuban and Apirudi Sombuntanond. 2000. "Kitchakan thorakhamanakhom thai." [The Thai telecommunications business] Working paper, Bank of Thailand.

Rattaphong Sonsuphap and Prajak Namprasanthai. 2003. *Thaksino's model: Patirup khwam mangkhang su than amnat thai.* [Thaksino's model: Converting wealth to power] Bangkok: Uxpress.

Riggs, Fred W. 1966. *Thailand: The Modernisation of a Bureaucratic Polity.* Honolulu: East-West Center Press.

Sakkarin Niyomsilpa. 2000. *The Political Economy of Telecommunications Reforms in Thailand.* London and New York: Pinter.

Sangsit Piriyarangsan et al. 2003. *Setthakit kan phanan thang lueak choeng nayobai.* [Policy alternatives for the gambling industry] Bangkok: National Lottery Bureau and Political Economy Centre.

Shin Satellite. 2003. *Rai ngan pracham pi.* [Annual Report] Bangkok.

Somchai Jitsuchon. 2003. "Poem khwam mankhong setthakit doi kan khachat khwam yakchon: Botbat khong phak rat." [Economc security

enhance-ment through poverty eradication: The role of government]
TDRI, 29–30 November.

Somchai Phatharathananunth. 2001. "Civil society in Northeast Thailand:
The struggle of the Small Scale Farmers' Assembly of Isan." Ph.D.
diss., University of Leeds.

Somchai Sujjapong, 2004. *Seeing through the Economic Dimension of Thai
Fiscal Policy*. (In Thai). Ministry of Finance, 2003.

Somkiat Tangkitvanit. 2003. "Phon krathop khong kan plaeng kha sampa-
than pen phasi sanphasamit." [Effect of converting concession fees
into excise tax] Unpublished paper.

Somkiat Tangkitvanit. 2004. "Sai samphan thang kanmueang kap phon
thop thaen nai talat hun thai." [Political connections and returns in
the Thai stock market] Unpublished paper.

———— and Tharathon Rattanonrimitson. 2002. *Saphap talat thorakhamanakhom nai tang prathet lae prathet thai*. [State of the telecoms
market overseas and in Thailand] Bangkok: TDRI.

Somkid Jatusripitak. 2001. "Dual-track economics." Speech in New York,
in *The Nation*, 19 December.

Sorakon Adulyanon. 1993. *Thaksin Chinnawat asawin khloen luk thi sam*
(Thaksin Shinawatra, knight of the third wave). Bangkok: Matichon.

Surachart Bamrungsuk. 2001. "Thailand: Military professionalism at the
crossroads." In *Military Professionalism in Asia: Conceptual and
Empirical Perspectives*, edited by Muthiah Alagappa. Honolulu: East-
West Center.

Suthep Kittikulsingh. 1999. "Non-performing loans (NPLs): The
borrower's viewpoint." *TDRI Quarterly Review*, 14 (4).

TDRI. 2003. *Nueng pi raek khong kan chai lak prakan sukhaphap thuan na*.
[First year of the universal health insurance] Bangkok: TDRI.

Thaksin Shinawatra. 1979. "An analysis of the relationship between the
criminal justice educational process and the attitude of the students
towards the rule of law." Ph.D. diss., Sam Houston State University.

————. 1999. *Thaksin Chinnawat: Ta du dao thao tit din*. [Thaksin Shinawatra: Eyes on the stars, feet on the ground] Edited by Walaya.
Bangkok: Matichon.

————. 2001a. "Inaugural address." At 57th session of ESCAP, Bangkok,
23 April.

————. 2001b. "Next generation Asia." Speech to Fortune Global Forum,
Hong Kong, 9 May, reported as "Thaksin sees a new Asian Silk Road"
in *The Nation*, 10 May, available through www.thaigov.go.th/index-
eng.htm.

————. 2001c. "Speech." At the Foreign Correspondents Club of Thailand, 4 June, available through www.thaigov.go.th/index-eng.htm.

————. 2001d. "Thaksin looks to a global strategy." Speech at Institute of Southeast Asian Studies, Singapore, in *The Nation*, 24 August.

————. 2001e. "New vision of Thailand." Speech at the seminar "Thailand: Invest in Our Future", Imperial Hotel, Tokyo, 20 November, at: www.thaigov.go.th/news/speech/thaksin/sp20nov01.htm.

————. 2001f. "Sathanakan prathet thai kap kan thucharit khorapchan." [The Thai situation and corruption] Speech at workshop on prevention and suppression of corruption, Government House, 23 November, available through www.thaigov.go.th/index_t.htm.

————. 2002. "Keynote speech." At the 2nd International Conference of Asian Political Parties, Bangkok, 23 November, at: www.thaigov. go.th/news/speech/thaksin/sp23nov02-2.htm.

————. 2003a. "Kham klao nai okat mopmai lae chichaeng nayobai kan pongkan lae prap pram ya septit" [Speech presenting and explaining policy of drug prevention and suppression] Meeting hall, Suan Dusit Ratchapat Institute, 14 January, at: www.thaigov.go.th/index_t.htm.

————. 2003b. "Kham prasai khong Thaksin Chinnawat nai 'kan prachum yai saman pracham pi 2546' khong phak thai rak thai." [Speech of Thaksin Shinawatra at TRT annual general assembly 2003] Rangsit, 27 April.

————. 2003c. "ACD, and a more self-reliant Asia." Speech to the Asia Cooperation Dialogue, Chiang Mai, 22 June, in *Bangkok Post*, 25 June.

————. 2003d. "Thaksin feels need for speed." Speech to the Thailand chapter of the Young Presidents Organization, in *The Nation*, 21 August.

————. 2003e. "Keynote address." At 36th international general meeting of the Pacific Basin Economic Council, Seoul, 24 August. At www.thaigov.th/news/speech/thaksin/sp24aug03.htm.

————. 2003f. "Keynote address." At the Philippine Chamber of Commerce and Industry and the Philippine-Thai Business Council, Dusit Nikko Hotel, Manila, 8 September, at www.thaigov.go.th/news/speech/thaksin/sp08sep03.htm.

————. 2003g. "Thaksin 'pluk khwan' thairakthai pramoen suk lueak tang 'rao chana baep ying kwa thalom thalai'" [Thaksin cheers TRT, predicts the election, "we'll win by an avalanche"] *Matichon*, 28 December 2003, from website www.matichon.co.th.

Thitinan Phonsudhirak. 2003. "Thailand: Democratic authoritarianism." In *Southeast Asian Affairs 2003*, (Singapore: ISEAS).

Turton, Andrew. 1984. "Limits of ideological domination and the formation of social consciousness." In *History and Peasant Consciousness in South East Asia*, edited by Andrew Turton and Shigeharu Tanabe. Osaka: National Museum of Ethnology.

Ubolrat Siriyuvasak. 2001. "Obstacles to reform of broadcast media." *The Nation*, 27 August 2001.

Ukrist Pathmanand. 1998. "The Thaksin Shinawatra group: A study of the relationship between money and politics in Thailand." *Copenhagen Journal of Asian Studies*, 13.

————. 2002. "From Shinawatra group of companies to the Thaksin Shinawatra government: The politics of money and power merge." Paper presented at conference on crony capitalism, Quezon City, 17–18 January.

————. 2004. "Korani suksa klum thorakhamanakhom." [Telecom groups case study] Unpublished paper, Faculty of Economics, Chulalongkorn University, 29 January.

UN Commission on Human Rights. 2004. *Promotion and Protection of Human Rights: Human Rights Defenders. Addendum: Mission to Thailand.* E/CN.4/2004/94/Add.1. March.

Warr, Peter. 2004. "Boom, bust and beyond." In *Thailand Beyond the Crisis*, edited by Peter Warr. London: Routledge Curzon.

World Bank. 2001. *Thailand Social Monitor: Poverty and Public Policy.* Bangkok: World Bank.

Worawan Chandoevwit. 2003. "Thailand's grass roots policies." *TDRI Quarterly Review*, 18, 2.

Yos Santasombat. 1985. "Power and personality: An anthropological study of the Thai political elite." Ph.D. diss., University of California, Berkeley.

INDEX